D0064856

The Consequences of
School Desegregation

The Consequences of
School Desegregation

EDITED BY

Christine H. Rossell

AND

Willis D. Hawley

TEMPLE UNIVERSITY PRESS

PHILADELPHIA

LC
214.2
.C665
1983

Temple University Press, Philadelphia 19122
© 1983 by Temple University. All rights reserved
Published 1983
Printed in the United States of America

Main entry under title:

The Consequences of school desegregation.

Bibliography: p.
Includes index.
1. School integration—United States—Addresses,
essays, lectures.   I. Rossell, Christine H.
II. Hawley, Willis D.
LC214.2.C665   1983   370.19′342   83-6755
ISBN 0-87722-320-3

#9533492

194064
OCT 3 0 1984

Contents

Contributors

VALERIE J. COOK is associate professor of psychology at Peabody College of Vanderbilt University. Her research focuses on student diversity, nondiscriminatory assessment of children, and school organization and policy. She received her Ph.D. in school psychology from Teachers College, Columbia University.

ROBERT L. CRAIN is senior social scientist for the Rand Corporation and principal research investigator at the Center for the Social Organization of Schools of Johns Hopkins University. He has coauthored four books on the politics of school desegregation and effective desegregation strategies and has published a number of articles on desegregation and minority academic achievement. He holds a Ph.D. in sociology from the University of Chicago.

JANET EYLER is assistant dean of Peabody College of Vanderbilt University, assistant professor of education and research associate at Vanderbilt Institute for Public Policy Studies. Her research and writing emphasize political socialization, the politics of education, resegregation, and incentives for the improvement of quality of education. She holds a Ph.D. in social studies education from Indiana University.

WILLIS D. HAWLEY is dean of Peabody College, Vanderbilt University's School of Education and Human Development, and professor of education and political science at Vanderbilt. He is a principal investigator for the Educational Analysis Center for Educational Quality and Equality for the U.S. Department of Education. From 1979 to 1981 he was director of the U.S. Department of Education's Policy Development Center for Desegregation. His research and writings deal with desegregation, education policy, education research and development, organizational change, and the learning of political and social values. He received his Ph.D. in political science from the University of California at Berkeley.

RITA E. MAHARD is currently a doctoral student in social psychology at the University of Michigan and serves as consultant to the Rand Corporation. She has coauthored a variety of publications on such topics as school racial composition and black college attendance and achievement, and desegregation and minority achievement. She received her M.A. in sociology from the University of Michigan.

CHRISTINE H. ROSSELL is associate professor of political science at Boston University. She has served as consultant to the Rand Corporation, the U.S. Office of Education, and the U.S. Department of Justice. Her primary areas of research and writing include white flight and school desegregation, community social change, and the use of social-science research in educational equity cases. She received her Ph.D. in political science from the University of Southern California.

H. ANDREW SAGAR is assistant professor of psychology at Elizabethtown College. His research areas include school desegregation and race relations and abortion attitudes. He received his Ph.D. in social psychology from the University of Pittsburgh.

JANET W. SCHOFIELD is associate professor of psychology and senior scientist at the Learning Research and Development Center at the University of Pittsburgh. She has also held policy research positions with the federal government and has served as a consultant to both federal and local agencies. Her research and publications focus primarily on the development of students' racial attitudes and behavior. She holds a Ph.D. in social psychology from Harvard University.

LESLIE E. WARD is Legislative Program Evaluator for the State of Tennessee. Her primary research focuses on policy analysis and evaluation research. She received her M.A. in political science from Vanderbilt University.

Preface and Acknowledgments

Against the background of continuing public debate about busing and changes in state and federal policies, school systems throughout the country go about the business of racial desegregation. To say that the issue of desegregation is socially and politically divisive is to state the obvious. The conflict over school desegregation has been fed by an enormous amount of misinformation about what happens in desegregating communities and by beliefs that desegregation substantially complicates the already difficult job of providing quality public education to the nation's children.

This book seeks to clarify the national experience with school desegregation and to identify what is known about the potential benefits and costs of desegregation. The book is the work of several authors, but it is based on the efforts of many others. It is a synthesis of existing empirical research and in that sense is the work of hundreds of writers. More directly, the book derives from two extensive projects that have involved numerous people in addition to those listed as authors of this book.

The first of these projects is the National Review Panel on School Desegregation Research. The panel, funded primarily by the Ford Foundation, has produced several books and articles that have sought to identify what is known and not known about desegregation. Panel members are Willis D. Hawley and Betsy Levin (chairs), Mark A. Chesler, Robert L. Crain, Edgar G. Epps, John B. McConahay, James M. McPartland, Gary Orfield, Peter Roos, Christine H. Rossell, William L. Taylor, and Mark G. Yudof. Chapter 1, which discusses assumptions about the overall consequences of desegregation, draws heavily on the work of the panel and the research of other scholars, including some of the contributors to this book.

Chapters 2 to 5 synthesize the findings of existing research on the consequences of school desegregation for children and communities. These chapters present a revised version of the review of empirical research that comprises the fifth volume of the project, *Assessment of Current Knowledge about the Effectiveness of School Desegregation Strategies*, funded by the National Institute of Education and the United States Office for Civil Rights (Contract No. NIE-R-79-0034). The listed editors and contributors of this book drafted and revised significant portions of that volume. Other members of the study team for that project were Carol Andersen, C. Anthony Broh, Ricardo R. Fernandez, John B. McConahay, William Sampson, Mark A. Smylie, Rachel Tompkins, William T. Trent, Charles B. Vergon, and Ben Williams. This project benefited from the advice of a distinguished panel of scholars and practitioners who made suggestions and comments on every aspect of the study from the project design to the final report. The members of the advisory board were Mary Berry, Fred Burke, Norman Chachkin, Francis Keppel, Hernan LaFontaine, Sharon Robinson, Peter Roos, and Franklin Wilson. Chapter 6 is an expanded revision of the agenda for further research on school desegregation contained in the second volume of this project.

The authors of this book are grateful to several project participants who reviewed drafts of the assessment project and made substantial suggestions. The contributions of Thomas Carter, Rosie Feinberg, Jayjia Hsia, Lorenza Schmidt, and Susana Navarro are especially acknowledged. Marilyn S. Zlotnik served as coordinator of the project.

We are indebted to Ralph Bohrson and Edward Meade of the Ford Foundation who advised and supported the work of the National Review Panel on School Desegregation Research. We are also grateful for the thoughtful advice of Oscar Uribe, Mary von Euler, and Ron Henderson, who in their roles as project officers at the National Institute for Education (NIE) monitored much of the work reflected in these pages. Janice Potker of the U.S. Office for Civil Rights was helpful in coordinating our efforts with that agency. Bonnie Moore cheerfully typed, retyped, and, along with Mark A. Smylie, helped edit the final manuscript. To all these people, we are very grateful.

Although many contributed to this book, both directly and indirectly, the editors and contributors take full responsibility for any errors or omissions. Of course, the views set forth here do not necessarily represent those of the Ford Foundation or the U.S. Department of Education.

Christine H. Rossell
Willis D. Hawley

The Consequences of
School Desegregation

1

Introduction: Desegregation and Change

Christine H. Rossell and *Willis D. Hawley*

For more than 25 years, the issue of school desegregation has divided communities, states, and the nation. Today, the legally sanctioned dual school systems of the South have been dismantled, and the vast majority of Americans of all races and in all parts of the country acknowledge that school desegregation is, at least in principle, a desirable policy. Nevertheless, implementing school desegregation is controversial. It often brings latent conflict between different ethnic, racial, and socioeconomic groups to the surface. Americans typically have minimized such conflicts by keeping neighborhoods homogeneous, by regulating access to certain professions, and by planning their lives around private organizations, such as churches and clubs. School desegregation undermines the strength of these social barriers and brings children and families with different lifestyles, values, and privileges into direct contact. In other words, school desegregation, perhaps more than any other social policy, threatens to tear down the walls we build around our lives.

The purpose of this collection of essays is to examine what the research on desegregation has to say about how communities and school systems can respond to desegregation in positive ways. The focus here is on the problems and opportunities desegregation poses for social change and the quality and equity of public education. Our interest in education is *not* with the differences between effective and ineffective schools, but with how desegregated schools differ from other schools and how desegregated schools can be made more effective. We are not, in other words, concerned with all issues relevant to education in desegregated schools, but with those matters that are at issue because a school has been desegregated. This rules out some important research that relates to effective education, especially for low-income and minority children (see for example, Brookover, Beady, Flood, Schwietzer, and

3

Wisenbaker, 1979; Edmonds, 1979; Bloom, 1976; Murnane and Phillips, 1979).

Desegregated schools differ from segregated schools in many important ways that tax the administrative capacity of a school system. The implementation of desegregation uncovers problems that administrators and teachers are typically not prepared to deal with, either because the problem did not exist or they had not been held accountable for it prior to desegregation. Minority achievement falls into the latter categroy. As long as minorities go to their own schools, white parents and the media are not very concerned about the achievement gap between the races. When minority children sit next to white children, the achievement gap becomes of immense importance. School desegregation thus subjects the school system to uncomfortable scrutiny, new demands for educational excellence, and skepticism—especially among whites—about the possibility of quality integrated education. For many whites, the assertion that desegregation is a remedy for past injustices and a way of improving minority education implies that the quality of their children's education will suffer.

Desegregation not only raises new concerns about the quality of schools, it results in parental concern about interracial conflict. Normal concerns about safety are magnified when parents think of their children attending school in distant, unfamiliar, and even foreign neighborhoods.

Prior to desegregation, most school systems are highly segregated by race, class, and achievement at both the school and classroom level. To the extent that the races differ in class and achievement, administrators who are required to integrate their schools and classrooms will have to deal with student diversity that they did not have in a segregated school system. Unfortunately, teachers and administrators are taught and socialized to respond to student heterogeneity by organizing the student body into homogeneous groups. Students, left on their own, usually prefer to associate with peers most like them. Thus, the desegregated school system will have a natural tendency to resegregate.

The problems that school systems have in adapting to desegregation influence, and are influenced by, the problems communities have in adjusting to what is usually a demand for change *imposed* by the courts or by state and federal governments. The adjustment problems are not limited to the white middle class. Working-class Irish Americans fear that their children will leave the extended family structures that characterize South Boston, Hispanics in Houston fear for the loss of a language-strengthened culture that sustains a sense of community, and blacks in Nashville see no reason why a historically black high school should not be preserved as a symbol of the strength of the black community.

School desegregation reminds us of just how separate we are. The myth of the melting pot and social mobility are exposed. The neglect of our urban schools by an aging and suburbanizing population is dramatized. The importance of racial and ethnic discrimination in determining where we live and work, and the standards we accept in deciding whether justice is achieved and a good education is received are brought into focus. Desegregation is, therefore, a fundamental challenge to the beliefs and structures that sustain racial, ethnic, and class distinctions.

THE MYTHOLOGY OF DESEGREGATION

In response to the challenges desegregation poses to the world as we have known it, certain myths have arisen that have become reality for many. In 1982, for example, the U.S. Senate overwhelmingly passed legislation that included several "statements of fact" that are not supported by evidence, but which express widespread beliefs that affect our willingness and our capability to respond to the challenges of desegregation in positive ways. An examination of this mythology will set the stage for the analyses of research that make up the heart of this book.

The first finding in support of the Neighborhood School Act of 1982 (Senate Bill 951), asserts that:

> court orders requiring transportation of students to or attendance at public schools other than the one closest to their residences for the purpose of achieving racial balance or racial desegregation have proven to be ineffective remedies to achieve unitary school systems.

While the definition of a "unitary school system" depends on the characteristics of individual school districts and the provisions of individual desegregation plans, longitudinal studies of national and regional desegregation trends show that black-white racial isolation has declined to the greatest extent in the areas of the country most significantly affected by court-ordered mandatory school desegregation (Coleman, Kelly and Moore, 1975; Taeuber and Wilson, 1979a; Farley, 1981). Studies that examine the effectiveness of different school desegregation strategies find a significant increase in racial balance among schools and interracial contact among students in districts implementing mandatory student assignment plans (Foster, 1973; Rossell, 1978a; Rossell, 1979; Morgan and England, 1981; Smylie, 1983). In addition, this literature reveals that voluntary desegregation plans, including those that rely on magnet schools as the sole desegregation technique, are for the most part ineffective, at least over the short term, in achieving any substantial districtwide reductions in racial isolation in districts over 30 percent minority (Foster, 1973; Rossell, 1978a, 1979; Royster, Baltzell, and Simmons, 1979; Larson, 1980; Morgan and England, 1981; Smylie, 1983). Even in those districts that rely on a combination of mandatory and voluntary strategies, most desegregation is attributable to the mandatory reassignment of students, not to the voluntary components (Rossell, 1979; Royster, Baltzell, and Simmons, 1979). It should be emphasized, however, that these are short term analyses and the long term effectiveness of these strategies is not known.

The second finding of this legislation states that

> such court orders frequently result in the exodus from public school systems of children causing even greater racial imbalance and diminished public support for public school systems.

Yet most studies indicate that the magnitude of white flight from school desegregation is generally overstated. The research examined by Rossell in Chapter 2 is in general agreement that white enrollment decline accelerates upon implementation of mandatory student assignment plans. However, implementation-year losses vary among districts according to a number of factors that include whether the plan affects only the central city or includes the entire metropolitan area, the size of the minority student population, the proportion of the white student population assigned to schools outside their neighborhoods, and busing distance. After implementation, white loss begins to level out and busing distance ceases to be a factor. Central city school districts with large minority populations continue to experience white losses, but those losses are less than during the implementation year. Many suburban, metropolitan, and countywide school districts experience postimplementation losses that approximate preimplementation declines, and in some of these districts, implementation-year losses are made up by less-than-normal postimplementation declines in white enrollment. Despite the occurrence of white flight, the evidence indicates that no school district, even the worst case, is currently more segregated in terms of racial balance and interracial contact than it would have been if no mandatory student assignment plan had been implemented.

The impact of mandatory desegregation plans on public support for public schools is difficult to assess. Most of the studies of community attitudes have been conducted in districts experiencing the greatest disruption and protest. Overall, however, the research reviewed by Rossell in Chapter 2 finds that reductions in school segregation have been followed by reductions in racial intolerance in both North and South, and over time there appears to be no backlash against the principle of racial integration despite the racial confrontation and controversy surrounding school desegregation. National and community surveys of public opinion find increasing support for the principle of racial integration and racially balanced schools although whites, in the aggregate, are opposed to busing for desegregation. Some parents in some school districts that have experienced violence and controversy continue to have strong fears regarding the quality of education in desegregated schools. However, an overwhelming proportion of both black and white parents whose children attend desegregated schools report satisfactory experiences with desegregation and the quality of their schools.

The third "statement of fact" in this legislation states that

assignment and transportation of students to public schools other than the one closest to their residence is expensive and wasteful of scarce petroleum fuels.

There is no question that mandatory student assignment plans increase the operational costs of school districts over those costs that might be incurred if all students attended schools closest to their homes. The magnitude of such increases, however, is generally overestimated as a result of overestimates of the number of students who are reassigned and ride the bus to desegregated schools. The best estimates to date indicate that nationwide only 3 percent to 5 percent of all students who ride buses to school do so for the purpose of desegregation (Orfield, 1978a; Moody and Ross, 1980). And the best estimate of increases in transportation costs indicates that school expenditure on transportation is, on the average, no more than 2 percentage points higher after desegregation than before (Moody and Ross, 1980).

The fourth finding contained in the act claims that

there is an absence of social science evidence to suggest that the [benefits] of school busing outweigh the disruptiveness of busing.

This statement is also misleading. Of those few studies that have specifically examined the impact of riding the bus to schools or attending neighborhood schools, most show no effect, either positive or negative, on student achievement and attitudes toward schools (Davis, 1973; Zoloth, 1976; Natkin, 1980). The desegregation and minority achievement research analyzed by Mahard and Crain in Chapter 4 of this book indicate that (1) desegregation tends to improve minority academic achievement and does not harm white achievement, (2) the greatest gains in achievement occur when students are first desegregated in the early elementary grades, (3) gains are greater in schools where there is a critical mass of about 15 percent to 20 percent minority enrollment, (4) there appears to be no difference between achievement gains with mandatory student assignment and with voluntary desegregation plans, and (5) studies with stronger methodologies show greater achievement gains than studies with weaker methodologies.

As Schofield notes in Chapter 3, disruption in schools that results from desegregation can have a negative impact on student achievement. The achievement research suggests, however, that whatever the impact of disruption on achievement, it has not been very great. In addition, the large national studies that examine the impact of desegregation find that what disruption occurs tends to be short in duration and related more to the type of governance and the leadership style of school-level administrators and staff than to desegregation and busing (National Institute of Education, 1978; Gottfredson and Daiger, 1979).

The last finding of the Neighborhood School Act of 1982 contends that

assignment of students to public schools closest to their residence (neighborhood public schools) is the preferred method of public school attendance.

While it is clear that most parents prefer that their children attend schools near their homes, this finding implies that attending schools not closest to students' homes is undesirable because students' experiences in these schools have been unsatisfactory. This contention is not supported by the evidence. The only two national polls that permit one to examine parental opinion show that both white and black parents who send their children to desegregated schools, presumably outside their neighborhoods, are overwhelmingly satisfied with the experience (Harris, 1977, 1981). In addition, several studies of local public opinion indicate that black and white parents directly involved with school desegregation—those who send their children to desegregated schools—express more support for desegregation and express a higher opinion of the quality of desegregated schools than people not involved with desegregation (Serow and Solomon, 1979b; Sobol and Beck, 1980). Of course, these findings do not suggest that neighborhood schools are not preferred by parents and the general public. Rather, they indicate that parents' and children's experiences with desegregation have not been as bad as we are led to believe.

In summary, then, the national experience with desegregation is shrouded in myths that, while they may find anecdotal support in isolated instances, are generally not consistent with the available evidence. These myths help to justify opposition to desegregation and to legitimize the widely held view that desegregation is desirable in principle but unworkable in practice. Thus, as a nation we do not have to confront our prejudices or the fact of inequality. Undesirable as racial separation is, there are, if one accepts the mythology of desegregation, few workable alternatives. In this context, even advocates of desegregation often see the task before them as herculean, and the issue is debated in moralistic terms rather than in terms of policy options that might maximize the potential benefits and minimize the potential costs.

TOWARD AN EXPLANATION OF SYSTEMIC RESPONSES TO DESEGREGATION

Because anecdotes, misinformation, and a fundamental predisposition to maintain differences dominate the conventional wisdom about desegregation, relatively little effort has been expended to identify and understand the conditions under which desegregation works best. Thus, before turning to research about the effects of desegregation on students and communities, we must establish a framework within which we can begin to understand why desegregation strategies known to be successful are not implemented more widely, and how to structure school systems politically and organizationally so that they can respond more effectively to desegregation. Educational equity is, in significant ways, a product of changes in the practices and policies of school systems. These changes are manifest in the behavior of teachers and administrators, in the suitability of learning environments and instructional strategies, and in the increase in opportunities for rewarding interracial contact among students. The product of these changes, of course, can be benefits that accrue to students and ultimately to society.

We hypothesize that three general conditions are required if these changes are to be implemented and sustained: (1) information on how to achieve them, (2) a reallocation of power in the system, and (3) new resources (money, materials, personnel) to affect change. Our theory is summarized in a two-by-two grid (Figure 1-1) which assumes policymakers have the information to produce change and that information is a necessary, but insufficient, source of change. The diagram shows the outcome of high and low increases in school resources (on the left) and high and low reallocations of power (at the top). If the distribution of power within both the organization and the community continues into the postimplementation phase largely unaffected, there will be no incentive, or motivation, for the school system to achieve equity. If new resources are not generated or freed from other activities, then the school system will have no significant capacity to achieve equity. If the opposite is true, and power and resources are reallocated, then it is probable that new incentives and capacities for educational equity will be produced. If there is only a reallocation of power but no new resources are provided, continuous and debilitating conflict is probable. If new resources are applied to desegregation programs but power is not reallocated, then the changes in policy and program will be largely marginal—perhaps symbolically innovative, but short term and limited in scope.

Changes in incentives, capacity, and information are likely to produce long-term change for students and their community because they influence be-

FIGURE 1-1

Outcome of Changes in Power and Resources[a]

Reallocation of Power

	HIGH	LOW
HIGH Increase in resources	Significant, long lasting change	Minimal, symbolic change reflected in superficial "innovations" and co-optation of change advocates
LOW	Short-run, non-institutionalized change, enduring conflict	No Change

havioral changes not only among administrators and teachers, but also among students and parents, all of whom are in turn influenced by community responses during and after implementation.

As Figure 1-2 illustrates, desegregation is a change process occurring at several levels at once: the community, the school district, the school, and the classroom. The major factors influencing the desegregation process are the characteristics of the community, the desegregation plan, the educational experience, and the individual student. All of these are interrelated.

The first goal of school desegregation is the instrumental goal of remedying unconstitutional segregation by reassigning students to other race schools. This is an instrumental goal because it is presumably the means by which the other goals are achieved. This is often forgotten by academicians, but never by the courts or school personnel, for it involves major changes in the pupil assignment process and the reassignment or hiring of staff members to carry out this task. The manner in which this is done can influence white flight, the extent of interracial contact, and academic achievement, sometimes in conflicting ways that require policymakers to make trade-offs.

The second goal of school desegregation is improving the academic performance of minority children. This is probably the most important goal as far as many academicians and most school professionals and parents are concerned. By presenting school desegregation as a means of improving the poor education of minority children, however, school professionals and the media contribute to white flight. For if school desegregation is primarily intended to rectify the poor education of minority children, why would white parents want their children to go to the schools minority children attend?

One goal of school desegregation that is usually ranked relatively low in importance by parents and educators is the improvement of race relations among students. Most principals and teachers do not feel it is their primary job to train children in social relations. Ironically, the research suggests that academic achievement, and later occupational success, is significantly enhanced by good race relations, both in the school and the community. The nature of race relations among students presumably has an important effect on the willingness of parents and communities to accept school desegregation and to be responsive to people of other races and backgrounds.

A fourth general goal of desegregation is to avoid resegregation and ensure equity within schools. The differences among races and ethnic groups often are reflected in the structures and processes of nominally desegregated schools.

A KNOWLEDGE BASE FOR MORE EFFECTIVE DESEGREGATION

The research reviews that constitute the next four chapters are the most extensive yet published. They include virtually all of the empirical research related to the ways the four goals of desegregation just noted can be attained.

FIGURE 1-2

The Analytical Model

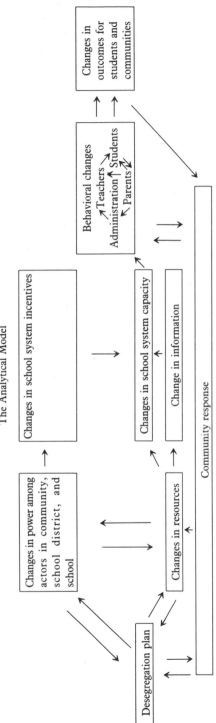

The contributors do not provide definitive solutions for all problems. They do provide a knowledge base upon which better policies could be developed, define the boundaries of our current knowledge, and indicate what further research needs to be done. Taken together, the analyses below address five important questions of concern to policymakers and academicians.

1. How can a school system be most effectively desegregated so as to maximize racial balance and minimize resegregation?
2. How can academic achievement be maintained and improved?
3. How can better race relations be attained?
4. What must educators know in order to be more effective in desegregated settings?
5. How can discipline and order be maintained in an equitable and just way?

While the issues that dominate concern over desegregation may change, it seems unlikely that desegregation will cease to be a significant concern of public policy. School districts are in constant flux; they are desegregating and resegregating on a continual basis. Courts, and some state and local agencies, will continue to insist that governmentally sanctioned segregation be remedied. It does, however, seem probable that the values embodied in demands for desegregation will be increasingly challenged not so much with respect to their legitimacy, but with respect to their centrality. The knowledge base we have will affect both the nature of these challenges and the nation's response to them.

2

Desegregation Plans, Racial Isolation, White Flight, and Community Response

Christine H. Rossell

DESEGREGATION PLANS AND RACIAL ISOLATION

Some school districts desegregate under a board order, some under a court order; some allow parental choice, others do not. Few studies have even attempted an analytical distinction between these types of plans and even fewer have attempted to determine which result in the greatest degree of school desegregation.

Figure 2-1 is a simple two-by-two grid in which the source of the order to desegregate is at the top and divided into two cells, "board-ordered" (that is, internal) and "court" or "HEW-ordered" (that is, external). The degree of parental choice is on the left and is divided into two cells: no choice (mandatory ressignment) and choice (voluntary ressignment). (The resulting four cells are numbered only for indentification purposes.) Many long-term obeservers of school desegregation have confused these different types of plans. There are board-ordered desegregation plans that allow parents no choice as to whether they will participate in the desegregation plan as long as their child is to remain in the public school system (for example, the Berkeley and Seattle desegregation plans). By contrast, there are court-ordered desegregation plans that have allowed parents a choice as to whether their child is to be reassigned to a desegregated school or to remain in their neighborhood school (for example, southern court-ordered plans from 1954 to 1970 and, more recently, those of San Diego, Houston, and Milwaukee); that is, they are voluntary. The amount of desegregation achieved depends on whether a plan is voluntary or mandatory, not on whether it is court-ordered or board-ordered.

Confusion over this abounds in the literature. When Bullock (1976a) notes that coercion is necessary in order to achieve effective desegregation in southern school districts, he is talking about some type of external order, whether

Christine H. Rossell

FIGURE 2-1
Types of Desegregation Plans

Source of Order

Parental *Choice*	Board (Internal)	Court or HEW (External)
No (mandatory reassignment)	1	2
Yes (voluntary reassignment)	3	4

by HEW or the courts. Because he makes no distinction between mandatory and voluntary reassignment, (cells 2 and 4 in Figure 2-1), his conclusions are ambiguous.

Bullock and Rodgers (1976) find that reductions in racial isolation in Georgia school districts are greater when the source of the order to desegregate is the Department of Health, Education and Welfare (HEW) than when it is the courts, again making no distinction between voluntary and mandatory reassignment. Rossell's (1978a) study of 113 school districts throughout the United States suggests that in both the North and South the vast majority of school desegregation plans are court-ordered rather than HEW-ordered. As Table 2-1 indicates, court-ordered plans on average produce slightly greater reductions in racial isolation than HEW plans and much greater reductions than board-ordered plans.[1] This is because on average they are more likely to require mandatory reassignment of both black and white students. The relative disadvantage of HEW in reducing racial isolation compared to the courts is undoubtedly due to the fact that HEW is limited by various Congressional amendments that forbid it to "racially balance" schools. In addition, as Bullock (1976a) demonstrates, withholding funds is not as great a threat to school boards as going to jail for contempt of court.

All external sources of desegregation orders, however, produce greater reductions in racial isolation than internal (board ordered) sources. School boards, on their own initiative, accomplish relatively little desegregation because they tend to be political compromisers. They balance the demands of the black community and the threat of a future court order with the demands of the much more powerful white community and thus produce a token plan. In Rossell's (1978a) study, of 113 school districts only one (Berkeley) mandatorily reassigned white students to minority schools during the period studied (1964–1975). Since that time, only one other school board in that sample (Seattle, Washington) has done so.[2]

TABLE 2-1
Variation in School Desegregation in the Year of Implementation and in Fall 1975

Type of Plan	% of Sample (N = 13)	Median Year	% Blacks Reassigned			% Whites Reassigned			Change in Segregation[a]			Fall 1975 Segregation Level[a]		
			X̄	Min.	Max.	X̄	Min.	Max.	X̄	Min.	Max.	X̄	Min.	Max.
Northern court-ordered	15.9	1973	25	2	83	6	0	24	−24.1	−1.9	−53.0	34.1	0.9	71.5
Northern HEW-ordered	1.8	1972	22	2	42	3	2	4	−23.9	−6.2	−41.6	42.2	17.0	67.4
Southern court-ordered	16.8	1970	18	4	47	3	0	10	−27.5	−6.3	−53.0	47.7	12.5	79.8
Southern HEW-ordered	2.7	1970	15	4	21	2	0.3	4	−28.5	−4.6	−45.0	57.8	39.8	88.5
Northern board-ordered city-wide plans	8.8	1970	19	9	42	2	0	16	−13.7	−4.4	−32.9	29.5	2.3	52.1
Partial or token board-ordered plans[b]	28.3	1969	3	0.1	10	0	0	2	− 6.5	3.5	−21.9	58.9	21.3	91.4
Northern control group	24.8	1971	0	0	0	0	0	0	− 0.7	3.5	− 5.5	59.6	36.0	91.1

Notes

[a]Measured by index of dissimilarity.
[b]All but one of these school districts (New Orleans) are northern.

Source: C. H. Rossell, School desegregation and community social change, Law and Contemporary Problems 42, 3 (1978): 156.

One major issue of concern to desegregation analysts has been whether voluntary desegregation plans (whether board-ordered, or HEW- or court-ordered) can be made attractive enough to effectively reduce racial isolation. Rossell (1979) finds that voluntary desegregation plans, even those including magnet schools, cannot reduce racial isolation by more than a few percentage points in school districts over 30 percent minority. In school districts less than 30 percent minority, however, magnet schools can produce significant desegregation simply because such school districts need only a small proportion of white volunteers in order to become desegregated. Even within these two categories, however, the ability of voluntary plans to desegregate effectively varies among school districts. In Montgomery, Maryland, a school district less than 30 percent minority, Larson (1980) found that voluntary magnet schools, by themselves, were unable to significantly reduce segregation. On the other hand, in Los Angeles, a school district above 30 percent minority, voluntary minority transportation to white schools produced more desegregation than did the mandatory plan, because the effectiveness of the latter was greatly reduced by white flight (Ross, 1981).

In the end, although mandatory desegregation plans produce more white flight, the evidence to date indicates that at least in the short run the net "benefit," defined as the proportion white in the average minority child's school, is greater than in a voluntary plan.[3] Armor (1980) argues, however, that ultimately a voluntary plan, because it produces less white flight, not only in the implementation year but in postimplementation years, will produce the same or a greater proportion white in the average minority child's school. At this point, however, there are not enough data to test this argument.

Individual Response to Mandatory School Desegregation

A large body of research is synthesized in this paper, but that research is less than definitive in explaining individual behavior in response to mandatory desegregation. School desegregation is not accepted by 90 percent of the white population if it is defined as the busing of school children for the purpose of "racial balance," "school desegregation," or "school integration" (Harris, 1976). Obviously, many whites oppose desegregation because they are prejudiced, but this explanation by itself explains too little. Racism permeates our entire society, but only a minority of whites actually participate in protest demonstrations or flee when a school district desegregates. Surveys indicate that individual racism is only weakly related to an intention to leave a desegregated school system (McConahay and Hawley, 1978; Giles, Gatlin, and Cataldo, 1976a).

When schools are desegregated, many parents believe that the ratio of costs to benefits changes. The costs people experience are both economic and psychological, and it is perceived costs rather than objectively measured costs that influence behavior. Some of the costs perceived by individuals are as follows.

1. The quality of education their child is receiving is declining or will decline.
2. Their child will be subjected to greater physical violence or emotional harassment.
3. Their child will be exposed to and probably influenced by values regarding academic achievement or social and sexual behavior that are not in the child's interest.
4. They will lose influence over their child's education.
5. Their property values will decline.

The decision to act on an assessment that desegregation will increase the costs and decrease the benefits of sending one's child to public school depends on several factors. Hirschman (1970) has developed some concepts that provide a framework for reviewing individual reaction to a controversial social change policy such as school desegregation. Individuals can react in three ways. First, they can remain "loyal" to their neighborhood or community. Loyalty may lead some people who believe that desegregation will reduce the quality of education to stay in their newly desegregated public schools anyway.

They may also engage in "voice." The most costly form of voice is the forming of citizen groups whose goal is to influence policymakers. The means commonly used include letter writing, marches, picketing, attendance at school board meetings, boycotts and similar activities. Because the costs of an organizing effort are great and the returns uncertain, this option will only be taken by a minority of citizens, primarily by those who cannot afford an alternative to the public school system.

The least costly form of voice for citizens is the vote. As a result, it is hypothesized that the vote will be a frequently adopted option for expressing dissatisfaction with a school desegregation decision because of its low cost compared to exit or group protest and because of its availability.

The third option for citizens is exit from their community. People will consider "exit" from the public schools when they perceive that the cost of seeking another option (private schools or suburban public schools) is lower than the cost they experience, or expect to experience, by staying in the public schools. In other words, exit occurs when the benefits of a move from the public schools outweigh the costs.

Community Response to Mandatory Desegregation

Rossell (1978c) has isolated four stages in the process of achieving mandatory school desegregation and, as a consequence, community social change. These include, both before and after implementation, (1) group protest demonstrations and individual protest voting, and (2) white flight. After implementation they include (3) attitudinal change and (4) behavioral change such as the election of blacks and residential integration.

In policy analytical terms, the negative consequences for social change in the community that result from the attempt to rid the community of school desegregation by protest demonstrations and voting and from the attempt to rid the individual of desegregation by exiting, are the indirect costs of the policy. The desired benefits of school desegregation are that it will influence people to have less prejudiced attitudes and to act in a less prejudiced manner in all aspects of community life.[4]

This review summarizes the research in each of the above areas, paying special attention to desegregation plan characteristics that can effectively increase interracial contact, minimize resegregation, and reduce protest and racial prejudice. The concepts and four stages of community social change outlined above will serve as the organizing framework.

THE EFFECT OF DESEGREGATION ON PROTEST DEMONSTRATIONS AND PROTEST VOTING

Although school desegregation provokes some degree of controversy in virtually all communities, significant protest occurs only in communities that have an environment conducive to it. This section describes research findings on the characteristics of protest demonstrators and the community social environment necessary for protest, the correlates of protest voting, and the effect of protest demonstrations and voting on school desegregation outcomes.

Characteristics of Protesters

While there have been numerous studies, both national and local, of the characteristics of those opposed to school desegregation, little systematic research has been conducted to determine who actually participates in protest activity. In analyzing protest, we are confronted with a paradox. Protest against school desegregation is a form of political participation. On the one hand, research findings suggest that those most opposed to school desegregation are lower-class, uneducated, racist, and southern. On the other hand, research into political participation indicates that those of higher social status tend to participate more than others in political activity.

The findings of four studies that analyze systematically the individual characteristics of protesters reflect the conflict between these two tendencies. A study of seven Florida county school districts, by Giles, Gatlin, and Cataldo (1976b, cited in Cataldo, Giles, and Gatlin, 1978, p. 37) found that among those who complied with the desegregation plan, the proportion of protesters increased as income, educational level, and occupational prestige rose; and that there was little difference between southerners and northerners. No other study has found this to be the case. Hayes' (1977) study of Indianapolis's desegregation plan, for example, found no direct or indirect relationship between protest and such individual characteristics as sex, income, and education.

Taylor and Stinchcombe (1977) found Catholics, less educated individuals, and younger people more likely to be mobilized for boycotts. Data collected in a 1976 and 1977 survey of Louisville-Jefferson County by McConahay and Hawley (1978) indicate that those in the upper working class (with high school degrees) are more likely to protest than either those with the least education or those with the most. In addition to this curvilinear relationship between class and participation in protest activity, their data suggest that while, in general, the working class participates in protest activity more than the middle class, protest leaders tend to come from the middle class. Moreover, the middle class participates at a much higher rate than the popular description of protesters would have led us to expect.

All of the above studies, as well as Begley and Alker (1978), have found participation in protest activities to be related to feelings of anomie, authoritarianism, racial prejudice, and opposition to school desegregation. Giles et al. (1976a) also found participation in protest by those of relatively high social status to be related to class prejudice. All of these factors affect the psychological costs of participation in protest or in the desegregation plan.

Protest Demonstrations and the Community Social Environment

Virtually all of the studies are in agreement that protest, because it is a deviant form of behavior, requires a supportive social environment, particularly at the neighborhood level, before it will manifest itself (Kirby, Harris, and Crain, 1973; Hayes, 1977; Taylor and Stinchcombe, 1977). The characteristics of the particular desegregation plan may also play a role in creating an environment supportive of protest. At the aggregate level, protest is positively related to the extent of white student reassignments to formerly black schools (Rossell, 1978b). Hence, as the likelihood that school desegregation will affect any given white increases, and as the costs increase (for example, change in school, greater distance from familiar neighborhood, and so on), the likelihood that entire white neighborhoods may be affected, and united in opposition, increases. This unity reduces informational costs, as well as the psychological costs of participating in an otherwise "deviant" act.

Rossell (1978b) also found that during the year preceding the implementation of court-ordered desegregation, public pronouncements for or against school desegregation by the political, business, and civic elite had little effect on protest. Public statements by city leaders may be ineffective because such techniques rarely influence what is important: the social support of the neighborhood environment and the tangible costs and benefits of the plan.

The fact that there has been a tendency for leadership statements in support of desegregation to be negatively related to the extent of the desegregation plan—the less the extent of white reassignments, the more positive the statements by leaders (most of whom are white)—may be the source of much confusion in the literature over the role of leaders. Studies that find leadership support of school desegregation to facilitate peaceful implementation may be confusing the effort of leadership support with the effect of a token plan.

Still, in the absence of any strong support by city leaders of school desegregation plans that require extensive reassignments, particularly of whites, it is difficult to say that such support would not reduce protest and violence. All that can be said with certainty is that there is no conclusive evidence.

Protest Voting

Only two studies (Lezotte, 1976; Rossell, 1975a) have specifically examined the effect on local elections of the process of implementing school desegregation, and both generally substantiate the principles of alienation theory, although with a new twist. This research indicates that in school districts that desegregate under court order, the voter turnout for school elections decreases after the implementation of desegregation, but there is no increase in dissent voting.

By contrast, school districts that have desegregated under a board order (that is, without a court order) evidence another pattern: the greater the desegregation, the higher the voter turnout and the greater the incidence of dissent voting in both school board elections and tax referenda (Rossell, 1975a). Presumably this relationship is due to the fact that the more extensive the desegregation plan, the more controversial and publicized it becomes. This attracts dissenting voters to the polls to punish their elected representatives.

While dissent voting is temporary (occurring immediately after the school desegregation decision is made and only rarely continuing past the year in which the plan is implemented), in the long term there is an increase in the voter turnout for school board elections in school districts where the median educational level is high, and desegregation has been extensive, but not court-ordered (Rossell, 1975a). Thus, in these communities the long-term effect of non-court-ordered school desegregation is to stimulate political participation.

The Effect of Protest on Desegregation Plans

Because protest demonstrations and protest voting are positively correlated with the extent of the desegregation plan, it follows that protest is generally not effective in preventing desegregation. Kirby et al. (1973) and Rossell (1978b) find that demonstrations begin after the decision to desegregate has been made—sometime during the middle of the school year before the plan is implemented—and peak during the opening week of school. They rarely occur before a decision is made because the information costs are too great, and they seldom persist past the year in which the plan is implemented because the likelihood of success is low. Rossell (1975a) finds that protest voting follows a similar pattern, although it will sometimes continue after the year of implementation.

Demonstrations

While there is no evidence that protest can prevent the implementation of a school desegregation plan, demonstrations may adversely affect desegregation efforts in two ways. First, there is some evidence they may accelerate white flight. Rossell (1978b) has shown that the degree of white flight in the year that desegregation is implemented is positively related to the level of protest in the first six months of the last school year before implementation, regardless of the extent of the desegregation plan. Thus, protest may reduce further the white enrollment needed to promote interracial contact.

Second, protest may negatively affect the behavior of students in the schools and, ultimately, educational outcomes. In Pontiac, Michigan, the U.S. Commission on Civil Rights (1973) found the drop in the number of student incidents to coincide with the decline in adult protest against the desegregation plan. Similarly, Richard, Knox, and Oliphant (1975) charted daily attendance in the Boston school system during the first year of the implementation of the school desegregation plan (1974–1975), and found that sharp drops in school attendance followed adult street disturbances. Moreover, as indicated in Weinberg's 1975 review of school desegregation research, community racial conflict and student disturbances may reduce the likelihood of minority achievement gains in desegregated schools.

Protest Voting

Because protest voting, like demonstrations, is positively related to the extent of desegregation, it follows that it, too, is not very effective in preventing implementation. As one might expect, defeats of school tax referenda have not been found to influence court or board orders. Much of the money used for desegregation programs comes from the federal government anyway (with the exception of that used for additional transportation).

Defeat of school board members in regular or recall elections clearly has a greater potential for affecting the characteristics of a desegregation plan than defeat of tax referenda. Yet Rossell's (1975a) study of 69 northern school districts found that in only one, Rochester, New York, did the defeat of incumbent school board members actually result in a desegregation plan being permanently rescinded. The defeat of the incumbent school board members in the Denver, Lansing and Detroit school district elections resulted in each plan's temporary rescission, but all were later ordered into effect by a federal court. Ironically, the district court in the Denver case (*Keyes* v. *School District No. 1*; 303, F. Supp. 279, 285 [D. Colo. 1969]) found that the rescission of the previous board's plan by the newly elected antibusing board was evidence of intentional segregation.

There are several plausible explanations for why dissent voting does not prevent the implementation of a desegregation plan. First, like demonstrations, dissent voting typically occurs after the decision to desegregate, and it is much more difficult to rescind a plan that has already been adopted than to avoid making the decision in the first place. Moreover, as suggested above, it is unlikely any court or school board would rescind a decision made on legal or educational grounds because the voters fail to approve a tax increase. Second, the decision to desegregate is obviously made in response to the presence of segregated schools. Therefore, if the board plan is rescinded, it is quite likely that a court will find this to be intentional segregation. If the dissent voting is in response to a school board's failure to appeal a court decision (as in the Pasadena recall election of 1970), it is unlikely that an appeal taken by a new antibusing school board will be successful. Finally, like demonstrations, protest voting is temporary. Therefore, its effect on the district's tax revenues will also be temporary, and its effect on the composition of the school board is significant only if there is a successful recall election where all the probusing members can be defeated at one time.

Summary

The research on protest indicates that the following propositions characterize this stage of social change:

1. Protest usually begins after the decision to desegregate the schools has been made and rarely continues past the implementation year.
2. The greater the proportion of white students reassigned to formerly black schools, the greater the degree of protest.
3. Participation in protest demonstrations has a curvilinear relationship to socioeconomic status. That is, protesters are more likely to come from the upper working class than the lower class or middle class.
4. Protest leaders tend to be middle class.
5. Protest demonstrations are dependent on a supportive community social environment, particularly at the neighborhood level. Moreover, there is no evidence that traditional methods of leadership influence (for example, public pronouncements) would reduce the level of protest.
6. Court-ordered desegregation results in a decrease in voter turnout for board elections but no change in dissent voting.
7. Increases in the turnout for board elections appear to be permanent in school districts with a high educational level that have implemented extensive desegregation without a court order.
8. Neither protest voting nor protest demonstrations are effective in preventing school desegregation once the decision has been made.
9. Adult protest demonstrations are related to student disturbances within the schools and to declines in student attendance.
10. Protest demonstrations increase the amount of white flight from public schools.

SCHOOL DESEGREGATION AND WHITE FLIGHT

The ineffectiveness of protest demonstrations and protest voting in preventing desegregation, once the decision has been made, will impel some people to attempt to avoid school desegregation even though the community is still forced to undergo it. The extent of this avoidance, however, cannot be predicted from the amount of community opposition to school desegregation or to busing. White flight depends not only on attitudes, but also on the availability of options for avoiding desegregation and the costs of avoidance in comparison to the perceived costs of compliance. These costs will vary greatly according to the characteristics of the plan and of the individual.

This section describes the impact of school desegregation (1) on residential out-migration and in-migration; (2) on white public school enrollment in the year that the plan is implemented and the causes of variation in this; (3) on long-term white enrollment; and (4) on interracial contact in both the long and the short run.

The best way to determine the effect of desegregation on white flight is to conduct a survey of predesegregation attitudes toward racial integration issues, behavioral intentions with regard to moving or withdrawing children from the public schools (in the absence of any knowledge of future desegregation), and postdesegregation attitudes, behavioral intentions, and actual behavior. The only such study that exists is a case study of Boston[5] analyzed in Estabrook (1980) and Ross (1977) which, although well designed, is not fully completed and which, because of the peculiarities of Boston and the original goals of the study, may be limited in its generalizability. The costs of a comparative study of several urban school districts, using such a methodology, would be astronomical. Thus, the comparative studies that are available are aggregate analyses, and the surveys, with the exception of Estabrook (1980) and Ross (1977), are postimplementation case studies.[6]

Residential Out-Migration and In-Migration in Response to School Desegregation

White flight from the public schools may take two forms: the transfer of students to private schools within the district and the movement of families out of the school district. Intuitively, the former would seem less damaging to a community than the latter, in part because the likelihood of returning to the public schools is much greater, but also because these individuals will remain a part of whatever community social change occurs. A counterargument can be made, however, that transfer to private schools within the school district is more damaging than movement to the suburbs because at least with the latter there is the possibility that the families who move out will be replaced by families who may put their children in the public schools. When families transfer to private schools, no such replacement can occur.

Unfortunately, most of the research makes no distinction between the two forms of white flight since the dependent variable is usually aggregate change in white public school enrollment. There are, however, five case studies of four different school districts that are able to make this distinction because of their use of survey sampling techniques or analysis of the local housing market. These studies indicate that, in most cases, there is little residential relocation in response to school desegregation. Three of the studies are of countywide plans so this finding should not be surprising, since the costs of relocation are greater in these districts than in city school districts. According to Lord (1975) only 0.2 percent of the Charlotte-Mecklenburg county school population moved to neighboring Union county. Studies of Louisville (McConahay and Hawley, 1978; Husk, 1980; Cunningham, 1980) have found little residential relocation, but these analyses were only of the postimplementation years. Since white flight is greatest in the year of implementation, this methodology may underestimate the amount of residential relocation that occurred, although it reveals useful information about the long-term effects.

The most important of the case studies is Estabrook's (1980) survey analysis because it is the only one that uses a quasi-experimental panel survey design. Her analysis (1980, p. 202) indicates that of those white residents in the sampled Boston neighborhoods who withdrew their children from the public schools after desegregation, 55 percent transferred their children to parochial schools while 45 percent moved to the suburbs during the implementation of desegregation. Orfield (1978b), by contrast, found almost no white flight to the suburbs in his analysis of the Los Angeles housing market in 1978, the year that desegregation was implemented.

All of the studies, including the two of citywide school districts (Boston and Los Angeles), support the theory that whatever the motivating factor, whites calculate the costs and benefits of their actions and tend to choose the course of action with the lowest costs. This is particularly illuminated by the surveys in Louisville (McConahay and Hawley, 1978) and in Boston (Estabrook, 1980), which found that of the families who withdrew their children from the public schools, those who moved to the suburbs rather than transferring to parochial or private schools were most likely to be those for whom moving was less costly—that is, renters, young people, and those without children. They also tended to be more pro–school desegregation. As a result of this tendency for those most supportive of desegregation to move, longitudinal nonpanel surveys will consistently underestimate positive attitudinal change.

The conclusions of two aggregate national studies (Clotfelter, 1976a; Frey 1977) of the effect of school desegregation on white suburbanization are not relevant because both analyzed white migration during the period from 1960 to 1970.[7] There was very little desegregation during this time and virtually no mandatory reassignment of white students.

Over the long term, nonentrance may become more of a problem than flight. For one thing, nonentrance obviously has lower relocation costs. Furthermore, information on public schools is easier to obtain for parents who already have their children in public school than for parents who do not; thus, the latter have an additional disincentive to placing their children in the public school system. Surveys of Louisville-Jefferson County (Mc-Conahay and Hawley, 1978; Husk, 1980), Nashville-Davidson (Pride, 1980), and Boston (Rossell and Ross, 1979), confirm that the long-term loss is greater among those with preschool children than among those whose children are already enrolled in the public school system.

On the other hand, the Cunningham (1980) and Husk (1980) study of Louisville (derived from their joint research project) indicates that *residential nonentrance* is a small and insignificant factor, at least in countywide school systems. Although an estimated 312 families moved out of the school system in 1975–1976 to avoid school desegregation, they were apparently replaced by families with school-age children, since the decline in white public school enrollment in Louisville-Jefferson County can be accounted for by the increase in private school enrollment and the declining birth rate. Husk (1980) found, however, that most of those white families who moved into Jefferson County placed their children in private schools rather than public schools.

The Effect of Desegregation on White Public School Enrollment in the Year of Implementation

Early Studies Finding No White Flight From Desegregation

Most of the early national aggregate analyses covering the period from 1967 (or earlier) to 1972 found little or no white flight as a result of school desegregation after controlling for the other causes of declining white enrollment. This is because there was little desegregation before 1970. Urban economists suggest that the decline in white public school enrollment that began in the 1960s (long before the advent of mandatory school desegregation plans) is in large part a function of the post–World War II white suburbanization trend.

In addition, the declining white birth rate has on its own caused a reduction of almost 1 percent in overall white school enrollments since 1968. The yearly decrease is now almost 2 percent. The black school-age population has only recently begun to decline because of a declining birth rate (U.S. Bureau of the Census, 1976; Sly and Pol, 1978).

Although the studies analyzing this period are limited in usefulness because there was little mandatory desegregation, problems with individual studies are instructive as to how analysis of this subject should be conducted. First, all studies that look at a single change measured over a four-, five-, or ten-year period may be misleading if they do not distinguish between pre- and postdesegregation enrollment losses (Farley, 1975; Fitzgerald and Morgan, 1977; Becker, 1978; Coleman, Kelly, and Moore, 1975a). Second, change in percentage white should not be used as a dependent variable, as has sometimes been done, because it can make minority in-migration look like white loss

(Mercer and Scout, 1974; Rossell, 1975b). Third, samples should be analyzed both in their entirety and as separate groups so that the effect of each technique is apparent. Jackson's (1975) reanalysis of James S. Coleman's early white flight study (data from 1967 to 1972), found no relationship between school desegregation and white flight when the entire sample was analyzed together and other variables were controlled. This suggests that Coleman found a relationship only because he divided his sample into large and small school districts. (The effect was found only in large districts.) Overall, there seems to have been no statistically significant desegregation effect during this period, primarily because of the small number of plans with mandatory white reassignments.

In addition to these national aggregate analyses, there are several regional case studies or comparative case studies (Giles et al., 1976b; Bosco and Robin, 1974) that also found little or no white flight. The most widely cited of these is the Giles et al. (1976b) study of seven Florida school districts, from which have come numerous articles. There are, however, two problems with it that limit its utility in estimating the extent of white flight attributable to school desegregation. First, because it is a study of seven countywide school districts in Florida that desegregated between 1969 and 1971, it does not fit the typical northern or southern experience where the central city school district desegregates while the surrounding suburbs remain segregated.

Second, and most important, it is not a study of the effect on white enrollment of implementing a desegregation plan. By classifying as "rejectors" those parents whose children were enrolled in public schools in 1971–1972, but not in 1972–1973, Giles et al. failed to analyze the implementation year in every school district in their sample, because all had desegregated in 1971 or earlier.

The significance of this is twofold. First, by analyzing only postimplementation years, they underestimate the amount of white flight that may have occurred, since it is greatest in the implementation year. Second, the relationship between racism and white rejection may be underestimated. Parents who decide to try school desegregation for a year or two and then end up withdrawing their children often have reasons for doing so—for example, failure of a child to adjust, grade problems, problems with transportation—substantially different from those of a parent who rejects desegregation outright without even trying it (that is, the implementation year effect). The study by Giles et al. is nevertheless, a useful contribution to our understanding of the characteristics of desegregation plans that cause variations in white flight, as long as it is understood that the study is of postimplementation years only.

Early Studies Finding White Flight from Desegregation

Perhaps the most publicized and controversial study finding a relationship between school desegregation and white flight during the period examined in the studies cited above (no later than fall 1972) is that of James S. Coleman and his associates. There are two Coleman white flight studies, and most of the criticisms are of the earlier study. This study, presented at the American Educational Research Association meeting in April 1975, analyzed the effect of change in segregation from fall 1968 to fall 1969 on change in white enrollment from fall 1970 to fall 1972. This particular time-lag method is inappropriate for analyzing this phenomenon, since most school desegregation occurred in the later, rather than in the earlier, period. The effects of present and future desegregation are thus confused. In addition, the entire sample was never analyzed as a whole. If it had been, the statistically insignificant relationship found by others would have become apparent.

Munford's (1973) study of 30 school districts in Mississippi ordered to desegregate in the fall of 1969–1970 has been cited occasionally as demonstrating no white flight from desegregation. This is not the case. It unequivocally demonstrates extraordinary white flight from desegregation at the time of implementation. What may be misinterpreted as an optimistic finding is that this flight does not always continue after the implementation year and is not always related in the same way to the racial balance in the schools.

Although most of the early studies were flawed in methodology or in their measurement of variables, the differences in conclusions are due not to these problems but primarily to variations in the time period and the sample analyzed. Had everyone understood this, there probably would have been much less controversy.

Later Studies Finding White Flight from Desegregation

The later Coleman study (1975b) is different from the earlier one. First, it covers the period from fall 1968 through fall 1973, thus including for the first time Memphis's desegregation which produced the largest white enrollment loss in the United States. Second, a different method of analysis was employed. In the later study, a pooled cross-sectional change analysis was used to analyze the effect of desegregation on white enrollment change in the same year. The analysis indicates that a substantial desegregation plan results in a doubling of the normal proportional white enrollment loss (an additional 6 percent) in the year of implementation.

All of the later studies by the researchers discussed above have concluded that school desegregation does indeed accelerate white flight in the year of implementation. Farley, Richards, and Wurdock's (1980) study of the 100 largest metropolitan areas through fall 1974 suggests that most cities will have a doubling of their normal white loss rate (from 4 to 8 percent) with a reduction of twenty points in their index of dissimilarity.

Clotfelter's 1979 reanalysis of Coleman's data, using the same pooled yearly cross-sectional change analysis, found that an increase in white exposure to black students in any one year has a strong negative effect on white enrollment in that year if the proportion black in the average white child's school is more than 7 percent. For districts with less than 7 percent black in the average white child's school, change in interracial exposure has no significant effect on white enrollment.[8]

Rossell's (1978a) study of the impact of school desegregation reassignments on white enrollment in 113 school districts through fall 1975 uses a quasi-experimental methodology that permits the analysis of effects peculiar to the period before, during, and after desegregation. The average desegregation plan—30 percent blacks reassigned, 5 percent whites reassigned, with a reduction in segregation of 30 percentage points—results in an additional reduction of 5 percentage points in the white enrollment in city school districts less than 35 percent black, 2 percentage points in countywide school districts less than 35 percent black, 8 percentage points in city school districts greater than 35 percent black, and 6 percentage points in countywide school districts greater than 35 percent black. What distinguishes this study from others is the separation of black reassignments to white schools from white reassignments to black schools as independent variables. All other comparative school district studies combine black and white reassignments when measuring changes in segregation. As will be discussed later, failing to distinguish between these different policy measures can produce misleading results.

Armor (1980) attempts to correct for this in his analysis of 52 northern and southern school districts that desegregated under court order. His incorrect assumption is that school districts that desegregate under court order will all have mandatory white reassignments. As indicated above there are numerous instances, some very recent—such as San Diego (1977) and Milwaukee (1976)—in which courts have allowed plans that call for no mandatory reassignments of whites. Moreover, there is extraordinary variation in the proportion of whites reassigned in different court-ordered desegregation plans. Because Armor does not calculate the proportion of whites reassigned, or even how much desegregation has been accomplished, he is unable to determine why the white enrollment loss in the court-ordered school districts in his sample varies from an additional 2 percentage points in Springfield, Massachusetts, to an additional 36 percentage points in Jackson, Mississippi, after the implementation of desegregation. There are also problems with Armor's methodology that make his findings somewhat suspect. These are discussed in Rossell (1981, pp. 26–29, 76).

The latest comparative analysis of the relationship between school desegregation and white flight is that conducted by Taeuber and Wilson (1979b). Because of the methodological problems discussed in Rossell (1981, pp. 26–29, 76), this study (and its conclusion that school desegregation does not produce white flight) is uninterpretable and is excluded from further tabulations, such as the table shown below and the review of research findings.

Table 2-2 indicates the average additional white enrollment decline in a school district for desegregation plans with both black and white reassign-

TABLE 2-2

Implementation Year Findings on Additional
White Enrollment Decline Due to Desegregation by
Percentage and Number of Studies

| Type of | | Districts > 35% Black | | | |
Reassignment		10–8%	7–4%	3–1%	0
Average 2-way	%	63	38		
reassignment[a]	N	(5)	(3)		
Average 1-way	%	30	30	30	
reassignment[b]	N	(1)	(1)	(1)	
		Districts < 35% Black			
		10–8%	7–4%	3–1%	0
Average 2-way	%	29	43	29	
reassignment[a]	N	(2)	(3)	(2)	
Average 1-way	%	30		30	30
reassignment[b]	N	(1)		(1)	(1)

Notes
[a] − 30 points index of dissimilarity
  30 percent blacks reassigned
  5 percent whites reassigned

[b] − 3 points index of dissimilarity
  8 percent blacks reassigned

ments and with black reassignments only in two types of school districts: those above 35 percent black and those below 35 percent black. Since most studies use an aggregate measure of change in school segregation and do not differentiate between black and white reassignments, they had to be reinterpreted and their desegregation measures converted to black and white, or black only, reassignments. This was done by means of the equation predicting change in segregation from black and white reassignments in Rossell (1978a). The average desegregation plan with black and white reassignments entails a reduction in segregation of 30 percentage points, 30 percent of blacks reassigned and 5 percent of whites reassigned. The average black-only desegregation plan entails a reduction in segregation of 3 percentage points and 8 percent of blacks reassigned.

The studies that have been conducted at the school level indicate that the average big city school system above 35 percent minority can expect that 35 to 50 percent of those white students reassigned to minority schools will not show up (Rossell, 1980; Rossell and Ross, 1979). Pride (1980), using a cohort retention rate technique similar to that used in Armor (1980), found the white cohort loss rate was as high as 49 percent in two elementary schools located in black areas in Nashville. The average white loss rate for schools in black areas, however, was 24 percent. For cluster schools in white areas, by contrast, the average white loss rate was 7 percent.

Causes of Variations

In most comparative white flight studies, the only characteristic of the plan that is measured is the change in district segregation. Thus, we typically have little or no information about how other aspects of a plan affect individual calculations of costs and benefits and, ultimately, behavior. Such characteristics as the source of the desegregation order, the type of reassignments (for example, black reassignments to white schools and white reassignments to black schools), as well as other plan characteristics are usually not included in the analysis.

White versus Black Reassignments

Numerous case studies have noted that white flight is greater when whites are reassigned to minority schools than when minorities are reassigned to white schools (Lord, 1975; Lord and Catau, 1976; Lord, 1977; Pride and Woodard, 1978; Pride, 1980; Giles et al., 1976a; Rossell and Ross, 1979). In addition, one comparative national analysis using multiple regression (Rossell, 1978a) also has demonstrated the disparate effect of white and black reassignments. Although Taeuber and Wilson (1979b) criticize the calculation of estimated white reassignments in Rossell (1978a) (see Rossell, 1981, pp. 77–78), Rossell and Ross's (1979) analysis of loss rates in Boston schools from 1974 to 1979, which used actual white reassignments obtained from the Boston School Department, produced essentially the same results. Both studies show white reassignments to produce two to three times as much white flight as black reassignments. Hence, studies such as Colemen et al. (1975a, 1975b), Farley, (1975), Farley et al. (1980), Armor (1980), and Taeuber and Wilson (1979b), which lump both types of reassignments into one aggregate measure of change in segregation, will often produce misleading results, particularly when these are related to other characteristics of the plan.

There are very similar white "no-show" rates wherever white students are reassigned to black schools regardless of whether it is done in the year of implementation or a later year (Rossell and Ross, 1979; Giles, Gatin, and Cataldo, 1974; Husk, 1980). In short, every time you reassign white students you lose a portion of them. Thus, it may be that the reason that the white enrollment loss rate declines in most school districts in the years after implementation is simply that they do not reassign students after that.

The Interaction Between School Desegregation and Proportion Black

Virtually all of the aggregate studies have determined that a school district or school with a large proportion of students who are black will have more white flight with a given desegregation plan than will a school district with a small proportion of students who are black. Whites will perceive the probable costs and possible risks to be greater in the first case.

Rossell (1978a), Giles et al. (1976a), and Giles, Cataldo, and Gatlin (1975) argue that the tipping-point theory, which orginated in studies of residential succession, does not adequately explain the pattern of white flight that occurs when the central school administration, either on its own or under court order, reassigns students for the purposes of desegregation.

Although there is some confusion in the literature, school desegregation resulting from residential succession and that resulting from administratively controlled desegregation are different phenomena. In the blue-collar, northern residential succession model, blacks begin moving into a neighborhood and, as a result, the neighborhood school becomes increasingly black primarily because whites who move out are not replaced by other whites. Thus, the unwilling white family is exposed to two types of desegregation—residential desegregation and school desegregation—as a combined economic and social threat. There is no administrative control of this process, and thus it may begin to accelerate after reaching a certain proportion black, usually estimated to be 30 percent, although there is no agreement over this.[9] Cities typically have few, if any, resources with which to stabilize this process, and rarely do any try. Therefore, it is not unreasonable for a white parent to assume that once this process of residential succession begins, both the neighborhood and school ultimately will become all black.[10]

With administratively controlled school desegregation, by contrast, desegregation occurs immediately and only in the school, not in the neighborhood. In addition, although the white family may be unwilling to desegregate, it at least has a guarantee of racial balance. Indeed, white families living in racially changing neighborhoods often have a *reduction* in the proportion black in their school because the school is racially balanced to conform to the citywide proportion, rather than to that of the neighborhood.

The studies of school desegregation and white flight have found either a first-order interaction effect between school desegregation and the proportion black (or minority) (Coleman et al., 1975a, 1975b; Farley, 1975; Farley et al., 1980; Pride and Woodard, 1978; Pride, 1980; Rossell and Ross, 1979; Rossell, 1980) or a threshold effect (Giles et al., 1975; Giles et al., 1976b; Rossell, 1978a) in the year of implementation. A first-order interaction effect means that the greater the proportion black and the greater the desegregation, the more white flight there is. With a threshold effect, however, the rate of white rejection increases at a specific percentage minority, but not after that.[11] For example, Giles et al. (1975) found that the rate of white rejection increased when a school became 30 percent black and also when it became 50 percent black but did not increase for increases in the percentage black between 30 and 50 percent or above 50 percent. Rossell's (1978a) study of 113 school districts found a threshold effect at 35 percent black in the school district, at which point white flight increased substantially.[12]

Phasing-In Desegregation Plans

Some school districts phase-in their desegregation plans over two or three years, either by grade level or geographic region. For example, in fall 1974 Boston implemented a partial desegregation plan affecting only certain neighborhoods. In fall 1975 this was expanded to include the rest of the city's neighborhoods. Some school districts desegregate one grade level (for example, high schools or only elementary schools) in the first year, and then expand the plan to the other two grade levels in later years. The school district's rationale for doing this is that the task of desegregating an entire school system in one year is so difficult that implementation will go smoother if it can be spread out over several years.

There is evidence, however, that phased-in plans that include mandatory white reassignments may cause greater white flight than plans that are implemented in their entirety in one year (Rossell, 1978a; Armor, 1980; Morgan and England, 1982). Phased-in plans usually publicize the desegregation expansion planned for the next stages, alerting parents to their child's impending reassignment. Parents thus have more time to locate alternative schooling, housing, or jobs outside of the desegregating school district.

Metropolitan Plans

Most studies and experts agree that metropolitan plans, or countywide plans, all other things being equal, will have less white flight in response to school desegregation than city-only plans. There are three reasons for this. First, because countywide plans incorporate suburban areas (where blacks typically are underrepresented), they will have a smaller proportion of students who are black in their school system than most city school districts. Second, there will be a diminished opportunity for residential relocation to a more segregated school district, and thus the decline in white enrollment will be less in the desegregating school district (see Coleman et al., 1975b; Farley et al., 1980; Armor, 1980; Rossell, 1978a). Third, countywide school districts will contain more of the suburban amenities that prompted middle-class suburbanization in the first place, and thus the "pull" factors stimulating movement to areas outside the school district will not be as strong as in city school districts.

Southern versus Northern School Districts

The evidence is inconclusive as to whether southern city school districts have a greater decline in white enrollment than northern school districts with the same desegregation plan. Coleman et al. (1975a, 1975b) found such an effect, but Clotfelter (1979), in reanalyzing Coleman's data, did not. Determining a North-South difference is made extremely difficult because of the problem of multicollinearity: southern school districts tend to be countywide, and almost all northern school districts are only citywide. Since countywide school districts have less white flight, the effect of southernness is observed.

Board-Ordered versus Court-Ordered Plans

As indicated at the beginning of this essay, such terms as mandatory and voluntary desegregation are often confused with court-ordered and board-ordered desegregation. "Mandatory" and "voluntary" refer to the degree of parental choice, whereas "court-ordered" and "board-ordered" refer to the source of the order to desegregate.

Many observers have assumed that court-ordered desegregation, all other things being equal, leads to greater white flight than board-ordered plans. There is simply no evidence to substantiate this. Because the proportion of students reassigned—particularly white students—is much greater in court-ordered plans than in board-ordered plans, and because few board-ordered plans include mandatory white reassignments, the white flight resulting from these two types of plans cannot be compared. Berkeley, the only school district in Rossell's (1978a) study with a board-ordered plan that mandatorily reassigned a significant proportion of white students to black schools, actually had a greater proportional white loss than Pasadena, the most extensive court-ordered plan in the same sample. This suggests that the characteristics of the plan—for example, whether there is parental choice regarding reassignments—are much more important in influencing white flight than the source of the order.

Elementary versus Secondary School Desegregation

Evidence that white flight is greater with elementary school desegregation than with secondary school desegregation is found in three case studies of school loss rates—one of Denver (Rossell, 1978a) and two of Boston (Massachusetts Research Center, 1976:20; Rossell and Ross, 1979)—and one national meta-analysis (Morgan and England, 1982). Although elementary school desegregation produces more educational and social benefits than secondary school desegregation, the psychological costs to both black and white parents are greater.

Social Status and White Flight

Parental income and, to a lesser degree, education are related to the degree of white student withdrawal from desegregated schools. Parents who withdraw their children in response to school desegregation tend to have more options, because of a higher income and educational level, than those who stay (Giles et al., 1976b; Lord, 1975; Pride and Woodard, 1978; Pride, 1980; Rossell, 1980). Not only do these parents have more options for exiting, but they accord more importance to the risk of a possible decline in educational quality.

Parental Attitudes

Only one study examining attitudes has been able to find a relationship between white flight and racism (Cusick, Gerbing, and Russell, 1979). This does not mean, however, that racism is not an important factor. The relationship between white flight and racism is obscured by the fact that all whites tend to have some degree of racial prejudice, and those with the most racial prejudice tend to be the least able to afford to withdraw their children. In order to detect a relationship between racism and white flight from school desegregation, one would have to control for the availability of alternatives to the public schools—and the ability to use them—and have more variation in racial prejudice than currently exists (for example, a substantial number of whites with no racial prejudice).

Minority School Educational Quality

The few studies examining school characteristics suggest that such nonracial characteristics of the minority receiving school as the quality of the physical plant, the average school reading scores, the median socioeconomic status, and the suspension rate have no relationship to white flight (Pride and Woodard, 1978; Rossell, 1980). It is not that whites do not care about school quality, but probably that the cost of obtaining this information is so high that most will rely on the racial composition of the school, or another easily obtained piece of information, as a surrogate.

One easily obtained piece of information is school size. The larger the size of the school before desegregation, the greater the white flight in both the implementation and postimplementation year (Rossell, 1980). In addition, newly constructed schools, even in minority neighborhoods, all other things being equal, have less white flight than older schools (Massachusetts Research Center, 1976; Rossell and Ross, 1979).

School District Size

Only one comparative analysis has found school district size to be a variable affecting the extent of white flight (Coleman et al., 1975a, 1975b). Other research suggests that the proportion black, and to a lesser degree, the average busing distance, are the important causal variables. Although these factors tend to be greater in large cities, they are also found to be high in many medium and small school districts, and in such instances to produce significant white flight.

Busing Distances

The research findings on the effect of busing distances on white flight seem contradictory. One important difference between the studies that do not find a white flight effect (Giles et al., 1976a; Pride and Woodard, 1978; Pride, 1980) and those that do (Massachusetts Research Center, 1976; Rossell 1980), is that the former are all of county school districts and the latter are all of city school districts. Moreover, a relationship between busing distance and white flight has been observed only in the implementation year. Parents who are willing to have their children bused a certain distance, or who do not have the means to withdraw them in the first year of desegregation, do not cite as a reason for doing so later that the bus ride is "too long." One reason may be that they have lower information costs regarding the effect of a bus ride—at least one study suggests that children actually like riding a bus (McConahay and Hawley, 1977a). There is an interaction effect between busing distance (at the time of onset or increase) and the proportion black in the receiving school (Giles and Gatlin, 1980; Rossell, 1980): when both perceived costs are incurred, the white flight effect is greater than the sum of the white flight effects from each in isolation.

Because of the cost of busing, school districts may be tempted to stagger school starting times in order to minimize the number of buses that have to be bought or rented. Pride and Woodard (1978) find that staggered school starting times will produce greater white flight as a result of the inconvenience to parents who have children going to school at different times.

The Role of Protest and City Leadership

Few studies have examined systematically the effect of protest and leadership support for desegregation on white flight, primarily because the costs of collecting such data are quite high. Even the Giles et al. (1976b) study, which has data on the protest activity of those parents interviewed, does not try to relate the amount of protest to the amount of white flight, although they note that protesters were no more likely to withdraw their children from the public schools than those who did not protest.

The two studies to systematically examine city leadership find it has no relationship to white flight. Giles and Gatlin (1980) demonstrate that compliers, potential avoiders, and actual avoiders do not differ in their perception of local school leaders' support or opposition to school desegregation. Rossell's (1978b) ten city study found, after controlling for the extent of school desegregation and the degree of protest, that leadership statements had no effect on white flight. The findings of both studies may be partly a result of the lack of leadership statements of any kind, and particularly in support of school desegregation.

The Role of the Media in Publicizing Protest

Newspaper coverage of school desegregation appears to have a significant effect on white flight. Rossell (1978b) found this to be true even after controlling for the extent of school desegregation reassignments, the proportion black, and the level of protest. The more negative the coverage of desegregation during the predesegregation school year, the greater the white flight. Protest demonstrations (as reported in the press) during the first six months of this year can increase white flight by symbolically illustrating the perceived costs of school desegregation.

The Long-Term Effect of White Flight

Most studies of the effect of school desegregation on white flight are of the implementation year. To measure the long-term effect of desegregation on white flight, a quasi-experimental design (pre- and postdesegregation observations and a control group) should be employed. Only Rossell (1978a) and Armor (1980) have done this. Nevertheless, four other studies employing different approaches also have produced some useful information on the long-term effects of desegregation (McConahay and Hawley, 1978; Coleman et al., 1975b; Farley et al., 1980; Cunningham, 1980; Husk, 1980; Pride, 1980).

Rossell's (1978a) analysis of the long-term effect in a sample of 113 school districts indicates that the effect in the year of implementation is offset in postimplementation years by lower-than-normal white enrollment losses. This decreased loss is especially pronounced in the fifth year of desegregation. Recent analysis of a subsample of this data set indicates, however, that desegregation still has a negative effect by the fifth year of desegregation in large, central city school districts. That, overall, desegregation had a positive effect on white enrollment loss was due to the countywide and suburban school districts that had desegregated.[13]

Coleman et al. (1975b) and Farley et al. (1980) also found school desegregation to have a nonnegative effect in postimplementation years. Roberts's (1978) analysis of 58 school districts found that if desegregation reassignments were 20 percent of the enrollment (that is, average desegregation), the district would lose an additional 8.5 percent of its white enrollment in the short run, but gain an additional 6.1 percent over the long run. All of these analyses may overestimate the positive long-term effects because they make no distinction between black and white reassignments. As noted above, black reassignments have a much less negative effect on white flight than have white reassignments.

The McConahay and Hawley (1978) survey of Louisville-Jefferson County in 1976 and 1977 indicates a dramatic decline in the proportion of white children who will be withdrawn from the public schools in the second and third years of the plan. It is estimated that between 10 and 15 percent will be withdrawn in the year of implementation; the proportion who will be withdrawn at the end of the first year because of busing is less than 2 percent. By the end of the second year, 1976–77, the proportion of parents saying that they would withdraw their children from the public schools because of busing was down to less than 1 percent. This indicates almost no effect, given the divergence between intent and action.

Nevertheless, as indicated above, there may be some significant nonentrance effects. One type of nonentrance occurs if residents do not enroll their children in the public schools when they reach school age. Rossell and Ross (1979) have found that Boston residents are still enrolling their first graders at a lower rate than before desegregation. Pride (1980) finds very much the same thing in his cohort retention analysis of Nashville-Davidson. Husk's (1980) cohort survival analysis of Louisville, on the other hand, shows declining white flight since school desegregation in 1975.

McConahay and Hawley (1978) find that almost 16 percent of the parents in Louisville-Jefferson County with children too young to attend school indicated at the end of the first year of the desegregation plan that they did not intend to send their children to the public schools because of busing. Assuming that these children are evenly distributed over the five preschool years and that there is a divergence between intent and action, each year about 1 to 2 percent of the eligible white children will not be enrolled when they reach school age. The study does not, however, provide information on differences between neighborhoods; the nonentrance effect in some neighborhoods may be offset by less-than-normal losses in others.

The Armor (1980) study of 54 court-ordered districts is one of the few to conclude that court-ordered, mandatory central city and county school desegregation has a long-term negative effect on white enrollment in school districts where there is at least 20 percent minority and suburbs are available. He estimates that at the end of the fourth year of desegregation, these school districts will still have a loss rate that is twice their normal rate. As noted above, there are problems associated with using 1970, 1960, or 1950 census data to predict annual changes a decade later. The further along in time one gets the less accurate such predictions should be.

Overall, the findings of this research suggest that school desegregation has different long-term effects in different kinds of school districts. There is still a negative effect in the fifth year of desegregation in large, high proportion black, central city school districts (Rossell, 1978a; Armor, 1980; Coleman, 1977; Ross, Gratton, and Clarke, 1981). The overall positive effect of desegregation on white enrollment found in some studies may be produced by the lower-than-normal white enrollment losses often found in some countywide and suburban school districts in the fourth and fifth year of desegregation, or may be a consequence of combining black and white reassignments into a single measure of change.

The Effect of White Flight on Desegregation

There is no good evidence on the effect of white flight on educational results in the classroom. We know, however, that the parents most likely to withdraw their children are those who have the highest levels of income and education and that, in Los Angeles, the white schools with the highest achievement scores had the greatest white enrollment losses. Clearly, this is not beneficial, but because we do not know how much the socioeconomic status of a child's classmates contributes to his or her achievement, it is difficult to say what is the net educational effect of the loss of high-achieving, high-status white students.

The impact of white flight on the instrumental goal of interracial contact can, however, be measured by using an index of black exposure to whites that reflects white flight and thus measures the net benefit.[14] Rossell (1978a) finds that even the most extensive desegregation plan involving mandatory white reassignments produces greater interracial contact than no desegregation, and this net benefit continues for at least four years after the implementation of desegregation. Recent additional analysis conducted by Rossell in Boston indicates that, although white flight was extensive in the year of implementation, and still continues, though at a lower rate, the level of interracial contact in Boston in fall 1979 was almost twice as high as it would have been if no desegregation had occurred.

Coleman et al. (1975b, p. 75) found very much the same thing. Their equations show that school districts that desegregate have, at the end of a ten-year period after desegregation, a level of interracial contact that is still twice that of school districts that have not desegregated, despite a relatively greater decline in white enrollment during this period.

Rossell (1979) finds that although magnet-mandatory school desegregation plans produce significantly greater white flight than voluntary desegregation plans, they also produce more than twice the interracial contact. Unfortunately, these data do not allow for the testing of long-term effects. As indicated above, Armor (1980) argues that if mandatory plans were compared to voluntary plans, rather than to no plan at all, ultimately the voluntary plans would produce greater interracial contact because they would produce less white flight over the long term. To date, there is not sufficient evidence to support this claim.

Summary

The research on school desegregation and white flight indicates that the following propositions characterize the phenomenon of white flight:

1. The case studies find that most flight from desegregation takes the form of relocation to private schools within the district, rather than residential relocation outside the district.
2. The average court-ordered desegregation plan—about 30 percent black students and 5 percent white students reassigned, with a reduction in segregation of 30 points—results in an additional white enrollment loss of 8 to 10 percentage points in the year of implementation in school districts above 35 percent black.
3. White reassignments to formerly black schools result in two to three times the white enrollment loss of black reassignments to white schools.
4. Most studies find white flight to be a function of a first-order interaction effect

between school desegregation and proportion black. Two studies show a threshold effect at 30 or 35 percent black.

5. White flight has no relation to the educational quality and social status of the minority receiving school.

6. The greater the busing distance, the greater the white flight, but only in the implementation years.

7. There is greater white flight from elementary school desegregation than from secondary school desegregation.

8. Phased-in plans may result in greater white flight than plans implemented in one year because the more advance notice white parents receive, the more white flight results.

9. Negative newspaper coverage of desegregation during the year before implementation increases white flight.

10. The greater the extent of protest demonstrations during the year before desegregation, the greater the white flight.

11. Those who withdraw their children from the public schools because of school desegregation tend to be of higher income and educational level than those who do not. White schools with higher achievement levels have greater loss rates with desegregation than those with lower achievement levels.

12. Metropolitan desegregation plans have less white enrollment loss than do city school district desegregation plans.

13. The long-term effect of school desegregation on white flight appears to be neutral or positive in countywide and suburban school districts.

14. There is a tendency for families already residing in the school district not to enroll preschool students when they reach school-age because of school desegregation, but it is difficult to estimate the long-term effect of this.

15. School desegregation continues to have a negative long-term effect on white enrollment change in large, central-city school districts above 35 percent minority.

16. The more extensive the school desegregation plan the greater the net benefit in terms of the instrumental goal of interracial contact (the proportion white in the average black child's school), despite implementation year losses in white enrollment. Moreover, this net benefit is evident as long as four years later and the effect is greatest in school districts with enrollments at or above 35 percent black, despite the fact that it is these districts that experience the greatest white enrollment loss upon desegregation.

17. Magnet-mandatory desegregation plans produce more interracial contact, despite greater white flight, than magnet-only plans, at least over the short run.

SCHOOL DESEGREGATION AND COMMUNITY ATTITUDES

This section describes (1) the findings of national surveys on racial attitudes and opinions; (2) the distribution of attitudes in a small number of desegregated communities; (3) voting behavior in a small number of desegregated communities; and (4) the effect of the climate of opinion in the community on student attitudes. The notion that school desegregation might bring about a positive change in attitudes toward racial issues is based on the research findings of two decades of social psychological research. This cognitive dissonance research indicates that when people are forced to change their behavior so that behavior is congruent with attitudes, attitudes will change in order to conform to behavior. A significant component of the theory that explains these research findings is that the greatest attitudinal changes will occur when the least force is used. Thus, the extent and direction of attitude change is likely to depend not only on the characteristics of the individual involved, but also on the degree to which force is associated with the desegregation process. It is likely that the greater the protest demonstrations and white flight in the first stage of desegregation, the more slowly attitudes will change in the second stage.

The National Surveys

Despite predictions of a backlash against forced desegregation, national surveys on attitudes toward racial integration over the last decade have indicated a trend toward increasing acceptance of the principle of integration. The National Opinion Research Center has conducted national surveys on racial attitudes since 1942. One survey question periodically repeated is whether white and black students should attend school together. In 1942 the proportion of respondents agreeing was 30 percent; in 1956, 48 percent; in 1963, 63 percent; in 1970, 74 percent; in 1972, 86 percent; and in 1976, 83 percent (Sheatsley, 1966; Taylor, Sheatsley, and Greeley, 1978).

Taylor, Sheatsley, and Greeley (1978) have charted trends in responses to the questions in the Treiman scale of racial tolerance.[15] Their data indicate that in the South, the greatest reduction in racial intolerance occurred between 1970 and 1972—shortly after the greatest reduction in school segregation, which was between 1969 and 1971.[16] While it cannot be concluded from this that there was any relationship between the two, it seems reasonable to conclude that desegregation failed to produce a backlash. Moreover, the smaller reduction in school segregation in the North and West is paralleled by a similarly small decrease in racial intolerance.

Sheatsley's (1966) analysis of the 1956 and 1963 NORC surveys attempted to distinguish between cause and effect in examining school desegregation and subsequent attitude change by establishing that the areas in the South that were integrated first were not areas where majority opinion was in favor of integration—only 31 percent of whites in these areas were in favor of integrated schools. By 1963, after substantial desegregation, this figure had increased to 58 percent. At the same time, only 38 percent of whites approved of integrated schools in those southern communities that had only token desegregation, and only 28 percent approved in those school systems that remained highly segregated. However, the conclusion that school integration resulted in an increase in prointegration attitudes in the desegregated school districts must be treated with some caution since the analysis did not interview the same people before and after desegregation in the same desegregating communities.

The NORC surveys also indicate that racial attitudes are stable over time, despite violent confrontations and outbreaks of racial hostility. There may be a backlash, however, regarding methods and the speed with which racial goals are attained. Ross (1973) found a significant correlation between the incidence of racial confrontations reported on the front page of the *New York Times* and a negative response by whites as to whether blacks were pushing "too fast." As the number of racial confrontations increased, the proportion of whites responding "too fast" went from 30 percent in 1962 to over 50 percent in 1966. This suggests that, at least at the national level, there are attitudes regarding methods and the speed of desegregation that are responsive to short-term events even while there is increasing acceptance of the ultimate goal.

Community Attitudes

National surveys cannot provide us with information on variations in attitudes among and within communities. The most accurate method of determining the effect of school desegregation (or any policy) on the attitudes (or any other characteristic) of those living in a particular community is a quasi-experimental panel survey—observations, over at least a decade, of pre- and postdesegregation attitudes held by the same people within that community, as well as of a comparable control group of people unaffected by desegregation. Because of the technical problems and the costs involved in employing such a design, there is no such study.

Indeed, only four studies even include data on predesegregation attitudes or a control group (Estabrook, 1980; Ross, 1977; Abney, 1976; Serow and Solomon, 1979b), and almost all are limited in their external validity because each was conducted in a school district that had considerable protest and violence and significant white flight. Thus we have little variance with which to test the hypothesis that the characteristics of the first phase of social change will affect the second phase.

Despite their limitations, these studies have produced some useful information. First, they provide at least a tentative substantiation of the findings of the national surveys regarding the absence of a backlash against the principle of school integration (Estabrook, 1980; McConahay and Hawley, 1978; Slawski, 1976; Ross, 1977; Jacobson, 1978; Abney, 1976; Serow and Solomon, 1979b). They also indicate that the importance of busing as a "problem" begins to recede by the second year of implementation.

Some paradoxical findings, however, are produced by the fact that as the psychological costs of desegregation have been reduced by the decline in racial intolerance over time, the more tangible costs have escalated with the mandatory reassignment of whites. Hence, busing continues to be a symbol that whites overwhelmingly reject because of its association with mandatory white reassignments, regardless of how inconsistent this is with other attitudes, and although they may at the same time support specific plans that involve some busing. Slawski's (1976) Pontiac survey showed that in 1975, 84 percent of all white parents preferred that their children attend a school 25 to 50 percent black. This was an increase of six percentage points from the previous year. Despite this increased support for the principle of racial balance, only 13 percent of white parents supported "the desegregation plan using busing," even though it produced that racial balance. Similarly, McConahay and Hawley's (1977a) survey of Louisville-Jefferson County citizens showed that 50 percent of all whites thought it a "good idea" for children to go to schools that have the same proportion of blacks and whites as generally exists in the Louisville-Jefferson County area. Nevertheless, only 5 percent of the whites supported the school district's busing plan, which achieved exactly that racial balance.

Both black and white respondents in Louisville-Jefferson County greatly underestimated their neighbors' support for racially balanced schools. While 50 percent of the whites thought racial balance was a good idea, only 19 percent believed their neighbors thought so. Although 80 percent of blacks thought racially balanced schools were a good idea, only 55 percent thought their neighbors did. Weatherford's (1980) survey of Los Angeles demonstrates that the attitudes of whites toward busing for racial integration are significantly affected by the racial attitudes of their neighbors. Therefore, a partial explanation for the tremendous opposition to actual busing plans may be this false perception of overwhelming community opposition to racial balance.

The Ross study of Boston, and the McConahay and Hawley study of Louisville indicate that at the end of the first year, white parents whose school-age children participate in the desegregation plan support desegregation more than do parents of preschool children. Ross (1977) found that whites whose children were bused during Phase 1 (1974–75) of Boston's desegregation plan were generally more certain that black children benefited from integration and less certain about the negative effect of school desegregation on white children than those with preschool children. In Louisville, the proportion of parents intending not to enroll their preschool children in the public schools when they reached school age was four times greater for those with no school-age children than for those who already had some children in the public schools. Normally we would expect parents of preschool children to be more supportive of desegregation than parents of school-age children because, on average, they will be younger. If the reverse occurs, it may be because the parents with children participating in the program are justifying their decision to keep their children in the public school system or their inability to find alternative schooling by subconsciously changing their attitudes to conform to their behavior.

Abney's (1976) quasi-experimental survey in Jackson, Mississippi, suggests this possibility. The first survey was conducted in the summer, before school opened but after the court order. The second survey was conducted at the end of the first year of desegregation. In order to assess the effects of compliance on support for integration, Abney compared the attitude changes of parents who had kept their children in the public schools and parents who had transferred them to private schools. Support for integration was measured by the maximum number of blacks a parent felt he or she could tolerate in his or her child's class of 30 students. Among the parents who kept their children in the public schools, 13 percent would accept fewer blacks than they had the year before, 37 percent would accept the same number, while 28 percent increased the number of blacks they would accept in their child's classroom. The highest number cited was 15, which represented a 50–50 racial balance. Among those parents who transferred their children to private schools, 20 percent would tolerate fewer blacks than the previous year, 55 percent would accept the same number, and only 13 percent were willing to have a larger number of blacks in their child's classroom.

Serow and Solomon (1979b) conducted a survey of postimplementation attitudes in a countywide suburban school district in the South where desegregation was initially implemented in a subsample of 12 elementary schools in the school system. Both white and minority parents who had children in the desegregated schools gave significantly greater support to the principle of school desegregation, higher ratings to various methods of desegregation, and a higher evaluation of the success of the new desegregation program than parents whose children were in schools that had not yet been desegregated. Moreover, white parents rated their child's school experience as more successful than parents whose children were in schools that were yet to be desegregated, although the difference was not statistically significant.

Despite this evidence supporting the attitudinal change hypothesized by cognitive dissonance theory, some studies indicate that there are strong parental fears about the effect of school desegregation on academic performance. McConahay and Hawley (1978) found that in Louisville these fears have increased over time. For example, among the overwhelmingly white opposition to busing to achieve racial desegregation, there has been an increase between 1976 and 1977 (78 percent to 81 percent) in those who believe that busing reduces the quality of education. More disturbingly, in the same group there has been a substantial increase (from 38 percent to 51 percent) in the proportion believing that "the difference in learning ability between most blacks and most whites is so great that neither group benefits from going to school together." On the other hand, they also find that among those supporting busing to achieve racial desegregation (overwhelmingly black), the proportion who believe that busing adversely affects the quality of education has decreased from 32 to 22 percent and the proportion believing that "the difference in learning ability between most blacks and most whites is so great that neither group benefits from going to school together," has decreased from 12 to 5 percent. Similarly, Cunningham (1980) finds that although black parents in Louisville have had to bear most of the inconvenience of busing because black children are bused nearly all of their school years, they do the least complaining and maintain the most favorable attitudes toward the school system.

In spite of this apparent polarization and increase in racial prejudice on some issues, a majority of whites surveyed in the Louisville study feel that their relations with blacks in a variety of settings (for example, work, church, sporting events, and stores) are friendly or neutral, and there has been little change in this proportion. Moreover, there has been an increase since the first year of the plan in the proportion of whites believing that relations with blacks have improved in each of these areas.

A study by Sobol and Beck (1978) produced similar findings in a Dallas survey of black parents conducted in early 1977. The Dallas school system at the time had only desegregated four of its six subdistricts. One of those not desegregated was a 97 percent black subdistrict. Black parents in this district felt that mixed schools offered better educational opportunities than did segregated schools. Moreover, those black parents whose children were attending mixed schools were significantly happier with their schools than those parents who said their children were in segregated schools. The evidence, such as it is, suggests that black parents continue to support school desegregation even when they bear the brunt of the burden.

Community and Student Attitudes

Community attitudes can significantly affect the process of school desegregation. As noted above, the attitudes of adults are influenced by the attitudes of their neighbors. This is also true of children. Numerous studies have found strong positive relationships between parents' attitudes and those of their offspring. As children grow older, however, peer and community influences grow stronger, so that by adolescence the relationship between the attitudes held by parents and those held by children is much weaker. McConahay and Hawley (1976) surveyed fifth through twelfth grade students in Louisville-Jefferson County. The results indicate that at the end of the first year of desegregation (1976), support for the principle of racial balance among black students and black adults was almost identical, 90 percent in each case. Support among white students and white adults was also almost identical, with 51 percent in each category supporting the principle.

This strong similarity between the attitudes of students and of adult citizens is not solely attributable to parental influence, however. There is also a community influence. Most whites in Louisville (91 percent) opposed busing for desegregation. Ninety percent of the white students whose parents opposed busing to achieve desegregation also opposed busing. One the other hand, only 44 percent of the white students whose parents favored busing to achieve desegregation also favored it. The other 56 percent paralleled the white community attitudes. In other words, the children of those white parents who favored busing were exposed to environmental cross-pressures that influenced approximately half of them to conform to their social environment rather than to their parents' opinions.

Most blacks in Louisville (61 percent) favored busing for desegregation. Seventy-nine percent of the black students whose parents favored busing also favored it, but only 47 percent of the black students whose parents opposed busing also opposed it. The other 53 percent conformed to black community attitudes. It is quite clear therefore that children, as well as adults, are influenced by their community environment.

It is also quite likely that the interaction between parents' attitudes and children's attitudes works in both directions. That is, not only will a child be influenced by parental and social group opinions, but parental attitudes are likely to be reinforced or changed by the child's perception of his or her experience with desegregation. This in turn will influence the child's future perceptions. Thus, there is likely to be a rather complex process of interaction that is not analyzed in studies of the racial attitudes of children or their parents. Indeed, too many studies, by their failure to study this interaction, imply that the school is an isolated laboratory.

Summary

The research on community attitudes—most of which has been conducted in school districts experiencing high levels of protest and white flight—indicates that the following propositions characterize this phase of social change:

1. The reduction in school segregation in the last decade and a half has been followed by a reduction in racial intolerance in both the North and the South.
2. Over time there appears to be no backlash against the principle of racial integration despite racial confrontations and controversy surrounding school desegregation.
3. The prominence of busing as a problem begins to fade by the end of the first year of school desegregation.
4. Although there is increasing support for the principle of racial integration and racially balanced schools, whites are overwhelmingly opposed to busing for racial desegregation of the schools.
5. Both blacks and whites greatly overestimate their neighbors' opposition to racial balance in the public schools, and this is important because adult attitudes are influenced by their neighborhood attitudinal context.
6. In desegregated school systems, parents who have some children attending public school are more likely to intend to enroll their preschool children in the public schools than are parents whose children are all of preschool age. In Boston, residents with school-age children in areas affected by the first phase of desegregation were more likely to have a favorable evaluation of desegregation than were those without school-age children.
7. While a few studies show increased prejudice after desegregation, most show

no difference or more positive attitudes. None of the studies has been conducted later than the second year of desegregation and most are in school
districts that experienced violence and controversy.

8. Parents in some school districts that experienced violence and controversy
continue to have strong fears about the quality of education in desegregated
schools.

9. Both community and parental opinions have a strong influence on children's
attitudes toward specific desegregation issues.

THE EFFECT OF SCHOOL DESEGREGATION ON VOTING BEHAVIOR AND RESIDENTIAL INTEGRATION

This last section explores the relationship between school desegregation
and behavioral changes in other areas of community life. The evidence suggests that people use the same kind of personal cost/benefit analysis to guide
their behavior in this area as they do in the areas of protest, white flight, and
attitudinal change.

Voting Behavior

Taylor's (1978) survey of the Detroit metropolitan area, conducted in
1972, indicates that antibusing candidates are not highly regarded, although
people may vote for them initially. About 68 percent of the white respondents
agreed that "some political candidates have blown the busing issue out of
proportion," and 57 percent responded that "most black and white children
would do fine in school together if adults didn't stir up the situation." This
suggests that there is a large group of whites who believe that school desegregation should not become an issue in local politics and whose support for
candidates who make it an issue eventaully fades.

  Although there have been no systematic studies of election campaigns after
a school desegregation plan has been implemented, some recent elections do
provide some insight into voting behavior. Three years after the implementation of Phase I of desegregation in Boston, Louise Day Hicks, John J.
Kerrigan, and Pixie Palladino, the most vocal antibusing leaders in Boston,
were voted out of office at the same time that John O'Bryant, the first black
school board member, was elected ("It's no to Hicks . . . ," 1977). In fall
1981 three white moderates and two liberal blacks captured all five seats on
the school board ("Winds of change," 1981). This occurred in a city where
blacks make up only 20 percent of the population and an even smaller proportion of the registered voters, and elections are at-large. In Charlotte-
Mecklenburg, North Carolina, Sam McNinch, a prominent antibusing school
board member, was defeated for reelection in the 1974 school board elections
(Maniloff, 1978). Similarly, in the fall 1977 elections in Louisville-Jefferson
County, Todd Hollenbach, the incumbent county executive and author of a
voluntary alternative to the mandatory desegregation plan, was defeated by

a Republican candidate who was considered more liberal on that issue ("Hollenbach is defeated by McConnell," 1977).

These electoral results make sense in light of the findings of the attitudinal surveys. Although most whites reject busing for school desegregation, they are not opposed to the principle of integration. Once it is clear that the busing plan is not going to be rescinded, it is to the advantage of parents to elect candidates who are committed to minimizing the risks and maximizing the educational benefits of the integrated public schools.

Residential Integration

The hypothesis that school desegregation will lead to community integration is not necessarily dependent on a reduction in prejudice. Because extensive, citywide desegregation will include the additional cost of reassignment away from the neighborhood school unless the neighborhood attendance zone is residentially integrated, white and black families who are loyal to the public schools, or who cannot afford other alterations, have an incentive to live in integrated neighborhoods. Moreover, the racial stabilization and reduction in the proportion minority that can occur in schools in transitional neighborhoods under a citywide plan, may provide an additional incentive for some white families to remain in such neighborhoods. Realistically, we would not expect these changes to be large in any one year, given the amount of movement that occurs normally in a city, but because the incentives are clear and obvious, this effect may appear before many others, and its long-term consequences may be profound.

A national, aggregate analysis of the relationship between school desegregation and residential desegregation in order to assess change since 1970 is not feasible until the 1980 census is available. Only a few citywide plans were implemented prior to 1970, and these were at the end of the 1960s rather than at the beginning. Although the school districts that implemented extensive desegregation exhibit a fairly large reduction in residential segregation between 1960 and 1970—almost twice as much on the average as other school districts—one cannot satisfactorily differentiate cause and effect. Even when the 1980 census is available, if the effects are small they could be swallowed up at the school district level.

The only systematic study available on the relationship between school desegregation and residential integration is Pearce's (1980) study of seven matched desegregated-segregated pairs of school districts. Two of the desegregated school districts are suburban (Riverside and Racine), two are central city school districts (Springfield and Wichita), and the other three (Charlotte-Mecklenburg, Greenville, and Tampa-St. Petersburg [Hillsborough and Pinnellas County districts]) are countywide or metropolitan school districts. Her data indicate that between 1970 and some year after 1975 (the year chosen depended on the availability of data) the desegregated school districts had significantly greater reductions in residential segregation than their segregated pair with no greater increase in the proportion black.[17]

There is also some unsystematic evidence on this issue from a few case studies. Greenwood's (1972) article describes a study conducted in the Riverside school district (desegregated in 1966 by a one-way busing plan) that found fifty black families who had moved into white neighborhoods to be near their child's new school. Today, all but four of the school attendance zones are residentially integrated and do not need school busing.

This phenomenon is also documented by the Kentucky Commission on Human Rights. Although the Louisville-Jefferson County school district (which includes the city and suburbs) experienced little white out-migration, the increase in the proportion of black students living in the suburban county (still within the school district) between 1974, the year before the plan was implemented, and 1977, the end of the second year of school desegregation, was greater than for the entire preceding twelve-year period. Student enrollment data indicate that 86 percent of this increase took place in areas where blacks would be exempt from busing because they would be in a minority (Foushee and Hamilton, 1977; Kentucky Commission on Human Rights, 1980a, 1980b).

Apartment occupancy rates in 1979 indicate that blacks are still moving in increasing numbers to white areas, and that school desegregation has had a positive effect in reducing apartment housing segregation since 1975 and, as a result, in reducing the amount of busing needed for school desegregation (Kentucky Commission on Human Rights, 1980b). Nevertheless, this movement has not been large enough to bring full housing integration or eliminate altogether the need for busing.

While it is difficult to determine motives without a survey, there are some significant features of the Louisville-Jefferson County desegregation plan and public housing program that suggest an explanation. First, according to the plan, any student who lives in, or moves into, a school attendance district in which he or she is in the racial minority is exempt from being reassigned away from that school. Furthermore, this aspect of the plan was publicized in a pamphlet widely distributed by the Kentucky Commission on Human Rights (1975) that listed the Jefferson County schools where blacks would be exempt from busing if they moved into the neighborhood. Second, in 1975 white residents of the East End in suburban Jefferson County distributed their own pamphlets encouraging black homeseekers to move into that area, presumably in order to "naturally" integrate those schools and thus avoid busing. Finally, in 1976, the Community Development Cabinet of Louisville and the Jefferson County Housing Authority merged their programs so that city families eligible for Section 8 rent subsidies would be allowed to search for housing in the suburbs and vice versa.[18] Of the 1,413 black families that signed Section 8 leases between 1976 and 1979, one third moved out of the city to white suburban Jefferson County. Virtually all of the black families already living in the suburbs chose to remain there. Hence by 1979, 51.1 percent of all black families availing of Section 8 leases lived in Jefferson County (Kentucky Commission on Human Rights, 1980a).

Although it appears that school desegregation can stimulate housing desegregation, the case studies indicate that the net migration will be to white neighborhoods as long as both races perceive the costs of busing to be high but blacks value the benefits of a move into a white neighborhood more than whites value the benefits of moving into a black neighborhood. Under these conditions, it will be in the interest of both groups for residential integration to occur through blacks moving into white neighborhoods.

Summary

The evidence from these studies indicates that there may be some significant positive changes in the behavior of citizens in a community after its schools have been desegregated. It is also possible that this may appear before any consistent attitudinal changes are found. These behavioral changes are as follows.

1. Black and liberal white candidates are voted into office, and antibusing candidates defeated two to three years after implementation of a school desegregation plan.
2. Residential integration increases in school districts with systemwide desegregation plans.
3. The evidence from two case studies of districts with citywide busing plans (Louisville-Jefferson County and Riverside) suggests that this residential desegregation occurs because such plans motivate black families to move into white neighborhoods to be near the school to which their children have been assigned in order to avoid busing. In addition, whites have an incentive to accept them if their school becomes exempt from busing as a result.

CONCLUSIONS

The research discussed above suggests that mandatory reassignment of white students is necessary in order to effectively desegregate most school districts, at least in the short run. Indeed, the reason why there is segregation in the first place is that whites rarely *choose* to live with or go to school with those of another race. They have to be forced to do it. Mandatory reassignment, however, has varying costs both from an individual perspective and in terms of social change.

The research on protest demonstrations suggests that people participate in protest when they perceive the costs of desegregation to be higher than the costs of participation. Such a perception is a function of (1) social class—the working class has the fewest alternatives to desegregation, but the upper working class feels itself to be more efficacious and is thus more willing to participate in protest); (2) racial prejudice and alienation on the part of the participants, which increase the psychological costs of desegregation; (3) the costs associated with the actual characteristics of the desegregation plan, particularly whether whites are bused into minority neighborhoods; and (4) a supportive neighborhood environment, which reduces the psychological costs of participating in a normally "deviant" act. Furthermore, it is reasonable to assume that the third condition contributes to the fourth. The greater the proportion of whites reassigned to schools in black neighborhoods, the more likely it is that entire white neighborhoods will be affected and thus become united in opposition.

Demonstrations can have serious consequences for student achievement and race relations either directly through their effect on attendance and in-school behavior, or indirectly through their effect on white flight and community attitudes. Nevertheless, protest demonstrations and protest voting are rare after the implementation year and are not successful in preventing desegregation once the decision has been made.

From a practical standpoint, the first instrumental goal of school desegregation is behavioral compliance. Whites overwhelmingly oppose busing for school desegregation, for whatever reasons. Nevertheless, they do not act capriciously, but calculate the costs and benefits of various options available to them. The evidence for this is clear: most white flight from desegregation takes the form of a change to private schools within the district, rather than the more costly option, residential relocation; countywide or metropolitan desegregation plans produce less white flight than city desegregation plans because the costs of residential relocation are greater in the former; those who opt for residential relocation tend to be renters, to be young, and to have preschool children; white reassignments to formerly black schools, which have greater costs to whites than black reassignments, produce two to three times the white flight of the reverse; the greater the busing distance, the more white flight; staggering bus pick-up times produces greater white flight because it is inconvenient; and those most likely to withdraw their children from the public schools tend to be those with more options—that is, those who have higher levels of income and education.

The average court-ordered desegregation plan—about 30 percent black students and 5 percent white students reassigned, with a reduction in segregation of 30 percentage points—results, on average, in an additional white enrollment loss of 8 to 10 percentage points in the year of implementation in school districts above 35 percent black. A school or school district with a black proportion above 30 percent will have more white flight with a given desegregation plan than will a school district with a small proportion black.

Because information is scarce in the year before school desegregation (no one having tried it), most individuals rely on newspapers. As a result, unfavorable newspaper coverage of desegregation during the year before implementation increases white flight because it increases the perceived costs of staying. Phasing-in a plan may produce greater white flight than implementing a plan in one year because the more advance notice whites receive, the lower the costs to them of obtaining information on alternatives to the public schools. Similarly, in postimplementation years it is more likely that those who do not have children enrolled in the public schools will not enroll them than that those who have will withdraw them. This is because obtaining information on the public school system is more costly for the former group. As a result of the difficulty of obtaining information on the educational quality and social status of schools that receive minority students, there is no relationship between most nonracial indicators of school quality and white flight. In forming opinions, whites appear to rely on racial composition and other easily obtained information, such as school size and age, as surrogates for quality.

Despite the research and common sense that suggests that desegregation at an early age has fewer costs and greater educational and social benefits than desegregation at a later age, whites react as if the opposite were true. White flight is significantly greater when elementary school children are desegregated than when secondary school children are desegregated.

The long-term effect of school desegregation on white enrollment is obviously of critical importance. School desegregation continues to increase the long-term decline in white enrollment in many large central city school districts above 35 percent black. Even if it did not, however, the "normal" decline in white enrollment would ultimately have the same effect unless black enrollment declined at the same rate. School districts (for example, Inglewood, California) have been released from their court order when the white enrollment has become so small that minority students are simply being bused from one minority school to another. For the same reason, the black plaintiffs in the Boston case are currently negotiating a consent decree to change the plan from a mandatory to a voluntary one. Nevertheless, white flight and the normal decline in white enrollment have not been so great as to negate the gains of racial balancing in the vast majority of school districts. At the end of four years, interracial contact (defined as the proportion white in the average black child's school) in mandatorily desegregated school districts is still twice as great as it would have been if they had not desegregated. Thus, at the simple level of mixing blacks with whites, the limited information we have suggests that mandatory school desegregation has so far been successful.

The attitudinal success is less clearcut. This is because at the same time as the psychological costs of desegregation have been reduced by the decline in racial intolerance, the more tangible costs have escalated with the mandatory reassignment of whites. Hence, whites are overwhelmingly opposed to busing for racial desegregation of the schools even when this attitude is inconsistent with other racial opinions.

None of the attitudinal surveys has been conducted later than the second year of desegregation, and most are in school districts that experienced violence and controversy. Nevertheless, they show either no difference, or a positive change in attitudes that is greater for those whose children actually experienced desegregation. The research evidence also suggests that school desegregation may produce some significant positive behavioral changes. When it becomes clear that the busing plan is not going to be rescinded, it is in the interest of parents to elect candidates who want to maximize the benefits of integrated public education. As a result, minority candidates are voted into office, and antibusing candidates defeated two to three years after implementation of a school desegregation plan. In addition, because extensive, citywide desegregation will include the additional cost of reassignment away from the neighborhood school unless the neighborhood attendance zone is residentially integrated, white and black families who are loyal to the public school system or who cannot afford other alternatives, have an incentive to live in integrated neighborhoods. The case studies suggest that the net migration will be to white neighborhoods.

The research discussed in this review has suggested various strategies that policymakers might adopt to influence individual attitudes and behavior. Unfortunately, as Table 2-3 summarizes, these strategies do not have uniformly positive or negative effects. Mandatory reassignment of white students to minority schools, for example, reduces racial isolation but increases white protest and white flight. On the other hand, it also facilitates the election of minorities and may ultimately reduce racial prejudice and residential segregation. The voluntary reassignment of white students reduces white protest and white flight but has little short-term effect on racial isolation and an effect on residential integration only if blacks transfer to white schools. Desegregation in early grades holds the greatest promise for improving race relations, increasing minority achievement, and ultimately reducing racial prejudice, but produces the most white flight. While limiting busing distances will reduce white protest and white flight, in many school districts it will undoubtedly also place limits on the extent to which racial isolation can be reduced.

From a policy standpoint, the costs of school desegregation do not seem to be overwhelming in comparison to the possible benefits. But the findings concerning community response to school desegregation are, with the exception of those on white flight, based on a small number of studies. Thus, there is not enough variation across cases in the first phase of social change (the reaction to the decision) for us to adequately understand how it affects the second phase (the reduction in prejudiced attitudes and behavior).

There is need for more research in order to answer some important policy questions:

1. Does including a magnet school as a component in a mandatory desegregation plan reduce white flight, protest, and racial prejudice in comparison to a

TABLE 2-3

Consequences of Desegregation Strategies

Desegregation Strategies	Reduces Racial Isolation	Reduces White Protest	Community Consequences			Promotes Election of Minorities
			Reduces White Flight	Reduces Racial Prejudice	Reduces Residential Segregation	
Mandatory reassignment of white students (two-way busing)	Positive[d]	Negative[d]	Negative[e]	Positive[c]	Positive[c]	Positive[c]
Voluntary reassignment of white students (one-way busing)	Negative[d]	Positive[e]	Positive[d]	Indeterm.	Negative[c]	Indeterm.
Magnet-mandatory	Positive[d]	Indeterm.	Indeterm.	Positive[c]	Positive[c]	Positive[c]
Magnet-only	Negative[c]	Positive[d]	Positive[d]	Indeterm.	Negative[c]	Indeterm.
Court-ordered[a]	Positive[d]	Negative[d]	Negative[d]	Positive[c]	Positive[c]	Positive[c]
Board-ordered[b]	Negative[c]	Positive[c]	Positive[c]	Indeterm.	Negative	Indeterm.
Elementary desegregation	Positive[d]	Negative[d]	Negative[d]	Positive[c]	Positive[c]	Positive[c]
Limit on busing distances	Negative[c]	Positive[c]	Positive[c]	Indeterm.	Positive[c]	Indeterm.
Closing of oldest and largest minority schools	Positive[c]	Positive[c]	Positive[d]	Indeterm.	Indeterm.	Indeterm.
New schools in minority neighborhoods	Positive[c]	Indeterm.	Positive[c]	Indeterm.	Indeterm.	Indeterm.
Phasing in of mandatory white reassignments	Indeterm.	Indeterm.	Negative[c]	Indeterm.	Indeterm.	Indeterm.
Metropolitan plan	Positive[e]	Indeterm.	Positive[d]	Indeterm.	Positive[c]	Indeterm.
Leadership support for desegregation	Indeterm.	Indeterm.	Indeterm.	Indeterm.	Indeterm.	Indeterm.
Positive media coverage of desegregation	Positive[c]	Positive[c]	Positive[c]	Indeterm.	Indeterm.	Indeterm.
Strict school discipline	Indeterm.	Indeterm.	Positive[c]	Indeterm.	Indeterm.	Indeterm.
Excluding integrated neighborhoods from busing	Positive[c]	Indeterm.	Indeterm.	Indeterm.	Positive[d]	Indeterm.

Notes

[a] It is assumed that reassignments are mandatory.

[b] Board-ordered plans usually do not involve mandatory white reassignments. The consequences of this strategy are predicated on the assumption that white reassignments are voluntary.

[c] Tentative findings based on a few case studies.

[d] More certain findings based on numerous case studies or national studies.

[e] Virtually all of the research supports this.

mandatory plan without magnets? Do magnet schools stigmatize nonmagnet schools so that the latter experience greater than expected white flight?

2. Do magnet-only (voluntary) plans result in greater interracial contact than magnet-mandatory plans at the end of a decade?

3. Does the voluntary reassignment of white students have a different effect on racial attitudes than mandatory reassignment?

4. Do support for desegregation from civic leaders and an extensive positive media campaign reduce negative consequences and enhance positive ones?

In general, desegregation research needs to be less "macro-negative," and more "micro-positive." That is, research needs to be less concerned with whether desegregation has succeeded or failed and more concerned with understanding how contextual variables can be manipulated to make it achieve its goals. This is true regardless of which particular consequence of desegregation is being examined.

NOTES

1. This random probability sample stratified by size represents 84 percent of cities over 250,000, 46 percent of all cities from 100,000 to 249,999 and 8 percent of all cities from 50,000 to 99,999. The level of segregation is measured with the index of dissimilarity. The index of dissimilarity is used to measure the extent of residential or school segregation. When used to measure school segregation, this index takes as its standard the racial composition of a school district, and then compares the racial composition of the individual school to the racial composition of the school district. In each school (i), suppose there are w whites and n blacks. The entire school district contains W whites and N blacks. The index of dissimilarity (expressed as a proportion) is calculated as follows:

$$D = \frac{1}{2} \Sigma \left| \frac{n_i}{N} - \frac{w_i}{W} \right|$$

The computational formula involves adding up the whites in each school at or above the proportion black in the whole district, adding up the blacks in the same schools, dividing each sum by its respective school district population, and subtracting these sums from each other. If the index is to be expressed as a percentage, the resulting absolute value is multiplied by 100. The index then ranges from 0 to 100, with 0 being perfect racial balance and 100 being perfect segregation.

2. Taeuber and Wilson (1979a) have begun some preliminary analysis of the impact that various kinds of desegregation actions have had on school segregation within individual school districts. The preliminary analysis suggests that the sources of pressure to desegregate (HEW, Court, State-Local or Other) had little differential effect on the desegregation of blacks in the South. In places other than the South, the courts were most effective, followed by HEW and

the state or local sources. First, it should be noted that it is a mistake to collapse state and local initiatives into one category. The history of desegregation, particularly in the North, is characterized by numerous state battles to force local school districts to desegregate. To put them into one category is only a little more reasonable than putting HEW and local into one category. Secondly, most long-term observers of southern desegregation would agree that almost no school desegregation occurred in the South because of local initiative, and very little because of state initiative. If Taeuber and Wilson find little difference between HEW, the courts, and state or local pressures in the South, they have made a major redefinition of what constitutes the source of the order to desegregate, and this definition does not conform to that used by most other analysts.

   3. The equation is:

$$S_{bw} = \frac{\sum_{k} n_{km}\, p_{kw}}{\sum_{k} n_{km}}$$

where n_{km} is the number of minorities in each school and p_{kw} is the proportion white in each school. These values are multiplied and summed for all schools. The result is divided by the number of minorities in the school district to yield the proportion white in the average minority child's school.

   4. See Rossell (1978c) for a more detailed discussion of these phrases and the theoretical assumptions underlying them.

   5. The designer of the study and project director is J. Michael Ross.

   6. It should be noted at this point that there is a large body of literature extending back through the early 1960s that has been misinterpreted as evidence of the effect of administratively ordered school desegregation on white enrollment losses. These studies are, in fact, analyses of the effect of uncontrolled black population growth in white neighborhoods on the racial composition of the neighborhood and the neighborhood school. Hence, they will not be reviewed here as studies of administratively ordered school desegregation. Some illustrative examples are Wolf (1963), Stinchcombe, McDill, and Walker (1969), Molotch (1969), Wegmann (1975), Levine and Meyer (1977), and Sly and Pol (1978).

   7. Moreover, both studies have questionable measures of school desegregation. Clotfelter measures school desegregation as a dummy variable in which any school district in the South was desegregated and any school district in the North was not desegregated. Aside from the problem of using a dummy variable (which Frey also uses), there remains the fact that in 1970 the South was still highly segregated—about fifteen percentage points above the North as measured by the index of dissimilarity. Clotfelter used this same dependent variable in another study (see Clotfelter, 1976b).

   8. Clotfelter (1979) finds that whites are more sensitive to change in the proportion black in their school than they are to desegregation per se (that is, if there are few blacks in a school system, even massive desegregation will have no effect). Such standardized measures as the index of dissimilarity (Farley, 1975; Farley et al., 1980), or the standardized interracial exposure (r_{wb}) (Coleman et al., 1975b) by themselves cannot determine this. The unstandardized index,

however, suffers from simultaneity bias when it is used as an independent variable to analyze the effect of desegregation on white flight. That is, as whites leave a school, the proportion of black students goes up and the cause is confused with the effect. Clotfelter (1979) has developed a method for eliminating some of this bias. The equation for S_{wb} used by Coleman (Coleman et al., 1975b, p. 8), is as follows:

$$S_{wb} = \frac{\sum_k n_{kb}\, p_{kw}}{\sum_k n_{kw}}$$

This is the sum of the number of blacks in each school multiplied by the proportion white in the same school. The sum of this calculation for all schools is divided by the total number of whites in the school system. Clotfelter has weighted the measure by an estimate of white enrollment if there has been no white enrollment decline. This can be shown as:

$$S_{wb}^* = \frac{1}{w} \sum_i W_i \; \frac{B_i}{h(NW_i + W_i)} = \frac{1}{h} S_{wb}$$

where $h = (NW + W^*)(NW + W)$, W^* is white enrollment for the previous year, W is white enrollment in the year being analyzed, and NW is nonwhite enrollment in the year being analyzed. However, it should be noted that results virtually identical to Clotfelter's can be obtained by calculating the interaction effect between a standardized measure of desegregation and proportion black. (*See* Farley et al., 1980; Coleman et al., 1975b; Rossell, 1978a.)

9. The most recent research, conducted by Becker (1979) and analyzing the period from 1970 to 1976, indicates that, in fact, whites are now willing to move into minority neighborhoods even after they reach 30 percent minority, although the rate of in-migration is lower than in all-white neighborhoods.

10. This type of ecological succession does not go on in all integrated neighborhoods. Notable exceptions are those neighborhoods such as Hyde Park in Chicago, Capitol Hill in Washington, D.C., and the South End of Boston, where middle-class whites move into a predominantly black neighborhood. Nevertheless, my own observation is that such neighborhoods are also unstable, but in the reverse direction from white working-class neighborhoods. That is to say, blocks will quite rapidly become all white because the rents and housing prices begin to go up, and the blacks who move out are not replaced by other blacks.

11. Clotfelter, 1976b, 1979; and Giles, 1978 are exceptions. These studies found a second-order interaction effect—a curvilinear, exponential increase in white flight with greater proportions black in school districts or schools. Rossell (1980) looked for a second-order interaction effect in Los Angeles but did not find one. Two of the three studies finding an exponential increase in white flight with greater proportions black analyzed only southern school districts (Giles, 1978; Clotfelter, 1976b) and did not specifically examine school districts undergoing a desegregation plan.

12. The Giles, Cataldo, and Gatlin (1975) study and the Rossell (1978a) study are comparable even though one is of school effects and the other of school district effects since in racial balance plans the schools to which white students will be reassigned should have roughly the same proportion black as the district proportion.

13. Taeuber and Wilson (1979b) correctly note that the measure of metropolitan segregation used by Coleman et al. (1975b), Farley et al. (1980), Clotfelter (1979), and Rossell (1978a) is incomplete since the OCR school survey did not sample all school districts in metropolitan areas in any of its annual surveys, except 1976. Surburban districts were far more likely not to be sampled because of the emphasis on districts with greater minority representation and size.

14. See note 3 for the equation.

15. The five questions in the Treiman scale are (1) "Do you think white students and Negro

students should go to the same schools or separate schools?"; (2) "How strongly would you object if a member of your family wanted to bring a Negro friend home to dinner?"; (3) "White people have a right to keep Negroes out of their neighborhoods if they want to and Negroes should respect that right"; (4) "Do you think there should be laws against marriages between Negroes and whites?"; and (5) "Negroes shouldn't push themselves where they're not wanted." See Treiman (1966).

16. See Rossell (1978c, p. 171) for a detailed visual description of these trends.

17. Pearce used the index of dissimilarity to measure segregation. In order to complete this analysis, an index of net benefit, such as S_{bw} (see note 3), should be calculated for each school district. Although it does not appear to be the case for these school districts, it is possible for a school district to be racially balanced residentially according to the index of dissimilarity but to have few whites left because of massive white flight. The S_{bw} index will measure both racial balance and the extent of white contact with blacks (i.e., the proportion white in the average black family's block). The study has other problems as well, but it is not clear that the findings are significantly changed by them.

18. Under Section 8 of the 1974 Housing and Community Development Act, a family with an income no greater than a specified amount related to family size may be eligible for a rental subsidy whereby the federal government pays the difference between 25 percent of the family's income and the fair market rent. The family must find its own housing in the private market, but the dwelling must meet certain physical standards and pass annual inspections.

3

Desegregation, School Practices, and Student Race Relations

Janet Ward Schofield and *H. Andrew Sagar*

*T*he goal of this chapter is to summarize what the empirical literature suggests about the impact of various desegregation strategies on the development of positive social relations between black and white children. This chapter focuses on black-white relations, in spite of the fact that Hispanic children are an increasingly important minority group in American schools, because there is so little research on factors that influence the development of social relations between Hispanics and other racial and ethnic groups.

Although the *Brown* v. *Board of Education* decision, which laid the basis for the desegregation of American schools, was based on the constitutional principle of equal protection (Read, 1975; Wisdom, 1975), many social scientists and educators were quick to point out the possible beneficial effects of desegregation. In particular, it has frequently been argued that school desegregation can lead both to increased academic achievement on the part of minority group members and to improved relations between minority and majority group members. In the years since the *Brown* decision, a tremendous amount of research has been conducted to assess the impact of desegregation on the academic performance of both white and black children (Crain and Mahard, 1978; Stephan, 1978; St. John, 1975; Weinberg, 1977). However, much less attention has been given to the social experiences of children in interracial schools and to the impact of these experiences on intergroup attitudes and behavior.

Perhaps one reason why so little attention has been paid to the social learning that occurs in interracial schools is that for most parties closely involved with the schools, traditional academic achievement is a matter of infinitely higher priority. The performance of a school district is usually judged by the academic achievement of its pupils. The proportion of students going on to college and the way local students score on nationally normed tests of academic aptitude and achievement are typical of the sorts of indicators normally used to judge how well educational institutions are performing. The widespread resistance to desegregation on the part of whites clearly suggests that they do not give the opportunity for interracial contact in schools high priority. Similarly, many blacks give low priority to increased opportunity for friendship with whites (Clark, 1973; Goldman, 1970).

Although many of the parties concerned with desegregated schools tend to be relatively uninterested in how interracial schooling affects intergroup relations, there are some compelling arguments in favor of giving more thought to the matter. First, the fact is that social learning occurs whether it is planned or not. Hence, an interracial school cannot choose to have no effect on intergroup relations. It can only choose whether the effect will be planned or unplanned. Even a *laissez-faire* policy concerning intergroup relations conveys a message—the message that either school authorities see no serious problem with relations as they have developed or they do not feel that the nature of intergroup relations is a legitimate concern for an educational institution. So those who argue that schools should not attempt to influence intergroup relations miss the fundamental fact that whether schools consciously try to influence such relations or not, they are extremely likely to do so anyway, in one way or another.

Because of the pervasive residential segregation in our society, students frequently have their first relatively intimate and extended interracial experiences in schools. Hence, whether their racial hostility and stereotyping grow or diminish may be critically influenced by the particular experiences students have there. While there may still be considerable argument about the desirability of close interracial ties, there is a growing awareness of the societal costs of intergroup hostility and stereotyping. It is clear that under many conditions interracial contact can lead to increased intergroup hostility. Hence, unless interracial schools are carefully planned there is a real possibility that they will exacerbate the very social tensions and hostilities that many initially hoped they would diminish.

A number of trends all suggest the importance of turning from an almost exclusive concentration on the academic results of schooling and focusing at least some attention on nonacademic results such as its effects on intergroup relations. First, the long-held assumption that academic achievement was the major determinant of occupational success has been seriously questioned. Hence, numerous investigators have begun to study nonacademic personal characteristics, such as interpersonal competence (White, 1966) or system awareness (Tomlinson and TenHouten, 1972), that appear to be related to occupational success and that may well be influenced by the schooling one receives. The ability to work effectively with outgroup members would seem to be an increasingly important skill in a pluralistic society that is striving to overcome a long history of discrimination in education and employment.

Second, intense concern over the flare-up in the late 1960s of youth-related social problems such as drug abuse and politically motivated violence focused public attention on the vital importance of the attitudes and attributes of individuals for society as a whole. That drug use, dropping out of "the system," and ideologies sanctioning violence were especially prevalent on elite college campuses served to underline the fact that high academic achievement is not necessarily synonymous from society's point of view with desirable individual behavior.

Third, Jencks et al. (1972) as well as others have suggested that more attention should be paid to structuring schools so that they are reasonably pleasant environments for students. This viewpoint emphasizes that in addition to being agencies that prepare students for future roles, schools are also the environments in which many people spend nearly one-third of their waking hours for a significant portion of their lives. This line of argument suggests that even if positive or negative interracial experiences do not cause change in interracial behaviors and attitudes outside the school situation, positive relationships within the school setting may be of some value.

Finally, there is the possibility that the social relations between students in interracial schools may affect their academic achievement and their occupational success (Katz, 1964; Crain, 1970; McPartland and Crain, 1980; Pettigrew, 1967; Rosenberg and Simmons, 1971; U.S. Commission on Civil Rights, 1967). For example, Katz's (1964) work suggests that the academic performance of blacks may be markedly impaired in biracial situations that pose a social threat. Katz argues that hostility or even indifference from whites is likely to distract black children from their work and to create anxiety that interferes with efficient learning. He also argues that social acceptance of black children by white children will tend to increase black children's academic motivation if the whites are performing better than the blacks, as is often the case. There are studies that suggest that interracial social acceptance does not necessarily lead to improved academic performance by blacks (for example, Maruyama and Miller, 1979, 1980). Yet it seems reasonable to argue that a very negative interracial atmosphere might well lead to a decline in achievement for white and black students alike. A massive National Institute of Education (NIE, 1978) sponsored study on violence in American schools found that around 4 percent of a large sample of American high school students reported having stayed home from school in the previous month because they were afraid. The study suggests that, in general, desegregated schools have only slightly higher levels of violence than other schools. Nonetheless, if the interracial atmosphere were particularly tense in a school, the students might well respond by staying home just as they respond to other sources of fear. Such absenteeism, if prolonged and widespread, could hardly do anything else but have an adverse affect on students' achievement.

Although far less has been done on the impact of desegregation on intergroup relations than on its impact on academic achievement, there is still a sizable body of research on this and closely related topics. This research can be roughly grouped into three basic categories. First, there are numerous studies that do things like (a) compare the attitudes of students in a segregated school to those of students in a similar desegregated school, or (b) look at changes in student attitudes and behavior associated with the length of time children have been desegregated. Such studies generally give relatively little information about the nature of the schools studied. Rather, they misleadingly tend to talk in terms of assessing the effect of desegregation as if it were operationalized similarly in a wide variety of circumstances. Such studies often contain analyses that examine the impact of student background variables like race or sex on reactions to desegregation. However, they generally do not directly address the impact of specific policies or programs on students. Thus, for example, such studies are unlikely to try to relate characteristcs of the schools to student outcomes.

A second type of research in this area investigates the impact of particular, very narrowly defined innovations on intergroup relations within desegregated schools. This type of research is generally experimental and allows one to assess with some confidence the result of implementing the specific innovation being studied. The most thoroughly researched technique is the use of small interracial cooperative learning teams. However, there are also occasional studies of other innovations such as the use of multiracial curriculum.

The third basic type of research of relevance to the topic at hand consists of the large correlational studies that attempt to relate a whole battery of school policies and practices to particular results. Perhaps the most widely known of these studies is Forehand, Ragosta, and Rock (1976). There are, however, a number of other studies of this type such as, for example, Slavin and Madden (1979). In addition, there are a few other correlational studies, like Serow and Solomon (1979a), that focus on assessing the impact of a much smaller number of practices on various aspects of intergroup relations.

Because the focus of the first kind of research described above is so different from that of the other two types of research, this chapter will examine studies attempting to assess the effect of desegregation before turning to a review of research that assesses the impact of particular school policies or practices.

RESEARCH ON "THE EFFECT" OF DESEGREGATION

The purpose of this review is not to argue that desegregation "works" or "doesn't work." Rather, it is to see what we know about which techniques work in promoting positive relations between students in desegregated schools. One might then ask, "Why bother to look at all at studies that attempt to assess the effect of desegregation as if it were a uniform strategy rather than immediately turning to research that explores the impact of varying types of desegregation and different school practices?" The answer is twofold. First, although these studies were generally not constructed to look at different desegregation strategies, they constitute the largest set of studies potentially relevant to the topic being explored. Thus, to reject them out of hand without seeing what, if anything, can be learned from them seems unwise. Second, even if these studies do not themselves contain comparisons of direct relevance to this paper, there is always the possibility that a meta-analysis of the literature will yield review-generated comparisons of interest. In discussing meta-analysis of research domains, Cooper (1980) distinguishes between study-generated comparisons and review-generated comparisons. The former emerge when a specific study looks at the impact of a particular variable. The latter emerge when a body of studies is analyzed and the results of studies having something in common are compared to the results of studies that differ in a specified way. For example, one could take 20 studies of "the effect" of desegregation, group them by the age of the children studied, and then ask whether the studies performed with elementary school children are more likely to yield positive results than those done with older children. This could be done even if none of the individual studies looked at the effect of age on student outcomes.

Thus, it seemed wise to start this review by looking to see what could be learned from studies that deal with the effect of desegregation on intergroup attitudes and behavior. Given this decision, the first question to arise is, "What are the relevant studies?" Fortunately, in the past decade or so there have been eight separate reviews of the effect of desegregation on intergroup attitudes and behavior (Carithers, 1970; Cohen, 1975; McConahay, 1978, 1979; St. John, 1975; Schofield, 1978; Slavin and Madden, 1979; Stephen, 1978).[1] While one of these reviews is quite old, the rest have all been published relatively recently. Thus, rather than repeating the searches of previous reviewers, I decided to use the reference sections of these eight reviews as the basis for the core set of studies to be explored. The appendix contains an outline of the procedure used to decide which of the papers cited in the eight reviews would be included in the core literature for this review. The potentially relevant studies cited in the reviews are all listed in the Appendix with reasons, where applicable for their elimination from the present review. A list of the studies that survived the elimination procedures discussed above, along with some summary information on the studies' characteristics and results, appears in Table 3-1.

In order to discover material not available at the time of even the most recent reviews, a search of *Psychology Abstracts, Sociology Abstracts,* and the ERIC system was conducted for the years 1978 through 1981. Many of the citations culled from these sources overlapped with those obtained from the most recent reviews. Although this search produced several dozen papers on race relations in classroom settings and on particular techniques for improving such relations, only three papers that could appropriately be added to the core literature were found. These studies also appear in Table 3-1.

One striking feature was how few of the studies contained specific information on the impact of desegration on Hispanic students. Only one or two studies were found that looked at the overall effect of desegregation on intergroup attitudes in schools including Hispanics. The major available source of data on this topic is a study performed in Riverside, California (Gerard, Jackson, and Conolley, 1975). A few other papers touch on this question or related ones, such as whether the structure of Hispanic children's intergroup attitudes is similar to that of blacks and whites (Green and Gerard, 1974; Jacobson, 1977; Stephan, 1977). Such studies are, however, few and far between.

Analysis of the Core Literature on "The Effect" of Desegregation

The original bibliography based on the earlier reviews of the literature included over 100 references. However, this large number of studies shrank rapidly as items were eliminated for the reasons already discussed. Substantial shrinkage was not surprising since in originally compiling the potential core every study of even marginal relevance was listed. However, the rather small number of studies remaining after this elimination process is surprising. In fact, after the elimination process only eight published studies and six dissertations remained in the core literature for assessing the effect of desegregation on intergroup relations. Three studies that were published since the most recent reviews were added to this core, bringing the total to seventeen.

Careful examination of these studies suggested that it would be very difficult, if not impossible, to try to perform any sort of formal meta-analysis. The reasons for this are many. First, these studies do not provide enough information to allow us to compare changes in the attitudes and behavior of black and white children or the school and community environments in which such changes occur. Although most studies do give information on whether a desegregation plan is voluntary or court-ordered, only two studies, both conducted in the same southern school district, examined court-ordered desegregation.

Second, there is great variation in the dependent variables from study to study. Some studies have focused on attitudes toward desegregation, others have looked at attitudes toward the racial outgroup, and still others have examined sociometric choice. Even within these categories, the actual study designs and dependent variables are so diverse that cumulation is difficult.

Mistaken assumptions contained in these studies also make it difficult to generalize from them. For example, many studies using sociometric choice assume that choice and rejection are strongly negatively correlated. Yet the work of Patchen and his colleagues suggests that, contrary to what one might expect, friendly and unfriendly cross-race attitudes and contact are independent of one another (Patchen, Davidson, Hofmann, and Brown, 1973;

TABLE 3-1

Summary of Core Study Characteristics and Outcomes

Study	First Data Collection (approx.)	Grades	Type of Desegregation	Community or Official Response[a]	Time Since Desegregation (end of study)
Armor (1972)	1968	7–12	voluntary for blacks (token)	?	1–5 years
Armor (1972)[d]	1969	7–12	voluntary for blacks (token)	?	1–5 years
Barber (1968)	1967	8	voluntary for blacks (token)	—	first year
Crain and Weisman (1972)	1966	1–12	neighborhood	?	long-term
Friedman (1980)	late 1970s	K–3	neighborhood ?	?	?
Gerard and Miller (1975)	1966	1–6	reassignment of blacks	mixed	long-term
Green and Gerard (1974)	1966	1–6	reassignment of blacks	mixed	first year
Koslin, Amarel, and Ames (1969)	1968	1, 2	neighborhood	?	long-term
Lachat (1972)	1971	12	neighborhood	0	long-term
Lachat (1972)	1971	12	neighborhood	+	long-term
Lombardi (1962)	1958	9, 10	voluntary for blacks (token)	0	first year
McWhirt (1967)	1965	10	? not specified	?	first year
Schofield (1979)	1976	8	voluntary for all	+	1–5 years
Seidner (1971)	1970	3	voluntary for blacks	?	?
Shaw (1973)	1972	4–6	reassignment of blacks	0	first year
Shaw (1973)	1972	4–6	reassignment of blacks	0	first year
Silverman and Shaw (1973)	1971	7–12	reassignment of blacks	—	first year
Silverman and Shaw (1973)	1971	7–12	reassignment of blacks	—	first year
Singer (1966)	1964	5	neighborhood	?	long-term
Speelman and Hoffman (1980)	preschool 1, 5	not specified	not specified	?	6 months
Webster (1961)	1959	7	reassignment of blacks	?	first year

Notes

[a]"0" indicates very low-key or neutral response; "?" indicates no information in report.

[b]Parentheses indicate questionable appropriateness of control group.

[c]Parentheses indicate nonsignificant trend of mixed results.

[d]Studies are listed more than once if they looked at more than one distinct independent or dependent variable.

Design[b]					Outcome[c]		
Pre-Test	Control Group	Time Trend	Independent Variable	Dependent Variable	Blacks	Whites	Combined
	X	X	current deseg./seg.	attitude toward integ.	−		
		X	length of time deseg.	peer interaction	−		
	X		current deseg./seg.	racial attitude		−	
	(X)		prior deseg./seg.	peer interaction	+		
	X		current deseg./seg.	racial attitude		+	
X	X	X	current deseg./seg.	sociometric status	(−)	0	
X	X		current deseg./seg.	racial attitude	(−)	0	
	(X)		current deseg./seg.	racial attitude	+	(+)	
	(X)		current deseg./seg.	racial attitude		−	
	(X)		current deseg./seg.	racial attitude		+	
X	(X)		current deseg./seg.	racial attitude		0	
	X	X	current deseg./seg.	racial attitude	0	0	
	X	X	prior deseg./seg.	peer interaction			(+)
	(X)		current deseg./seg.	peer interaction	0	0	
		X	length of time deseg.	sociometric choice	0	0	
		X	length of time deseg.	sociometric rejection	(+)	−	
		X	length of time deseg.	peer interaction			0
		X	length of time deseg.	attitude toward deseg.			(+)
	(X)		current deseg./seg.	racial attitude	(+)	(+)	
	X		current deseg./seg.	racial attitude		0	
X	(X)		current deseg./seg.	racial attitude	+	−	

Patchen, Hofmann, and Davidson, 1976). Another mistaken assumption that makes it difficult to generalize from these studies is that intergroup relations cannot improve except at the expense of intragroup relations. Although this is true in some situations, such as lunchroom seating, there is no reason to believe that attitudes toward outgroup members can improve only if ingroup members are abandoned or valued less than previously.

Finally, these studies also vary markedly in methodological rigor. In compiling this list, I was careful to include any studies from the original bibliography that met some quite minimal standards of methodological rigor and direct relevance to the issue under discussion. The extent to which more rigorous methodological standards for inclusion in any meta-analysis would cut down on the number of studies available for inclusion is suggested by McConahay (1979, p. 1) who writes, "In my own review of over 50 published and unpublished studies done between 1960 and 1978, I did not find even one true experiment and only four of the quasi-experimental studies had enough methodological rigor to make them worth reporting in any detail" (the four mentioned were Gerard and Miller, 1975; Schofield and Sagar, 1977; Shaw, 1973; Silverman and Shaw, 1973).

In summary, the literature designed to see whether desegregation per se leads to changes in race relations has little to contribute to our understanding of what specific desegregation strategies are likely to produce improved race relations. The fact that there are relatively few studies combined with the lack of information about the types of schools studied and the wide variety of rather different dependent variables employed makes any formal meta-analysis aimed at assessing different desegregation strategies virtually impossible.

STUDIES LINKING SCHOOL POLICIES AND PRACTICES TO STUDENT RACE RELATIONS OUTCOMES

A broad search of the literature was performed to locate research relevant to this part of the review. Many such studies were culled from the bibliographies of the eight reviews cited earlier. Others were located using *Psychological Abstracts, Sociological Abstracts*, and the ERIC system. Finally, others were obtained through searches of the recent editions of journals and the programs of the national meetings of the American Psychological Association, the American Sociological Association, and the American Educational Research Association.

The studies reviewed in this section include (a) experimental studies looking at the impact of one or a few specific techniques designed to affect race relations; (b) "shotgun" correlational studies that search for the links between a wide array of dependent and independent variables; and (c) smaller correlational studies that, like the experimental studies, tend to look at the impact of a few specific strategies on race relations. It is crucial for the reader to keep in mind the uncertainty of inferences about the direction of causality in correlational research. Whereas experimental research, if well executed, generally leaves one feeling fairly confident about the causal direction of empirical relationships, correlational research does not. Thus, in interpreting the meaning of the correlational studies, the reader must constantly make judgements about the extent to which the causal connections suggested by the researcher are more likely than alternative connections.

Unfortunately, there are even fewer carefully performed studies that allow statistical assessment of the effectiveness of school practices in promoting positive race relations than there are studies of "the effect" of desegregation. Thus, in organizing the following discussion I have often been forced to draw on research and theory that *seems* to have implications for the topics under discussion but that was not developed with that purpose in mind. This means that much of what follows is more speculative than I would like. Yet the only alternative to that seems to be to say that with the exception of one or two well-researched practices, we have little or no quantitative research helpful in determining the likely impact of school practices on race relations.

Before proceeding to a discussion of how various school practices are likely to influence relations between students, it is important to emphasize that the review will focus on their likely impact on this one very specific area. Many of these practices may have an important impact on other variables. Failure to discuss this impact here is a consequence of the particular focus of this review. Obviously, in deciding whether or not to adopt any particular practice, a broader perspective that weighs gains and losses in a variety of dimensions would be required.

A Framework for Viewing School Practices

One of the most frequently employed perspectives on desegregation and intergroup relations was suggested by Gordon Allport (1954) over a quarter of a century ago. This perspective, sometimes called contact theory, argues that in order for increased contact to lead to improved relations, three conditions are necessary. The first of these is equal status. The second is cooperation, and the third is the support of authorities for positive intergroup relations. Contact theory has been criticized for lack of clarity, and some researchers have argued that, for example, equal status is not a *sine qua non* for improved intergroup relations but merely one possible way of achieving this goal (Amir, 1976; Riordan, 1978). Nonetheless, the contact theory variables seem to provide a useful conceptual framework within which to examine the impact of many of the school policies or practices that have been studied.

To my knowledge, there are only two studies that have carefully compared race relations outcomes in desegregated school environments that approximately fulfill Allport's contact conditions to outcomes in interracial school environments that do not. Lachat (1972) studied racial attitudes in an all-white school, in a racially mixed school that approximated the Allport contact conditions (the integrated school) and in a racially mixed school that did not meet the Allport conditions (the desegregated school). Although there was a considerable amount of voluntary segregation in informal social activities in the integrated school as well as in the desegregated one, the white students in the former school were almost twice as likely to hold positive attitudes toward blacks as students in the latter (71 percent versus 37 percent).

In the second study, Schofield and Sagar (1977) found different trends in interracial interaction in different grades of a school. In the seventh grade, where classes were racially and academically heterogeneous and policies stressed cooperation, racial mixing in the school cafeteria increased over time. In the eighth grade, characterized by academic tracking, racially homogeneous classes, and an emphasis on individual accomplishment, racial mixing in the cafeteria decreased over time.

Although studies like those mentioned above are a clear advance over earlier studies that made little or no effort to characterize the nature of the desegregation experience and to link differential experiences to differential outcomes, they do have one important theoretical and practical limitation. Since the school experiences compared differ on a number of dimensions, it is impossible to disentangle the effect of any one variable. For example, the very different outcomes in the two grades studied in the Schofield and Sagar research could be due to the racial isolation caused by tracking in one grade; to the unequal status of blacks and whites in the tracked grade; to the greater emphasis on cooperation in the untracked grade, and so on. Thus, while these studies lend some support to Allport's original contention, they do not help the theorist or practitioner to decide whether one or all of the Allport conditions must be present for the observed effects to be produced.

To explore this question and to begin to untangle, insofar as it is possible, the effect of particular policies or programs, I will now discuss what research suggests about the impact of a vaerity of policies and programs. The topics covered are naturally limited by the available research. They will be roughly grouped under the three conceptual variables identified by Allport. These groupings are for heuristic purposes only. In some cases, one could argue that a specific practice fits as well under one variable as another. In spite of these occasional ambiguities, however, contact theory provides a useful framework for integrating the various studies.

PRACTICES INFLUENCING EQUAL STATUS OF MINORITY AND MAJORITY GROUP MEMBERS

There are three very different views in the desegregation literature of how "equal status" should be defined. A brief discussion of these views will be presented here, not as a way of deciding which definition is closest to Allport's (1954) original conceptualization, but rather as a way of laying out several aspects of status, all of which seem likely to have an important effect on the outcome of intergroup contact. Kramer (1950) succinctly captured two of the three aspects of equal status by differentiating between status *within* and status *outside* of the contact situation. Many theorists—Pettigrew is, perhaps, the best known—have argued that Allport's original arguments concerned equal status *within* the contact situation. These theorists tend to focus on equal access to roles within formal organizational structures, and they believe that equal status of this sort can be obtained even if the status-linked background characteristics of the majority and minority group members are very different.

In sharp contrast, researchers like St. John (1975) and Armor (1972) emphasize the ways in which inequality in socioeconomic status or other personal characteristics can undercut the attainment of equal status within the contact situation. For example, St. John writes (1975, p.98): "Black and white children may be unequally prepared to be successful students or may be accorded unequal status in the peer group because of differential family background." According to this view, even if the school is carefully structured to give black and white children equal formal status, inequalities due to differential socioeconomic status or academic performance may create serious problems.

Cohen (1975) goes even further, arguing that even when blacks and whites are accorded equal formal status *and* have similar background characteristics, race itself operates as a diffuse status characteristic to create the expectation that whites are more competent. She argues that these expectations lead whites to behave in a dominant rather than an "equal status" manner in interracial interactions.

Cohen's view of equal status is notably different from Pettigrew's in two important ways. First, whereas Pettigrew tends to focus on access to various *positions* in the formal and informal status structure of an organization, Cohen focuses more on the *interaction patterns* that emerge. Indeed, one could even argue that the type of behavior that Cohen studies could reasonably be conceptualized as a desirable consequence of carefully planned interracial contact as well as a possible mediating variable leading to other outcomes such as a reduction in stereotyping. Second, Pettigrew (1969) clearly states that equal status can prevail within a contact situation even when major differences in family background exist between black and white students. Cohen's argument, on the other hand, suggests that even if blacks and whites come from similar backgrounds, are equally capable, and are given equal formal status, being black or white in and of itself creates expectations that lead to unequal participation and influence in peer interactions.

Pettigrew's view of equal status suggests that close attention be paid to aspects of a school's organization and structure that affect the formal roles of blacks and whites within the school and the opportunities of each group to influence decisions within it. This viewpoint encourages consideration of factors like the racial composition of the school and its staff, which clearly have great potential for affecting power within the school, as well as practices like tracking and ability grouping within classes, which may resegregate students into groups that differ in status.

The work of individuals like St. John and Armor implies that one also needs to pay close attention to the possible impact of factors such as similarity in achievement or socioeconomic status on the evolution of relations between students. The socioeconomic status and the achievement levels of black and white children at any point in time in a school district are given facts over which policymakers have no control. Yet policymakers often have some choice about the way in which students with different background characteristics will be assigned to specific schools. Since some flexibility about patterns exists in many situations, it seems worth considering what is known about the probable results of different strategies.

Finally, Cohen's work suggests that close attention should be paid to children's expectations since these expectations can lead to white domination of interracial interaction even when the children involved have equal formal status in the contact situation and similar levels of ability.

Racial Composition of the Student Body

The racial composition of a school is, of course, heavily influenced by the demographic characteristics of the area in which it is located. Nonetheless, when desegregation plans are being formulated there is often the potential for some flexibility in deciding what the desired racial mix of a school or set of schools should be.

It seems very likely that the final racial mix of any school will affect the potential for equal formal status of the different racial and ethnic groups within it. If any group is a very small minority in the student body, it will naturally have difficulty in making its presence felt in establishing an effective power base. Such problems are most likely exacerbated for members of racial minority groups for two reasons. First, many racially mixed schools view their mission as one of assimilation (Sagar and Schofield, 1983). The assimilationist ideology holds that integration will have been achieved when minority groups can no longer be differentiated from the majority group in any significant ways. This viewpoint thus tends to deny the value of aspects of minority culture that minority group members themselves may value. Second, minority group members have traditionally been powerless relative to majority group members. Indeed, such powerlessness is generally part of the sociological definition of the concept of minority group. Compounding this is the individual powerlessness in face-to-face interaction, which Cohen has documented and called an interaction disability. Thus, rather than winning a place in the status structure of a school, minority students who form a very small proportion of the students in desegregated schools may become "invisible" boys and girls whose presence makes no difference. This phenomenon is well illustrated in the following conversation among some white teachers on the first day of a token desegregation program in the school studied by Rist (1978).

> When Mrs. Brown said Donald (a new black student) would be no problem, one of the secretaries . . . said, "I don't think with this small number . . . that there should be any problems. Now if there were seventy-five or a hundred, it would be different. But I don't think twenty-eight will make any difference at all. We probably won't even know they are here." This comment was greeted with nods of agreement from the other teachers. [p. 83]

A number of studies suggest that if the proportion of minority students in a desegregated situation is quite small, relations between minority and majority group members may be adversely affected. For example, Koslin, Koslin, and Pargament (1972) found that when black students form less than 15 percent of the student body, they tend more to choose friends on the basis of similar racial group membership. Willie and McCord's (1972) study of black college students on predominantly white college campuses found quite strong norms against mixing with whites. Taking a similar position, Crain writes (cited in Roberts, 1980, p. 4), "When whites are the overwhelming majority in a school, blacks apparently engage in self-segregation in order to maintain their group identity."

When a group is proportionately very small, outgroup members have very little opportunity to interact with members of it even if they are inclined to do so. Rosenfield, Sheehan, Marcus, and Stephan (1981) found that the higher the percentage of minority students in a class, the more minority friends white fourth graders had.[2] This finding is quite consistent with other similar research as summarized by McConahay (1978). However, there are occasional studies that suggest that interaction with the outgroup is far from a direct linear function of the number of outgroup members available for interaction. For example, Roberts (1980) found that the percentage of black students reporting various types of interactions with whites was somewhat higher in schools that were more than 25 percent white than in schools that were less than 25 percent white. However, in schools between 26 percent and nearly 100 percent white, there were very few consistent differences in the reported frequency of such interactions.

Although there are indications that token desegregation may foster a tendency to ingroup preference among black students, there is also evidence suggesting that the strategy of creating schools in which the student body is roughly half black and half white, which stemmed from a concern for providing black and white students with equal status, also has some drawbacks. Specifically, a number of studies suggest that white hostility to blacks is highest in just such situations. For example, Bullock (1976b) found that white hostility to blacks was greater in such a situation than when the proportion of black students was markedly either higher or lower than 50 percent.

Similarly, Longshore (1981) concluded that white hostility to blacks was highest in desegregated schools that were between 40 and 60 percent black, arguing that in such situations whites are particularly hostile to blacks because they feel their control of the situation is threatened. When whites are either a clear minority or a clear majority, control of the situation is presumably less of an object of contention and whites' feelings are therefore less negative.

In contrast, Davidson, Hofmann, and Brown (1978) found no relation between racial composition of schools and their racial climate, which was conceptualized as a function of both the amount and kind of peer interracial interaction. This study concluded that the racial composition was not itself related to the interracial climate, but that the rate of change in racial composition was. A more detailed look at data from the same study does, however, suggest a more complex relationship between the racial composition of schools and various aspects of students' intergroup attitudes and behavior. Those interested in the intricacies of this issue are referred to Patchen (1982).

In summary, there is some evidence suggesting that token desegregation in which minority group members form a very small proportion of the student body is not particularly conducive to improved race relations for three reasons. First, black students may cluster together in such situations and thus have little contact with whites. Second, even if black students are open to intergroup contact in these circumstances, they are not present in a high enough proportion to give many white students an opportunity to interact with them. Third, small numbers seem likely to be conducive to a lack of power within the school. Thus, traditional status relations may be maintained because the minority group students lack the sheer numbers to become an influential force in the life of the school. However, increasing the proportion of black students to nearly half of the student body also seems likely to increase white hostility. Thus, on the basis of the research in this area, two quite different possibilities seem likely to be associated with reasonably good race relations—either schools that are roughly 20 to 40 percent black or schools that are over 60 percent black. Of course, these two strategies may differ considerably in their implications for other areas such as white flight and school climate.

Racial Composition of the Staff

There are, to my knowledge, no published studies that examine the effect of the racial composition of a school's teaching staff on race relations between students. One could argue that the modeling of positive interracial behavior by staff might well influence students. Indeed, a large-scale study by Genova and Walberg (1980) found a moderate positive correlation between staff modeling of positive intergroup relations and positive intergroup attitudes and behavior in high school students in several northeastern cities. Further, it seems unlikely that majority students will begin to perceive and react to other students in an equal-status manner if minority members are conspicuously absent from the staff. Finally, one well-designed study concluded that minority teachers were more equitable than majority teachers in their instructional grouping practice (System Development Corporation, 1980). Specifically, this study showed that minority teachers were more likely to treat minority and majority students in a similar manner when assigning them to possible work situations (alone, in a dyad, in a large group, and so on) than were majority teachers. In addition, the minority teachers tended to pay more attention to minority students in nonacademic contexts. To the extent that such practices help minority students feel comfortable and welcome in desegregated schools, therefore, the presence of minority faculty may well improve black-white relations.

Tracking of Academic Classes

Very little research has been done on the effect of academic tracking on race relations in desegregated schools. The few studies that do exist have somewhat unclear results. Slavin and Madden's (1979) reanalysis of the ETS data on desegregated high schools found no significant effect of tracking on the six race relations outcome variables they studied. The Schofield and Sagar (1977) study cited earlier suggested that tracking had a negative effect. Since the tracked and untracked grades also varied in other respects, however, the implications of this study for tracking are far from clear. Finally, the National Opinion Research Center (NORC, 1973) study of southern schools found that tracking had a negative effect on race relations in their elementary school sample and no consistent effect in high school. Yet the NORC study has such serious methodological problems that it seems best to give these findings relatively little weight.[3]

Given the dearth of direct evidence about the impact of tracking and the potential importance of policies about tracking, it seems important to see what theoretical work and other empirical evidence might bear on the issue. The first and most obvious question in trying to assess the potential effect of tracking on race relations is to what extent tracking will result in resegregation within a school. To the extent that race is correlated with actual or perceived academic performance, tracking will tend to create classes that differ in racial composition. It seems obvious that a tracking system that yields heavily black low-status tracks and heavily white high-status tracks can only reinforce traditional racial stereotypes. Such situations not only undercut opportunities for contact in classrooms but reinforce the traditional status order in society. Thus, it seems highly unlikely that such a system could improve race relations and reasonably likely that such a system might create problems.

Although a tracking system that results in virtually all-white or all-black classes seems bound not to improve race relations, the impact of a system that tracks while nonetheless maintaining some racial heterogeneity is more difficult to assess. Some considerations suggest that such a system might have positive effects, whereas others suggest negative effects. On the positive side is the large body of research in social psychology that suggests that perceived similarity fosters attraction between individuals (Newcomb, 1961; Schacter, 1951). To the extent that tracking leads to increased perceived similarity, it should then lead to more positive relations between classmates from different racial or ethnic groups. Indeed, a study by Rosenfield et al. (1981) suggests that the more nearly equal the socioeconomic status and academic achievement of whites and minority group children in a classroom, the more minority friends white students have. A rather different study of secondary schools found similar results (Olson, 1977). In this study, racial prejudice was lowest in classrooms where the achievement gap was smallest. Research conducted in Israel by Amir, Sharan, Bizman, Rivner, and Ben-Ari (1978) also suggests that there is more intergroup strain in junior high schools in which there is a great deal of academic heterogeneity than in schools in which members of the different ethnic groups have relatively similar levels of academic achievement. Close study of classroom life in an American school has suggested a number of ways in which great disparity in academic performance between blacks and whites can lead to strain and misunderstanding (Schofield, 1980, 1982). It seems reasonable to suggest, although there is less directly relevant research, that similar levels of achievement should be conducive to the weakening of stereotypes linking race and academic ability, since there is evidence suggesting that children perceive their classmates' academic performance quite accurately (Cohen, 1979; Snyder, 1981). A study by St. John and Lewis (1975) suggests that for blacks and whites, popularity with peers of both races is associated with high academic performance relative to one's classmates. Although this finding is not completely consistent with the idea that similarity produces attraction, it too suggests the possibility that black children who are not well above average in academic achievement might fare better with their classmates in tracked than in nontracked classrooms.

On the other hand, suggesting that tracking may have negative effects, there is evidence that racial balance within a school, defined as the proportional distribution of blacks and whites across all classes, is related to positive race relations (Koslin, Koslin, Pargament, and Waxman, 1972). As long as race and achievement are correlated, tracking will of necessity lead to racially unbalanced classrooms. Although the reason for the relation between racial balance and race relations has not been empirically established, Koslin et al. argue that the existence of racially imbalanced classrooms is likely to make race more salient and to restrict intergroup contact. It should also be noted that to the extent that the racial imbalance is caused by tracking, unbalanced classrooms also create a situation in which the status of majority and minority group children in the school is clearly and often officially unequal.

In summary, research on the impact of academic tracking on race relations is sparse. Some factors suggest that, in certain situations, tracking might have some positive effects on race relations. Other factors suggest just the opposite. The one thing that is clear is that if tracking results in virtually complete resegregation within a school, there are no grounds for expecting it to improve race relations and there are solid grounds for expecting it to reinforce traditional stereotypes.

Ability Grouping within Classrooms

The one large study examining the effects of ability grouping within classrooms on relations between black and white children found no consistent statistically significant effects. Perhaps one reason why no consistent effects were found was the fact that such groupings may have quite different effects depending on the circumstances in which they are used and the way in which they are implemented. For example, Schofield and Sagar (1979) report on two very different types of ability grouping found in the same school. One teacher divided students in his five math classes into group 1 (the fast group) and group 2 (the slow group). The teacher made frequent references to the differences in the performance levels of the two groups. In all but one class, no black students were in group 1 and few, if any, white students were in group 2. Children were seated with others in their own group and movement around the class was strongly discouraged. Once placed in a group, children were rarely moved as the quality of their work changed.

A second teacher used ability grouping in a very different way. Children spent part, not all, of their class time with others in their group. Classes were divided into three or four ability levels. Thus, although the top group was primarily white and the bottom group was primarily black, a significant proportion of the students worked in mixed groups. Finally, the teacher rarely made overt invidious comparisons between groups and frequently moved children from group to group as their progress seemed to warrant. The first type of ability grouping not only virtually prevented any contact between black and white children but also highlighted achievement differences. The second type resulted in a great deal of intergroup cooperation and contact among academic equals of different racial groups and, relatively speaking, minimized status differences between black and white children.

Similarity of Academic Performance and Socio-Economic Status

Unfortunately, there is little research directly relevant to determining how race relations are likely to be affected by differences in academic achievement or socioeconomic status. Indeed, quite recently Hawley (1980, p. 41) wrote that "there is no published research on the effects of SES mixture on race relations in desegregated schools." There are, however, a few bits of related evidence. First, there are the studies discussed earlier that suggest that perceived similarity is conducive to attraction. This body of research suggests that to the extent that they are aware of the social class of their peers, children are attracted to those of similar background more than to those who differ from them greatly. Furthermore, even if social-class background itself is not important to students, the strong correlation between social class and achievement combined with the fact that similarity in achievement is conducive to the development of friendship between children of different racial or ethnic groups suggests that similarity in social class might be helpful in fostering positive relations.

On the other hand, there is evidence suggesting that whites with relatively high levels of education are likely to be less overtly and strongly prejudiced than whites who have less education (Campbell, 1971; Nunn, Crockett, and Williams, 1978; Selznick and Steinberg, 1969).[4] Making the reasonable assumption that children's racial attitudes are influenced by their parents' attitudes, one might then expect that white children from well-educated families would be more favorably predisposed than other white children toward their black classmates. Thus, rather than maximizing similarity of social class, one might try to ensure that white children from well-educated families are maximally involved in any desegregation plan. Whether their more favorable predisposition toward blacks in general would result in positive attitudes and behaviors in spite of the marked differences in average levels of achievement and socioeconomic status that would probably exist remains an open question. Furthermore, it is quite possible that black students mixed with whites from unusually educated backgrounds would be put in a position that would create powerlessness and feelings of hostility. A study by Davidson et al. (1978) clearly suggests that the racial climate is better in high schools in which either black or white students are of relatively high socioeconomic status than in schools where neither group is of high status. This study suggests that the presence of students of high status is more conducive to creating a positive intergroup atmosphere than equality of socioeconomic status. Further analysis of the data utilized in this study suggested that neither similarity of academic achievement nor similarity of socioeconomic status were related to positive race relations in desegregated high schools (Patchen, 1982).

Techniques to Alleviate the Impact of Race as a Diffuse Status Characteristic

As indicated earlier, Berger, Cohen, and Zelditch (1966, 1972) have developed a theory of status characteristics and expectation states that Cohen and her colleagues have applied to studying interracial interaction. In brief, their theory holds that the status order in society engenders expectations about competence that become widely held by members of both the higher-ranked and the lower-ranked groups. When members of these groups come into contact, these mutually held expectations about competence may lead to dominance and actually superior performance by the higher-ranked group. The theory further holds that expectations need not be conscious to influence behavior.

Cohen (1972) argues that in American society race is one of the status characteristics that lead to the self-fulfilling prophecy predicted by the theory. This argument gains strong support from Cohen's demonstration that white junior high school students working in biracial groups dominate interaction even in an experimental situation carefully constructed to eliminate all factors, aside from the students' expectations, that might promote dominance by either race. Katz (1964) and his colleagues had previously found similar dominance by white college students in biracial work groups. Cohen argues that in thinking about race relations in desegregated schools it is important to recognize that relatively comfortable friendly relations are not the same thing as equal status relations. She also holds that any useful definition of "good" race relations should include emphasis on equality in interaction.

Fortunately, research has not only documented the existence of an imbalance in influence that Cohen and her colleagues predicted on theoretical grounds but has also suggested ways of changing it. For example, Cohen and Roper (1972) reasoned that if expectation states help to account for white domination of interaction in biracial groups, then changes in expectations should lead to changes in such patterns. Hence, they used a specially designed training experience to influence black children's expectations about their own competence. Black children were taught how to build a radio and also instructed how to teach the skill to others. Then these children viewed a film of themselves constructing the radios. Next, some of the black children taught white children how to build the radios while others taught the skill to a black administrator. The white children who learned how to build the radio from a black child also saw a videotape portraying this same child in a teaching role. Then all these children plus some white children who had not had their expectations about black competence treated as described above participated in small biracial groups. The groups in which black children had taught whites how to make the radio showed a pattern of equal-status interaction. The other groups showed the familiar pattern of white dominance, however. Cohen and Roper (1972) concluded that unequal interaction patterns will persist unless the expectations of both groups are treated.

Another recent study replicated most of Cohen and Roper's results. Riordan and Ruggiero (1980) found that without a treatment of their expectations, black and white children were not equally influential in a biracial interaction even though the experiment controlled for socioeconomic status, age, and sex. As expected, whites tended to dominate the interaction. In this study, which used a more prolonged treatment than the Cohen and Roper study, the treatment of black expectations only and the treatment of black and white expectations both increased the influence of black children. Indeed, treatment of black expectations only led to equal status interaction. Treatment of both groups led to black dominance.

There are some data suggesting that white children tend to dominate Anglo-Chicano interactions just as they tend to dominate black-white interaction

(Robbins, 1977). There is also evidence that this pattern is malleable and can be altered by the expectation training techniques that Cohen and her colleagues have developed (Robbins, 1977).

Taken as a whole then, research in this area suggests that effective techniques are available for reducing the tendency of white children to dominate interaction just because they are white. The studies performed to date have concentrated on interactions involving nonacademic tasks. Such interactions occur in many school settings. Furthermore, it does not seem fanciful to think that some of the treatment techniques could be modified for use in academic classroom settings.

PRACTICES INFLUENCING COOPERATION BETWEEN MINORITY AND MAJORITY GROUP MEMBERS

There is much evidence suggesting that cooperation can and often does have positive effects on interpersonal and intergroup relations. As Worchel (1979, p. 264) points out: "Research has demonstrated that cooperation results in increased communication, greater trust and attraction, greater satisfaction with group production, [and] greater feelings of similarity between group members." Such evidence has led many theorists and researchers to suggest that inducing cooperation between children from different racial or ethnic groups may well help to foster improved intergroup relations in desegregated schools. Quite a large number of studies suggest that this is indeed the case.

There is also evidence, however, that significant cooperation does not often occur spontaneously between blacks and whites in interracial schools. Reports of voluntary resegregation on the part of students for both social and academic activities are legion (Collins, 1979; Cusick and Ayling, 1973; Gerard et al., 1975; Schofield and Sagar, 1977; Silverman and Shaw, 1973). Thus, schools hoping to improve race relations need to adopt strategies designed to *promote* cooperation. There has been a great deal of research on strategies for promoting cooperation on academic tasks. There is less research on the impact of cooperation in the nonacademic sphere on students' racial attitudes and intergroup behavior.

Cooperative Learning Techniques

In a large correlational study of the relation of various school practices to six different indicators of students' intergroup attitudes and behavior, Slavin and Madden (1979) found that the one practice that showed quite consistent positive effects was assigning black and white students to work together on academic tasks. It is interesting to note that a study by Roberts (1980) suggests that this practice is almost twice as common in schools that have many white students as in schools that are 25 percent or less white.[5]

Although the Slavin and Madden study suggests that in general, assigning students to work together does have a positive effect, it seems clear that some types of cooperative situations are more likely to promote positive relations than others. For example, there are studies that suggest that whites working in cooperative groups with blacks respond more positively to their black teammates when the group experiences success than when it fails (Blanchard, Adelman, and Cook, 1975; Blanchard and Cook, 1976; Blanchard, Weigel, and Cook, 1975). One of these studies suggests that whites show more attraction to a black work partner when he or she performs competently than when he or she performs poorly, although no parallel phenomenon was observed in the ratings of white partners (Blanchard, Weigel, and Cook, 1975). A similar study with white military personnel as subjects failed to replicate this finding, but it did suggest that relatively competent group members, whatever their race, were more favorably regarded than less competent ones (Mumpower and Cook, 1978). It is easy to see how friction might result if children of different achievement levels are required to work together and to share a joint reward for their product. Thus, it seems important to specify carefully the kind of cooperative situation one has in mind.

Most of the research on cooperative learning techniques for classroom use with academic subject matter has focused on one of five models: Teams-Games-Tournament (TGT); Student Teams–Achievement Divisions (STAD); Jigsaw, the Johnson's cooperative learning approach; and Small-Group Teaching. All five techniques have been researched in classroom settings and have books or manuals that explain their implementation. For further details on these and other techniques readers are referred to Slavin (1980a), Sharan (1980), Aronson and Osherow (1980), and Cook (no date).

In some of these techniques, like Aronson et al.'s (1978) work on the Jigsaw Method, cooperation between students on racially or ethnically mixed teams is induced through task interdependence; that is, no individual child can fulfill his or her assignment without the assistance of others. In other cases, like Slavin's STAD technique, cooperative behavior between students is induced through reward interdependence; that is, each child's grade partly depends on the success of other group members. Although these techniques differ in many ways, most have mechanisms that allow lower achievers to contribute substantially to the attainment of the group goals. In spite of the rather important conceptual differences in the way in which cooperation is induced in the different team learning programs, there is a very noticeable similarity in the outcomes resulting from their use. The great majority of studies suggest that use of these techniques leads to some improvement in intergroup relations even if the student teams are used for a small part of the school day for no more than two or three months.

Slavin (1983) has recently reviewed much of the literature on these small group-learning teams. Rather than repeat this analysis, I have borrowed directly from Slavin's work in constructing Table 3-2, which displays a summary of the results of over a dozen studies that examined the impact of various small group-learning techniques on race relations. As can be seen from this table, a large majority of such studies show positive effects. A very few show no consistent effect and none suggest an overall negative effect of these cooperative strategies on intergroup relations. Thus, it appears safe to say that these strategies are quite likely to have a positive impact on intergroup relations between black and white students.

In contrast to the general situation regarding school policies and practices, there are a few studies that explore the impact of cooperative work groups on peer relations in classrooms with Hispanic students. Specifically, a study by Geffner (1978, cited in Towson, 1980) of fifth-grade Anglo and Mexican-American students found that students liked each other in classrooms using cooperative learning techniques more than students in classes using a different innovative teaching strategy that did not involve cooperation or students in traditionally structured classrooms. Indeed, over time, students in the cooperative classes came to like their classmates more than previously, those in the innovative classroom showed no change, and those in the traditional classes decreased their liking for their classmates.

A number of other studies also support the idea that cooperative learning strategies have positive effects on intergroup relations in classes containing Hispanic children, although these studies rarely, if ever, find positive changes for all groups on all measures of liking and respect (Blaney et al., 1977; Gonzales, 1979; Weigel, Wiser, and Cook, 1975). For example, Weigel and his colleagues (1975) examined the impact of small interdependent work groups on the intergroup attitudes and behavior of white, black, and Mexican-American teenagers. Not surprisingly, cross-ethnic helping behavior was strikingly more frequent in the experimental classrooms than in the control classrooms. A statistically significant change in intergroup attitudes, however, was found only for white students' attitudes towards Mexican-Americans. White students in the experimental classrooms rated their Mexican-American classmates as favorably as their white peers. Such was not the case in the traditional classrooms.

It is worth mentioning that a number of studies have found that Cuban and Mexican-American children are generally more positively oriented toward cooperation than are either black or white Americans (Alvarez and Pader, 1979; Kagan, 1977, 1980; Kagan and Madsen, 1972; Knight and Kagan, 1977; Madsen and Shapira, 1970). This finding has led some researchers, such as McClintock (1974), to argue that Mexican-American children are likely to be at a disadvantage in traditionally organized American classrooms, which tend to emphasize competition. Thus it may be that cooperative strategies not only have a positive impact on intergroup relations in classes including Mexican-Americans but also are particularly well suited to these children's cultural background.

Cooperation in Extracurricular Activities

Some studies suggest that blacks are less likely than whites to participate in extracurricular activities in desegregated schools (Gottlieb and TenHouten, 1965; Gordon, 1967). These findings must be interpreted cautiously, however, since the black students in such studies are generally of lower socioeconomic status than their white peers, and certain exceptions to this generalization, such as the relatively high participation rates among black males in sports like basketball, must be noted. Furthermore, there is some evidence that the participation rate of both black and white students is influenced by the racial composition of their school or the rate of change in their school's racial composition (Darden and Jacob, 1981; Gottlieb and TenHouten, 1965).

The evidence on whether school desegregation changes participation rates in extracurricular activities is quite inconclusive. However, two things do seem clear about such activities in desegregated schools. First, unless schools plan carefully, extracurricular activities that provide opportunities for cooperation may well become completely or virtually resegregated. Second, cooperation in nonacademic activities can be used to foster positive intergroup relations. Let us examine these two propositions separately.

A number of studies suggest that unless schools take steps to prevent it, a great many extracurricular activities become typed as black or white. For example, Scherer and Slawski (1979) report that in a high school they studied, basketball and football were considered black sports and swimming was seen as a white activity. These perceptions made it difficult for interested students to get involved in activities that "belonged" to the other group. Similarly, Collins (1979) reports in a study of a high school that was 60 percent black that football and basketball became black sports and that white boys interested in basketball tended to compete on church-sponsored teams rather than on their school team. Over time the school cheerleading squad also became entirely black. St. John (1964), studying two schools that were about one-fifth black, found that black students were markedly underrepresented in some activities, like the school newspaper and the student council, and markedly overrepresented in boys' sports and on the majorettes squad. Although none of the activities were close to completely black, some were almost completely white.

It seems unwise to argue that ideally all types of students should participate in all clubs in exact relation to their proportion in the student body. Cultural differences between ethnic groups may lead to differences in interests that would naturally be reflected in differential rates of enrollment in some activities. Yet often it seems that the resegregation of extracurricular activities is much more than a reflection of different interests. Rather, once an activity is seen as belonging to a particular group, members of other groups who would like to join begin to feel uncomfortable and unwelcome. Such resegregation of extracurricular activities is especially unfortunate since many of

TABLE 3-2

Characteristics and Effects on Intergroup Relations of Cooperative Learning Field Experiments

Major Reports	Number of Students	Grade Level	Duration (weeks)	Level of Random Assign.	Kind of School	Ethnic Compos. (percent)	Type of Measure	Intergroup Relations Effects
Group Study, Group Reward for Learning Methods								
Student Teams-Achievement Divisions (STAD)								
Slavin, 1977[b]	62	7	10	class	Urban East	B–61 W–39	Sociometric	+
Slavin, 1979[a] Hansell and Slavin, 1981	424	7–8	12	class	Urban East	W–61 B–39	Sociometric	+
Slavin and Oickle, 1981	230	6–8	12	class	Rural East	W–66 B–34	Sociometric	Black-White Friendships 0 White-Black Friendships +
Teams-Games-Tournament (TGT) DeVries, Edwards and Slavin, 1978:								
Experiment 1	96	7	9	class	Urban East	W–70 B–30	Sociometric	0
Experiment 2	128	7	12	student	Urban East	B–51 W–49	Sociometric	+
Experiment 3	191	10–12	12	class	Suburban South	W–90 B–10	Sociometric	+
Experiment 4 (also reported as Edwards and DeVries, 1974)	117	7	4	student	Urban East	W–57 B–43	Sociometric	+
Group Study Methods								
Learning Together Cooper, et al., 1980	57	7	3	student	Urban Midwest	W–67 B–33	Sociometric	+
Johnson and Johnson, 1981	51	4	3	student	Urban Midwest	W–78 B–18 H–2 AI–2	Observation	+
Weigel, Wiser, and Cook Methods Weigel, Wiser, and Cook, 1975	324	7–10	Gr. 7– 28 wks. Gr. 10– 18 wks.	class	Urban West	W–71 B–17 H–12	Peer rating	Ratings of: Hispanics + Blacks 0 Whites 0

Notes: + = Cooperative learning group exceeded control group significantly ($p < .05$); 0 = No significant differences; W = Non-Hispanic whites; B = Blacks; H = Hispanic-Americans; A = Asian-Americans; E = European Immigrants; WI = West Indian Immigrants; AI = American Indians; AC = Anglo-Canadians.

Source: Adapted from _Cooperative Learning_ by Robert E. Slavin. Copyright © 1983 by Longman, Inc. Reprinted by permission of Longman, Inc., New York.

Task Specialization, Group Reward for Learning Methods

Study	N	Grade	Wks	Assignment	Location	Ethnic composition	Measure	Result
Jigsaw II Ziegler, 1981	146	6	8	class	Urban Canada	AC–44 E–36 A–12 WI–8	Sociometric Ethnic Attitudes	Friendships toward: Hispanics + Blacks 0 Whites 0 +

Task Specialization Methods

Study	N	Grade	Wks	Assignment	Location	Ethnic composition	Measure	Result
Jigsaw Blaney, et al, 1977	304	5–6	6	Non-random (matched)	Urban South-west	W–59 B–23 H–16 A–2	Socio-metric	0
Gonzales, 1979	326	9–12	10	Non-random (matched)	Calif. Rural Town	W–48 H–44 A–6 B–1	Ethnic Atti-tudes	Ratings of: Hispanics + Asians 0 Anglos 0
Gonzales, 1981	182	3–4	20	Non-random (matched)	Rural Calif. (Bilingual classes)	H–54 W–46	Ethnic Attitudes	0

these activities present good opportunities for cooperative contacts that differences in academic performance may not impede as much as they sometimes impede smooth cooperation in the classroom.

The potential for cooperative involvement in extracurricular activities to improve intergroup relations is suggested by Patchen's (1982) work, which found that participation in extracurricular activities had a stronger influence on interracial friendships than almost any of the numerous other variables in his study. Consistent with this result was Slavin and Madden's (1979) finding that participation on integrated athletic teams was one of the few variables correlated with a variety of positive intergroup attitudes and behavior.[6] The correlational nature of this study leaves the direction of causality unspecified. Given the clearly demonstrated positive effects of cooperative activity on intergroup relations, however, it seems reasonable to assume that at least some of the relation stems from the positive influence of joint athletic activity. Crain's (1977) work suggests that having winning athletic teams is negatively correlated with racial tensions in desegregated schools, indicating that under some circumstances, at least, athletics can improve relations between black and white students who are not themselves athletes. A number of studies have suggested that boys in desegregated schools engage in more positive interaction across racial lines than girls (Francis and Schofield, 1980; Jansen and Gallagher, 1966; Schofield, 1982; Schofield and Sagar, 1977; Singleton and Asher, 1977). One of the many possible factors contributing to this phenomenon is the greater involvement of boys in extracurricular activities, most especially sports. For example, St. John (1964) found that boys in a desegregated school were more active in extracurricular activities than girls primarily because of their involvement with athletic teams. Although there has recently been considerable controversy about increasing the involvement of girls in athletics, it is clear that boys' intramural and extramural athletics are still generally much more important in the social life of schools than are girls' athletics. Thus, boys often have opportunities for cooperative endeavors in a highly valued sphere that are either not open to girls or available but not highly valued. Indeed, one longitudinal study of a racially mixed high school football team clearly demonstrates the positive effects of cooperative involvement in team athletics on intergroup relations between boys, although it suggests that these effects are quite situation specific (Miracle, 1981).

Although team sports are a very visible cooperative extracurricular activity, they are far from the only one. Activities like the school newspaper, band, dramatic club, and choir also provide an opportunity for students to work together toward shared goals. The important question appears to be how to ensure that such activities, including sports teams, do not become segregated. Although to our knowledge there are no studies that empirically test the effectiveness of various strategies, there is some research that reports efforts that seem to make sense and that were generally acknowledged to be effective by those in the schools involved. For example, Schofield (1982) reports that to keep school clubs from being voluntarily resegregated, one school official monitored club lists and actively set about recruiting students to clubs to achieve greater racial balance. Often this recruitment involved encouraging several children who were already friends to join a particular group. Thus, fears about being the only white or black were eased. Furthermore, children in the racial minority in a particular club who dropped out of that club were contacted and encouraged to rejoin with their friends rather than to leave the activity altogether. This same school also made strong efforts to ensure that positions of special status in extracurricular activities were distributed fairly equally between whites and blacks. For example, in casting for the dramatic club play, the drama club advisors specifically decided to divide the leading roles equally between whites and blacks. Also, in one grade a student council open to anyone who was interested was formed. The council, sponsored jointly by a black faculty member and her white colleague, was generally acknowledged to have greatly improved relations between students (Schofield and McGivern, 1979). In a similar vein, Clement and Harding (1978) report that membership in a "Powderpuff Patrol," an organization designed to help teachers maintain order, created a sense of cohesiveness among the black and white sixth-grade girls who belonged to this group.

In summary, there is substantial evidence suggesting that cooperation in the pursuit of shared goals can have a positive effect on relations between students in desegregated schools. There are a number of well-researched techniques available for promoting cooperation in the classroom. Although its impact on nonacademic tasks has not been as closely studied, here, too, cooperation seems conducive to positive relations. Further, it is clear that the resegregation of widely valued extracurricular activities like athletics can lead to tensions and resentment. Thus, strategies that are effective in encouraging cooperative contact in such activities seem likely to lead to more positive intergroup relations.

PRACTICES RELATING TO OFFICIAL SUPPORT FOR POSITIVE INTERGROUP RELATIONS

The most salient authority figures for children in a school setting are undoubtedly their teachers and the school administrators, including the principal. The evidence to be reviewed here suggests that principals and teachers can have an important influence on the evolution of intergroup relations in their schools.[7] As will become apparent, some of this influence stems directly from practices directly related to their support for positive intergroup relations while some of it stems from practices that may be adopted for a wide variety of reasons.

Principal's Commitment

Much of the evidence suggesting that principals can have a significant impact on the evolution of intergroup relations in desegregated schools comes from intensive case studies of small numbers of schools (Noblit, 1979; Willie, 1973). Some large correlational studies, however, have come to a similar conclusion. For example, one analysis of the impact of the Emergency School Assistance Program found that black and white children in schools in which the principal felt the achievement of good intergroup relations was important were more likely to interact in the lunchroom and at recess than were children in schools in which the principal did not give this goal high priority (Wellisch, Marcus, MacQueen, and Duck, 1976).

A principal's ideological commitment can be translated into behaviors that influence children's behavior in several ways. First, principals are often able to make or to influence policy decisions that affect important aspects of students' school experiences. In one school, for example, the principal and vice-principals refused to let teachers set up academically tracked, racially homogeneous classes even though the teachers strongly desired such a policy (Schofield, 1977). Second, principals can help to set a general climate that may influence teachers' attitudes and decisions. Forehand et al.'s (1976) analysis of data from a large number of desegregated schools suggested that principals' racial attitudes had a direct influence on teachers' attitudes. Even if the principal does not directly influence teachers' attitudes, he or she may be able to influence their behavior in realms where teachers are free to make their own decisions since some teachers may hope to achieve their own personal goals by pleasing their principal.

Aspects of a principal's behavior quite unrelated to an ideological commitment to improving race relations may also have a major impact on changes in student race relations. For example, Cohen's (1979) research suggests that the amount of conflict with specific racial overtones may be highly correlated with the overall level of aggressiveness in a school. Comparing one school with high rates of both types of conflict to another elementary school that had little conflict of any sort, Cohen (1979, p. 22) argues that the low level of conflict in the latter school was "the result of a long and skilled campaign on the part of the principal working closely with his staff." Thus, a principal's overall ability to create a humane and well-disciplined school climate may itself affect race relations. Forehand et al. (1976) tends to support the view that intergroup relations are influenced by characteristics of principals beyond their commitment to intergroup relations and the behaviors following therefrom. The study found that teachers' ratings of their principal's overall effectiveness were correlated with reports by white students of positive racial attitudes and high levels of intergroup contact. Similarly, Patchen (1982) found that the more that students believed that mechanisms for solving problems, racial and otherwise, were available in their schools, the more positive were their attitudes towards schoolmates of the other race and the more they reported positive changes in their intergroup attitudes.

Teachers' Workshops

Inservice training for teachers has been widely used in desegregated schools (Acland, 1975). Unfortunately, there is not a lot of evidence suggesting that such training is generally effective in improving intergroup relations. In analyzing the impact of such workshops it seems crucial to distinguish between workshops aimed at affecting intergroup relations and those with quite different goals. Acland's (1975) research found that teacher inservice training that emphasized race relations was quite clearly related to a variety of positive student attitudes and behaviors, especially for white students. Other sorts of inservice training, not surprisingly, had no such impact. Slavin and Madden's (1979) research suggests that inservice teacher training focused on race relations does not have a powerful consistent effect. Indeed, such training was significantly associated with only one of the six student race relations outcomes studied for both white and black students. Thus, although Gay (1978) has outlined a variety of very useful and important things that teacher inservice training should accomplish, there is mixed evidence about the effectiveness of such workshops.

Multiethnic Texts and Minority History

Research suggests that multhiethnic texts may have some positive impact on race relations, but the evidence is neither overwhelmingly strong nor completely consistent. Forehand et al. (1976) found a correlation between the use of a variety of "race relations practices" and favorable racial attitudes in black and white elementary school students. Their variable, race relations practices, included the utilization of multiethnic texts and inclusion of information about blacks in the curriculum as well as five or six other components. The same study found a similar relation between these practices and the attitudes of white but not black high school students. However, Slavin and Madden's (1979) reanalysis of the high school data suggests that most of the relationship found in the Forehand et al. research was due to one component within the composite variable. This component, as discussed previously, was assigning students to work with those of the other race. When the effect of multiethnic texts was examined by itself, no statistically significant relation was found between the use of such texts and any of the six race relations outcomes examined for white and black students separately. It is worth noting, however, that 11 of the 12 correlations computed were positive. A study of Iadicola (cited in Cohen, 1975) found a negative correlation between the use of multicultural curricula and the extent to which white children tended to dominate blacks in peer interactions. However, the use of such curricula was so closely correlated with the racial composition of both the student body and the staff in the schools studied that it was impossible to determine which of these factors was responsible for the relationship found.

The one experimental study of the impact of multiethnic texts of which we are aware was performed in an all-white elementary school. This well-designed study (Litcher and Johnson, 1969) compared the racial attitudes of white second-grade students who used a multiethnic reader to those of similar white children who used a reader in which all the characters were white. At the end of the four-month experiment, the former group showed more positive racial attitudes on four separate measures than did the latter. Although this experiment quite clearly shows the multiethnic reader to have a positive effect on white attitudes, it is certainly possible that one would find the effect of a multiethnic reader to be greater in a segregated school where it is the children's main source of information about the outgroup than in a desegregated school.

Studies of the impact of courses on minority history on intergroup relations are few and far between. Furthermore, there have been rather conflicting results. Acland (1975) found a correlation between interracial interaction rates and courses on minority history and culture. However, Slavin and Madden (1979) found that the availability of minority history courses was significantly related to only one of the six racial relations outcomes examined for white students and to none for black students. As in the case of the multiethnic curriculum, however, the great majority of the correlations were positive in direction. Finally, one study that found high levels of interracial friendship associated with low levels of prejudice in teachers suggested that the fact that the less prejudiced teachers utilized aspects of minority culture in teaching more than did highly prejudiced teachers might help to explain the relation between teacher prejudice and student interraical friendships (Johnson, Gerard, and Miller, 1975).

Teacher Behaviors

Koslin, Koslin, and Pargament (1972) collected data on the racial attitudes of two successive sets of third-graders who were randomly assigned to a group of teachers in racially balanced schools. They found that teachers tended to have consistent effects on students' racial attitudes. That is, the teachers whose students had the most positive intergroup attitudes in the first year were the very same teachers whose students had positive attitudes in the study's second year. Although attrition problems in the sample of teachers led the researchers to consider these findings as tentative, they are nonetheless quite suggestive. How is it that teachers affect students' interracial attitudes? As is the case with principals, teachers may both set a general climate that influences others and engage in specific practices motivated by their racial attitudes that have predictable outcomes. For example, Genova and Walberg's (1980) study found a positive though modest link between racial fairness, exemplified in their measure by items such as "Teachers are equally friendly to students of all racial and ethnic groups," and students' intergroup attitudes and behavior.

Serow and Solomon (1979a) factor-analyzed various aspects of teachers' behavior and related the dimensions that emerged from that analysis to two aspects of interracial peer behavior: general positive intergroup interaction rates and joint intergroup effort. Although these two student behavior variables were not completely independent, the second emphasized task-oriented behavior whereas the first variable emphasized positive affect and social interaction. Serow and Solomon found a positive relation between the teacher's warmth and acceptance of children and general positive interracial interaction. Also, they found a negative relation between this aspect of peer behavior and both the teacher's emphasis on a businesslike atmosphere and his or her tendency to interact directly with students. Although these findings are suggestive, two additional findings must be kept in mind in interpreting them. First, as Serow and Solomon note, a businesslike atmosphere and high levels of teacher-student interaction may well depress overall student interaction. Thus, although students in such academically oriented classrooms may not learn specifically to avoid outgroup members, they tend not to interact much with other students in general. Second, neither teacher warmth nor the two teacher behavior variables that depressed general positive intergroup interactions influenced joint intergroup effort significantly. Rather, joint intergroup effort was related to the diversity of structure and activity in the classroom and the teacher's patience and persistence.

The Serow and Solomon study discussed above suggests that certain aspects of a teacher's behavior that may have little or no direct relation to the teacher's racial attitudes can influence intergroup relations in the classroom. It should come as little surprise to learn that there is also some evidence that teachers' racial attitudes are related to student outcomes. For example, in the analysis of their high school data, Forehand et al. (1976) found that teachers' racial attitudes were quite strongly related to white students' racial attitudes and to the amount of interracial contact reported by white students. Their data from elementary schools suggested a similar although weaker and less consistent pattern.

Gerard et al. (1975) found, as previously mentioned, a relation between teachers' prejudice and white children's acceptance of minority group children as friends. This influence may be transmitted through the teachers' classroom practices. Indeed, analysis of these researchers' data showed that teachers who were more prejudiced were less likely to assign children to work in small groups. The potential advantages of cooperative work within small groups have already been discussed. As was also mentioned above, highly prejudiced teachers were less likely to utilize aspects of minority culture in their teaching than were those low in prejudice.

Discussions of Race and Human Relations Activities Involving Students

One way in which some teachers try to improve relations between black and white students is by discussing race in their classes. Slavin and Madden (1979) examined the impact of class discussions on race of students' attitudes and behavior and concluded that such discussions had some positive effects on white students but no consistent one on black students. Specifically, two of the six outcome variables for white students were significantly correlated with such discussions. No significant correlations were found for black students.

Acland looked at the impact of programs specifically designed to improve relations between students and concluded that they were positively correlated with improved interracial interaction rates and attitudes. However, correlations between the presence of such programs and changes in behavior and attitudes were much more common for white students than for blacks. Acland does not describe the content of these programs in any detail. Thus, it is difficult to know whether these programs involved discussion of race or whether they tried to improve black-white relations in other ways, such as through stimulating cooperative involvement in projects of interest to both groups. Carbonari and Birenbaum (1980) describe a program based on, although not restricted to, increasing students' understanding of the stereotyping process that led to positive short-term attitude change in junior high and high school age students. On the other hand, Lessing and Clarke (1976) report that an eight-week "multimedia, multiple influence mode" intergroup relations curriculum had no significant effect on the racial and ethnic attitudes of white junior high school students in a suburb that was experiencing racial tensions.

In summary, taken as a whole, the scattered research that is available suggests a weak link between classroom human relations activities and students' attitudes and behavior. One interesting conclusion emerging from the System Development Corporation Study (1980) of human relations programs funded by the Emergency School Assistance Act was that programs provided directly to students had a greater impact on students' intergroup behavior and attitudes than did programs provided for parents or school staff.

Seating Patterns

Stuart Cook (1969) argues that one variable likely to have an important influence on the outcome of contact between two groups is the contact situation's acquaintance potential. He defines acquaintance potential as "the extent to which the situation provides opportunities for getting to know the other race as individuals" (1969 p. 211). Cook does not systematically lay out variables that influence the acquaintance potential of a situation. It seems obvious, however, that physical proximity plays a vital role. Unless students from two previously unacquainted and even hostile groups are physically close to each other, it seems unlikely that they will have much opportunity to get to know each other.

Teachers can easily affect the acquaintance potential in their classrooms through a variety of classroom practices. One of the most basic of these is the seating assignment policy. Seating assignment policy can be differentiated from policies about small-group work. Although it is true that students assigned to work together will most probably have to sit together, often students are assigned to nearby seats without being assigned to work cooperatively. For example, some teachers assign students to sit in alphabetical order whereas others let students choose their own seats.

When students are allowed to pick their own seats they often tend to sit next to those of the same race (Schofield, 1982). This, of course, greatly decreases the acquaintance potential of the desegregated classroom. In a study of an all-white school, Byrne and Buehler (1955) have shown that students who are assigned adjacent seats tend to become acquainted with each other. Also, Byrne (1971) demonstrated that the number of friendships a student forms in school can be increased if the teacher changes the assigned seating pattern during the course of a semester. The only study of which we are aware that yields quantitative data on the impact of seating policies in desegregated schools is consistent with the other studies just cited. Wellisch et al.'s (1976) study found more interracial mixing in informal settings like the lunchroom and the playground among elementary school children whose teachers used classroom seating assignment policies that resulted in a lot of cross-race proximity than among children whose teachers tended to group children by race. Patchen (1982) also found a positive relationship between proximity to other-race students in class seating patterns and a wide variety of positive interracial behaviors and attitudes. Seats were not assigned in all classes in this study, making the direction of the casual link between seating proximity and positive interracial attitudes somewhat ambiguous; but internal analyses of the data suggested that seating proximity did have an effect on intergroup relations.

SUMMARY AND CONCLUSIONS

Two strategies were used to explore the empirical literature potentially relevant to the issue of what approaches are likely to lead to improved relations between black and white children in desegregated schools. First, we examined studies that were designed to explore how desegregation itself influences children's intergroup attitudes and behavior. Second, we summarized the results of various studies that have looked directly at the impact of a variety of school practices and policies on children's attitudes and behaviors toward members of other racial or ethnic groups.

The first strategy, a review of the studies looking at the effect of desegregation on students' intergroup attitudes, was aimed at producing review-generated comparisons of studies of different types of desegregated schools that would lead to some conclusions about which types of desegregation are more effective than others. This part of the review did not produce many such conclusions for several reasons. First, an extensive search of the literature located only seventeen studies of sufficient relevance and rigor to warrant inclusion in this review. The number of studies useful for assessing the impact of desegregation on specific groups of students dwindles still further since some studies look at outcomes for blacks or whites but not for both. As an inspection of Table 3-1 will show, the studies that do exist rarely describe the schools in which they were conducted in sufficient detail to make review-generated comparisons of "types of desegregation" possible. In addition, approximately one half of the studies, including both studies of court-ordered desegregation, were conducted during the first year of desegregation, and a number of these were conducted less than four months after desegregation. Thus, a substantial proportion of the studies are of questionable utility for understanding the long-term effect of desegregation.

The dependent variables utilized in these seventeen studies vary greatly. Unfortunately, there is little reason to expect that the variables examined are highly correlated aspects of intergroup relations. Furthermore, a large proportion of these dependent variables were measured using "zero-sum" techniques that pick up only the changes in outgroup acceptance that occur at the expense of acceptance of ingroup members. Yet there is no reason to believe that improved intergroup relations come at the expense of intragroup relations. Indeed, there is some evidence to the contrary (Cohen, 1979). In sum, a number of characteristics of the existing literature on the effect of desegregation on children's intergroup attitudes and behavior make it virtually impossible to do a useful meta-analysis comparing the outcomes of various desegregation strategies.

The second section of this essay was based on a broad search of the empirical literature on the impact of various school practices and policies on student intergroup relations. Although some experimental studies were located, the vast majority of this research is correlational. Thus, readers must keep in mind that although this review tends to assume that the various policies cause the related outcomes, it is always possible, although more probable in some instances than in others, that this assumption is not accurate.

It is also important to mention that many of the correlational studies do not measures the variables they study in ways that maximize the likelihood of finding relations that do, in fact, exist between school practices and outcomes. For example, in the studies reviewed, both practices and outcomes were often measured as dichotomous variables. Such variables are far from ideal for use in correlational designs. Their attenuated range makes it possible for covariation that would be found with more sensitive measures to be almost completely masked.

For heuristic purposes, the various techniques on which there is some research were grouped in three broad categories drawn from Allport's (1954) contact theory. The first category, studies of practices that seem to affect the extent to which blacks and whites are likely to attain equal status in a desegregated school, is quite broad because of the complexity of the concept *equal status*. The studies examined practices relating to three types of status: formal status within the school, informal status linked to personal characteristics like socioeconomic background and academic ability, and status defined as dominance in ongoing interactions when both formal roles and personal characteristics linked to informal status are similar for all interactants.

Factors examined that are related to the first type of status were the racial composition of the student body and staff, academic tracking, and ability grouping within classes. There is evidence that token desegregation in which minority group members form a very small proportion of the student body is not particularly conducive to improved race relations. Some researchers argue that intergroup relations are, all things considered, likely to be best when all groups are represented in roughly equal numbers. However, there has not been a great deal of study of this proposition, and there are some studies that suggest that white hostility is greatest in just such situations. Unfortunately, there is virtually no direct quantitative evidence pertaining to the impact of a racially balanced faculty on student intergroup relations, although there are some reasons for thinking that a racially balanced faculty would have a positive effect. It seems obvious that a tracking system that yields heavily black low-status tracks and heavily white high-status tracks can only reinforce traditional stereotypes and resegregate desegregated schools. There is also some research that suggests that the effects of such a system are negative. The results of tracking systems that maintain some racial heterogeneity are harder to assess. On the positive side is the fact that black and white students similar in academic performance level are probably more likely to respond to each other favorably than are those very dissimilar in achievement. On the other hand, there is evidence suggesting that wide variations in the proportion of black and white students in the various classrooms of a school has a negative effect on intergroup relations. The one large study examining the effects of ability grouping within classrooms on relations between black and white children found no consistent effect. However, data from a qualitative study of a desegregated school suggests that this may be because different kinds of ability grouping within classrooms may have different and even directly opposite effects.

There is little or no research directly relevant to determining how race relations are likely to be influenced by differences in status-linked personal characteristics like academic achievement and socioeconomic status. There are some bits of evidence suggesting that similarity of blacks and whites on these dimensions might be conducive to better relations than large differences would be. Yet there is also research that clearly suggests that desegregation can lead to more positive intergroup relations even when differences in achievement levels and socioeconomic background are large (Schofield and Sager, 1977).

Cohen's theorizing and research has emphasized that it is important to move beyond attention to how smooth and friendly intergroup relations are to examine power and influence in interracial interactions. Her research shows that even when blacks and whites have similar formal status in a situation and similar background characteristics, whites tend to dominate interracial interaction. Fortunately, research has suggested techniques that are effective in reducing and even eliminating this imbalance.

The second general category into which various studies were grouped for consideration was that including practices that influence the amount of co-operation that occurs between students. There is a great deal of evidence suggesting that cooperation can and often does have quite positive effects on interpersonal and intergroup relations. Indeed, of all the techniques designed to improve intergroup relations in desegregated schools, the most heavily researched are those that foster cooperation in small task-oriented learning groups. There are several such techniques, which differ in a number of ways. All have been extensively researched in classroom settings and have books or manuals explaining their implementation. Experimental research suggests that all of these techniques have a positive effect on intergroup relations.

There is much less research on the effects of cooperation in nonacademic spheres on intergroup relations than there is on the effects of the various cooperative learning techniques. Yet two things do seem clear. First, unless schools plan carefully, extracurricular activities that provide good opportunities for cooperation may well become virtually resegregated. Second, cooperation in nonacademic activities can be used effectively to foster positive intergroup relations.

Studies of factors relating to the support of school authorities for positive intergroup relations were also examined. Holding teacher workshops that emphasize ways of improving race relations between students is one sign of support for positive intergroup relations. One large study, however, found no such effect. Research about the impact of multiethnic texts and minority history also has mixed results. However, the one *experimental* study of multiethnic readers found that they have a marked positive impact on white elementary school children's reactions to blacks. Class discussions of race and programs designed to improve intergroup relations also show a positive relation to at least some aspects of intergroup relations, although only one or two studies have examined these practices. There is reason to think that seat assignment policies fostering intergroup contact will have a positive impact.

It is interesting, although not surprising, to note that several aspects of teachers' and principals' behavior that do not seem to be directly connected to their attitudes about intergroup relations appear to have a sizable impact on such relations. For example, Serow and Solomon (1979a) found that an emphasis on academics and on direct teacher interaction with students was negatively correlated with the rate of interaction between groups. On the other hand, teachers' warmth and their acceptance of students were positively correlated with interaction between groups. Also, Cohen (1979) suggests that principals may influence the development of intergroup relations through policies that affect the general tone of personal relations at a school.

In summary, although the evidence is, in general, quite fragmented and spotty, this review has discussed a number of malleable practices and policies that research suggests may have an impact on the evolution of intergroup relations in desegregated schools. A knowledge of such policies and practices, taken in conjunction with an examination of their likely impact on other important outcome variables, should suggest ways in which educators can improve the education that children receive in desegregated schools.

APPENDIX

Procedure for Determining Inclusion of Studies in the Present Review

1. All citations in the reviews that related even tangentially to desegregation and race relations were part of the potential core. These papers were grouped into several categories:

a. works published in 1960 or earlier,

b. unpublished papers,

c. Doctoral dissertations; and

d. other published papers, books and large technical reports. All items in categories (a) and (b) were automatically eliminated from consideration. The early papers were eliminated since there have been such major changes in so many aspects of race relations in the intervening years that the relevance of these studies to the present-day situation seemed quite uncertain. Most of the unpublished papers were not given further consideration for the following reasons. First, some were not obtainable. Second, in general there appears to be a noticeable difference in quality between published papers and those that remain unpublished long after they were written. Only two of the unpublished papers cited in the reviews were less than five years old. These two papers were included in the potential pool of studies.

2. Studies were eliminated from further consideration in this section of the review if they were:

a. review articles rather than research reports (these were coded R for review);

b. more appropriately considered in another section of this review because they focused on specific techniques used to promote positive race relations or reported the results of large correlational studies of various techniques (these were coded S for specific techniques or C for large-scale correlational study);

c. conducted with children of preschool age or with college students or adults (these were coded A for age);

d. primarily of methodological rather than substantive interest (these were coded *M* for methodological focus);

e. studies of racial attitudes, personality variables, or social behavior that were tangential to the focus of the present review for a variety of reasons, such as failure to compare the attitudes of segregated and desegregated students (these were coded *I* for irrelevant);

f. seriously flawed methodologically for the purposes of this review (these were coded *P* for methodological problem. It should be emphasized that placement in this category does not imply that a study is so methodologically flawed that it is of no interest for any purpose. On the contrary, some of the studies coded *P* contain quite useful and interesting information. However, the structure of these studies is methodologically flawed for exploration of the impact of desegregation on intergroup attitudes and behavior); or

g. duplicate reports of research projects reported more fully elsewhere. In such cases, the more complete document was used even if it was unpublished (these were coded *E* for elsewhere).

The following are potentially relevant studies cited in previous reviews with the reasons, where applicable, for their elimination from the present review. Reviews citing each study are given in parentheses.

Doctoral Dissertations

Barber, R. W. The effects of open enrollment on anti-Negro and anti-white prejudices among junior high students in Rochester, New York. Unpublished doctoral dissertation, University of Rochester, 1968. (Schofield, Stephan, St. John.)

Evans, C. L. The immediate effects of classroom integration on the academic progress, self-concept and racial attitudes of Negro elementary children. Unpublished doctoral dissertation, North Texas State University, 1969. (P—Stephan, St. John.)

Garth, C. E. Self-concept of Negro students who transferred and did not transfer to formerly all-white high schools. Unpushlished doctoral dissertation, University of Kentucky, 1963. (I—Stephan, St. John.)

Herman, B. E. The effect of neighborhood upon the attitudes of Negro and white sixth grade children toward different racial groups. Unpublished doctoral dissertation, University of Connecticut, 1967. (I—Stephan, St. John.)

Lachat, M. A description and comparison of the attitudes of white high school seniors toward black Americans in three suburban high schools: An all white, a desegregated, and an integrated school. Unpublished doctoral dissertation, Teachers College, Columbia University, 1972. (Cohen, Schofield.)

Lewis, R. G. The relationship of classroom racial composition to student academic achievement and the conditioning effects of interracial social acceptance. Unpublished doctoral dissertation, Harvard Graduate School of Education, 1971. (I—St. John.)

Lombardi, D. N. Factors affecting changes in attitudes toward Negroes among high school students. Unpublished doctoral dissertation, Fordham University, 1962. (Schofield, Stephan, St. John, Carithers.)

McWhirt, R. A. The effects of desegregation on prejudice, academic aspiration and the self-concept of tenth grade students. Unpublished dcotoral dissertation, University of South Carolina, 1967. (Schofield, Stephan, St. John.)

Seidner, J. Effects of integrated school experience on interaction in small bi-racial groups. Unpublished doctoral dissertation, University of Southern California, 1971. (Cohen.)

Singer, D. Interracial attitudes of Negro and white fifth grade children in segregated and unsegregated schools. Unpublished doctoral dissertation Teachers College, Columbia University, 1966. (Carithers, St. John, Cohen, Schofield.)

Taylor, C. P. Some changes in self-concept in the first year of desegregated schooling. Unpublished doctoral dissertation, University of Delaware, 1967. (I—St. John.)

Useem, E. L. White suburban secondary students in schools with token desegregation: Correlates of racial attitudes. Unpublished doctoral dissertation, Harvard University, 1971. (P—St. John, Cohen.)

Walker, K. D. Effects of social and cultural isolation upon the self-concepts of Negro children. Unpublished doctoral dissertation, University of Miami, Florida, 1968. (I—St. John.)

Unpublished Papers

Omit all in this category written before 1976.

Aaronson, S., and Noble, J. Urban-suburban school mixing: A feasibility study. Unpublished manuscript, 1966. (St. John, Schofield.)

Bullock, C. School desegregation, inter-racial contact and prejudice. Final report to the National Institute of Education, Project no. 3–0182, 1976. (McConahay.)

Carrigan, P. M. School desegregation via compulsory pupil transfer: Early effects on elementary school children. Public Schools, Ann Arbor, Michigan, September 1969. (St. John.)

Chesler, M., and Segal, P. Characteristics of Negro students attending previously all-white schools in the deep South. Unpublished manuscript, Institute for Social Research, University of Michigan, September 1972. (Cohen.)

Coats, W. A longitudinal survey of desegregation in Kalamazoo, Michigan. Paper presented at the annual meeting of the American Psychological Association Annual Convention, Honolulu, Spetember 1972. (Cohen.)

Cusick, P., and Ayling, R. Racial interaction in an urban, secondary school. Paper presented at the annual meeting of the American Educational Research Assocation, New Orleans, February 1973. (Cohen.)

Fox, D. S. Free choice open enrollment-elementary schools. Unpublished manuscript, Center for Urban Education, New York, August 1966. (St. John.)

Gardner, E. B., Wright, B. D., and Dee, R. The effects of busing black ghetto children into white suburban schools. Unpublished manuscript, July 1970. (ERIC Document Reproduction Service no. ED 048 389.) (Schofield, Stephan, St. John.)

Hawley, W. Teachers, classrooms, and the effects of school desegregation on effort in school: A "second generation" study. Working paper no. 4763, Institute of Policy Sciences and Public Affairs, Duke University, 1976. (McConahay.)

Johnson, D. W., and Johnson, R. T. Effects of cooperation, competition, and individualism on interpersonal attraction among heterogeneous peers. Paper presented at the annual meeting of the American Psychological Association, San Francisco, September (S—Slavin-Madden.)

McPartland, J. The segregated student in desegregated schools: Sources of influence on Negro secondary students. Report no. 21, Center for the Study of Social Organization of Schools, Johns Hopkins University, 1968. (St. John.)

Morland, J. K. Race attitudes and race in public schools: A case study of Lynchburg, Virginia. Unpublished manuscript, 1976. (ERIC Document Reproduction Service no. ED 131 166 UD 061 567.) (McConahay.)

Office of Education, U.S. Department of Health, Education and Welfare. Follow-up study of student attitudes toward school reorganization of the public schools in a northern city. Final report, 1972. (Cohen.)

Orost, J. H. Racial attitudes among white kindergarten children from three different environments. Paper presented at the annual meeting of the American Educational Research Association, New York, February 1971. (St. John.)

Patchen, M., and Davidson, J. D. Patterns and determinants of interracial interaction in the Indianapolis public high schools. Unpublished manuscript, 1973. (St. John.)

St. John, N. H. School integration research: The Pittsburgh study. Unpublished manuscript, 1969. (St. John.)

St. John, N. H., and Lewis, R. Children's interracial friendships: An exploration of the contact hypothesis. Unpublished manuscript, Univserity of Massachusetts, 1973. (Cohen.)

Schofield, J. W. To be or not to be (black). Paper presented at the annual meeting of the American Psychological Association, Chicago, September 1975. (Schofield.)

Slavin, R. E. Multiracial student team instructional programs and race relations in desegregated schools. Paper presented at the annual meeting of the American Educational Research Association, Toronto, March 1978. (S—Slavin-Madden, McConahay.)

Walberg, H. An evaluation of an urban-suburban school busing program: student achievement and perception of class learning environments. Paper presented at the annual meeting of the American Educational Research Association, New York, February 1971. (Cohen).

Books, Articles, and Technical Reports

Amir, Y. Contact hypothesis in ethnic relations. *Psychological Bulletin*, 1969, *71*, 319–338. (R—Cohen, Slavin-Madden.)

Armor, D. J. The evidence on busing. *Public Interest*, 1972, *28*, 90–126. (St. John, Cohen, McConahay.)

Aronson, E., Blaney, N., Sikes, J., Stephan, G., and Snapp, M. The Jigsaw route to learning and liking. *Psychology Today*, February 1975, 43–50. (S—Schofield.)

Berger, J., Cohen, E., and Zelditch, M. Status characteristics and expectation states. In J. Berger, M. Zelditch, and B. Anderson (Eds.), *Sociological theories in progress*. Boston: Houghton Mifflin, 1966. (S—Cohen.)

Bradley, G. H. Friendship among students in desegregated schools. *Journal of Negro Education*, 1964, *33*, 90–92. (I—Carithers.)

Bullock, C., and Braxton, M. V. The coming of school desegregation: A before and after study of black and white student perceptions. *Social Science Quarterly*, 1973, *54*, 132–138. (P—Cohen.)

Cohen, E. G. Interracial interaction disability. *Human Relations*, 1972, *25*, 9–24. (S—Cohen.)

Cohen, E., Lockheed, M., and Lohman, M. The center for interracial cooperation: A field experiment. *Sociology of Education*, 1976, *49*, 47–58. (S—Cohen.)

Cohen, E., and Roper, S. Modification of interracial interaction disability: An application of status characteristic theory. *American Sociological Review*, 1973, 37, 643–657 (S—Cohen.)

Cook, S. W. Social science and school desegregation: Did we mislead the Supreme Court? *Personality and Social Psychology Bulletin*, 1979, 5, 420–437. (R—McConahay.)

Crain, R., and Weisman, C. *Discrimination, personality and achievement: A survey of northern blacks*. New York: Seminar Press, 1972.

Crooks, R. C. The effects of an interracial (pre-school) program upon racial preferences, knowledge of racial differences and racial identification. *Journal of Social Issues*, 1970, 26, 137–144. (A—Schofield, St. John, McConahay.)

Dentler, R. A., and Elkins, C. Intergroup attitudes, academic performance, and racial composition. In R. A. Dentler, B. Mackler, and M. E. Warshauer (Eds.), *The urban R's*. New York: Praeger, 1967. (P—Stephan, Carithers, McConahay - omit, St. John, Schofield.)

DeVries, D. L. , Edwards, K. J., and Slavin, R. E. Biracial learning teams and race relations in the classroom: Four field experiments using Teams-Games-Tournament. *Journal of Educational Psychology*, 1978, 70, 356–362. (S—Slavin-Madden.)

Erlanger, H. S., & Winsborough, H. H. The subculture of violence thesis: An example of a simultaneous equation model in sociology. *Sociological Methods and Research*, 1976, 5, 231–246. (I—McConahay.)

Forehand, G., Ragosta, M., and Rock, D. *Conditions and processes of effective school desegregation*. Final report, U.S. Office of Education, Department of Health, Education, and Welfare. Princeton, N.J. Educational Testing Service, 1976. (C—McConahay, Slavin-Madden.)

Gerard, H., Jackson, D., and Conolley, E. Social contact in the desegregated classroom. In H. Gerard and N. Miller (Eds.), *School desegregation*. New York: Plenum Press, 1975.

Gottlieb, D., and TenHouten, W. D. Racial composition and the social systems of three high schools. *Journal of Marriage and the Family*, 1965, 27, 204–212. (I—McConahay, St. John, Carithers.)

Green, J. A., and Gerard, H. B. School desegregation and ethnic attitudes. In H. Fromkin and I. Sherwood (Eds.), *Integrating the organization*. New York: Free Press, 1974. (Schofield, McConahay, Stephan.)

Herman, B. Interracial attitudes among 175 sixth grade students. *Curriculum Leadership*, 1970, 9(1), 30–35. (P—St. John.)

Jansen, V. G., and Gallagher, J. J. The social choices of students in racially integrated classes for the culturally disadvantaged talented. *Exceptional Children*, 1966, 33, 221–226. (I—Schofield.)

Justman, J. Children's reactions to open enrollment. *The Urban Review*, 1968, 3, 32–34. (P—St. John.)

Kaplan, H. K., and Matkom, A. J. Peer status and intellectual functioning of Negro school children. *Psychology in the Schools*, 1967, 4, 181–184. (I—McConahay, St. John.)

Koslin, S., Amarel, M., and Ames, N. A distance measure of racial attitudes in primary grade children: An exploratory study. *Psychology in the Schools*, 1969, 6, 382–385. (McConahay.)

Koslin, S., Koslin, B., Pargament, R., and Waxman, H. Classroom racial balance and students' interracial attitudes. *Sociology of Education*, 1972, *45*, 386–407. (S—St. John, McConahay.)

Kurokawa, M. Mutual perceptions of racial images: White, black, and Japanese Americans. *Journal of Social Issues*, 1971, *27*(4), 213–235. (I—Schofield, St. John.)

Lewis, R., and St. John, N. H. Contribution of cross-racial friendship to minority group achievement in desegregated classrooms. *Sociometry*, 1974, *37*, 79–91. (I—Cohen.)

National Opinion Research Center. *Southern schools: An evaluation of the effects of the Emergency School Assistance program and of school desegregation*. Vol 1. U.S. Office of Education, Department of Health, Education and Welfare. Chicago: NORC, The University of Chicago, 1973. (C—McConhay, Slavin-Madden.)

Patchen, M., Davidson, J., Hofmann, G., and Brown, W. Determinants of students' interracial behavior and opinion change. *Sociology of Education*, 1977, *50*, 55–75. (I—Schofield, McConahay.)

Patterson, D. L., and Smits, S. J. Reactions of inner-city and suburban adolescents to three minority groups. *Journal of Psychology*, 1972, *80*, 127–134. (I—Cohen, McConahay.)

Porter, J. D. R. *Black child—white child*. Cambridge: Harvard University Press, 1971. (A—St. John.)

St. John, N. H. De facto segregation and interracial association in high school. *Sociology of Education*, 1964, *37*, 326–344. (I—Carithers, St. John, McConahay.)

St. John, N. H., and Lewis, R. G. Race and the social structure of the elementary classroom. *Sociology of Education*, 1975, *48*, 346–368. (I—McConahay, St. John, Schofield.)

Schmuck, R. A., and Luzki, M. B. Black and white students in several small communities. *Journal of Applied Behavioral Science*, 1969, *5* 203–220. (P—St. John.)

Schofield, J. W., and Sagar, H. A. Peer interaction in an integrated middle school. *Sociometry*, 1977, *40*, 130–138. (S—McConahay, Schofield.)

Shaw, M. E. Changes in sociometric choices following forced integration of an elementary school. *Journal of Social Issues*, 1973, *29*(4), 143–157. (McConahay, Schofield.)⸍

Silverman, I., and Shaw, M. Effects of sudden mass school desegregation on interracial interactions and attitudes in one southern city. *Journal of Social Issues*, 1973, *29*(4), 133–142. (McConahay, Stephan, Schofield, Cohen: cites earlier version presented to APA.)

Singer, D. Reading, writing and race relations. *Trans-Action*, 1967, *4*(7), 27–31. (E—Stephan.)

Slavin, R. E. Effects of biracial learning teams on cross-racial friendships. *Journal of Educational Psychology*, 1979, *71*, 381–387. (S.)

Smith, M. B. The schools and prejudice: Findings. In C. Y. Glock and E. Siegelman (Eds.), *Prejudice U.S.A.* New York: Praeger, 1969. (P—St. John.)

Stephan, W. G. Cognitive differentiation and intergroup perception. *Sociometry*, 1977, *40*, 50–58. (I—Stephan.)

Trubowitz, J. *Changing the racial attitudes of children*. New York: Praeger, 1969. (I—Schofield.)

U.S. Commission on Civil Rights. *Racial isolation in the public schools*. Washington, D.C.: Government Printing Office, 1967. (C—St. John, Cohen, Schofield.)

Useem, E. L. White students and token desegregation. *Integrated Education*, 1972, *10*, 46. (E—McConahay.)

Useem, E. L. Correlates of white students' attitudes towards a voluntary busing program. *Education and Urban Society*, 1976, *8*(4), 441–476. (E—Schofield.)

Wade, K., and Wilson, W. Relatively low prejudice in a racially isolated group. *Psychological Reports*, 1971, *28*, 871–877. (P—Cohen, McConahay.)

Webster, S. W. The influence of interracial contact on social acceptance in a newly integrated school. *Journal of Educational Psychology*, 1961, *52*, 292–296. (Stephan, St. John, Cohen, McConahay, Schofield.)

Wellisch, J., Marcus, A., MacQueen, A., and Duck, G. *An in-depth study of Emergency School Aid Act (ESAA) schools: 1974–1975*. U.S. Office of Education, Department of Health, Education and Welfare. Washington, D.C.: System Development Corporation, 1976. (C—Slavin-Madden.)

Williams, J. E., Best, D. L., and Boswell, D. A. The measurement of children's racial attitudes in the early school years. *Child Development*, 1975, *46*, 494–500. (M—Stephan.)

Williams, R. L., and Venditti, F. Effect of academic desegregation on southern white students' expressed satisfaction with school. *Journal of Negro Education*, 1969a, *38*, 338. (I—Cohen.)

Williams, R. L., and Venditti, F. Effect of academic integration on southern Negro students' expressed satisfaction with school. *Journal of Social Psychology*, 1969b, *79*, 203–209. (I—Cohen.)

Willie, C., and Beker, J. *Race mixing in the public schools*. New York: Praeger, 1973. (P—Cohen.)

Works Published Before 1961

Omit all in this category.

Campbell, E. Q. *The attitude effects of educational desegregation in a southern community*. Unpublished doctoral dissertation, Vanderbilt University, 1956. (St. John, Stephan.)

Criswell, J. H. A sociometric study of racial cleavage in the classroom. *Archives of Psychology*, January 1939 no. 235. (St. John.)

Deutschberger, P. Interaction patterns in changing neighborhoods: New York and Pittsburgh. *Sociometry*, 1946, *9*, 303–315. (St. John, Carithers, McConahay.)

Dwyer, R. J. A report on patterns of interaction in desegregated schools. *Journal of Educational Sociology*, 1958, *31*, 253–256. (Carithers.)

Horowitz, E. L. Development of attitude toward the Negro. *Archives of Psychology*, 1936, no. 194. (Stephan.)

Kupferer, H. J. An evaluation of the integration potential of a physical education program. *Journal of Educational Sociology*, 1954, *28*, 89–96. (St. John.)

Lundberg, G., and Dickson, L. Inter-ethnic relations in a high school population. *American Journal of Sociology*, 1952, *58*, 1–10. (St. John, McConahay.)

Mann, J. H. The effects of inter-racial contact on sociometric choices and perceptions. *Journal of Social Psychology*, 1959, *50*, 143–152. (Schofield.)

Springer, D. V. Awareness of racial differences of preschool children in Hawaii. *Genetic Psychology Monographs*, 1950, *41*, 215–270. (St. John.)

Whitmore, P. G. A study of school desegregation: Attitude change and scale validation. Unpublished doctoral dissertation, University of Tennessee, 1956. (Stephan.)

Yarrow, M. R., Campbell, J. D., and Yarrow, L. J. Acquisition of new norms: A study of racial desegregation. *Journal of Social Issues*, 1958, *14*(1), 8–28. (St. John.)

NOTES

1. The Slavin and Madden (1979) paper differs somewhat from the other reviews cited here since it focuses on school practices that improve race relations and presents data rather than functioning exclusively as a review paper. The introductory sections of this paper, however, provide a good overview of previous work in the area. Hence, the paper's reference section was utilized to build the core bibliography for this project.

2. Since the classrooms studied ranged from 81 percent to 14 percent white, it is hard to tell whether whites would show the tendency to ingroup preference when they are a very small minority that previous research suggests blacks do. It is worth noting that although the number of white friendships with minority group students was related to the number of minority group students in the classes, white racial prejudice was not.

3. For a discussion of some of the methodological shortcomings of this study see note 84, p. 99, in McConahay (1978).

4. Two other factors generally considered to influence socioeconomic status, income and type of occupation, do not seem to have a very consistent effect on racial attitudes (Campbell, 1971).

5. Roberts' study suggests that the relationship between percent white in the student body and utilization of cooperative academic teams is not linear. Rather, schools that are one-quarter or less white are less likely than others to use this practice.

6. The Slavin and Madden study controlled for percent black in the student body, so their conclusion does not appear to be a mistaken one based upon a correlation between percent black in the student body and students' intergroup behavior.

7. Some of the practices discussed here are not under the complete control of principals and teachers. For example, if school boards refuse to appropriate money for multiethnic texts, teachers and principals cannot assign these texts. However, all of the practices are ones a school system can decide to implement. The attitudes of principals and teachers are obviously not practices in any strict sense of the word. Nevertheless, it seems worth discussing the impact of these attitudes since one might be able to find ways to take such attitudes into account in hiring staff for desegregated schools.

4

Research on Minority Achievement in Desegregated Schools

Rita E. Mahard and *Robert L. Crain*

T he research on the effects of school desegregation has focused primarily on minority achievement. Although such an emphasis may be undeserved given what we know about the weak link between achievement and life chances, it has occurred for two reasons. First, most people believe that school desegregation is an educational innovation designed to improve the cognitive ability of minorities. Second, achievement is relatively easily measured by standardized tests that are already part of the normal educational evaluation process of a school system.

Although plentiful, most of these studies are small, unpublished, and deal with single cities. These are, of course, not the only kinds of studies that can contribute to our knowledge of how desegregation works and how it can work better. Indeed, almost any laboratory or classroom study of student learning contributes valuable information about how to make desegregated schools more effective. A study in a single city, however, cannot test hypotheses about the relative effectiveness of different kinds of desegregation plans. A study in a single city cannot do this, since normally there is only one kind of desegregation plan present; but if we bring together a large number of these studies, using each one as an evaluation of a certain kind of desegregation, we can draw some overall conclusions.

There is a second literature that can also be useful. This is made up of large-scale national studies based on simultaneous achievement testing in a large number of schools. The Coleman report (Coleman et al., 1966) is the best known of these, but there are several others, and one book has attempted to pool the conclusions from all of these studies (Bridge, Judd, and Moock, 1979). These large-scale studies can be used to compare the performance of minority students in various kinds of segregated and racially mixed schools. They have, however, an important drawback: they pool together racially mixed schools that are newly desegregated with those that are "naturally" integrated—meaning that they have served an integrated neighborhood, or adjoining segregated neighborhoods, for a long time, and the students have not gone through the experience of a formal desegregation plan. Does this make a difference? We do not know, but the possibility of a self-selection bias means we must be cautious about assuming that the large-scale studies will tell us useful things about how to operate a desegregation plan.

With that caveat, let us consider the two main findings that have appeared consistently in these studies. First, minority students in predominantly Anglo schools score higher on achievement tests. Second, this does not seem to be because of the "whiteness" of the school but because predominantly white schools have student bodies with higher socioeconomic status. These two findings suggest that the best desegregation plan is one that creates predominantly white schools using white students from relatively affluent families. However, two studies found a slightly different pattern, and their findings are worth consideration. The first, by Wrinkler (1976), found that black students who came from segregated elementary schools into predominantly white junior high schools did not experience a gain in achievement. There were gains only for those desegregated in elementary schools. A second study (National Opinion Research Center, 1973) found that in newly desegregated southern high schools, achievement among black students tended to be lower in schools where blacks made up less than 20 percent of the student body. Male black students had especially low scores in these schools. We shall see that both of these findings are consistent with the literature we review here.

The National Assessment of Educational Progress (NAEP, 1981) provides a third source of information on the relationship between desegregation and academic achievement. Roy Forbes, director of the National Assessment, recently (1981) compared trends in the performance of blacks and whites in the Southeast, the most thoroughly desegregated section of the country, with performance trends in other regions. This analysis showed that changes over the last several years in achievement were generally more positive for southeastern youngsters, especially blacks, than for students in other regions. The most recent data on reading performance confirm the continuing progress of southeastern youngsters, both black and white. Thus, the historic differences in the performance of southern students and those from other regions are narrowing (NAEP, 1981), and this is not attributable to increased migration from North to South (Forbes, 1981). An additional analysis of the NAEP data (Burton and Jones, 1982, p. 12) shows further that the average difference in achievement between blacks and whites has declined steadily in the last decade, and that this is so "regardless of learning area [that is, subject of test] or age of assessment." Although the National Assessment data do not provide conclusive evidence that desegregation improves minority achievement, they do seriously challenge the claim that desegregation and compensatory education have failed.

Finally, we can draw upon studies made of individual students in desegregated situations. Recent studies (Patchen, Hofmann, and Brown, 1980; Patchen, 1982; Maruyama and Miller, 1979) make important negative contributions by failing to support one popular theory of desegregation's effects: that black students benefit from the "lateral transmission" of values or behavioral norms from white students. This research shows that actual personal contact with white students in desegregated schools is irrelevant to the performance of black students. If black students were somehow learning better study habits or developing more achievement-oriented values from associating with whites, we would expect achievement gains to be greater for those with white friends. By seeming to refute this line of argument, these papers bring an alternative hypothesis to the forefront: the teacher expectation theory of desegregation. This theory, derived from the work of Rosenthal and Jacobson (1968), argues that students perform better when teachers have higher expectations about their ability to learn. This suggests that the predominantly middle-class desegregated school benefits black students because the teachers pace their teaching to what they see as the average level in the class—which will be higher than the level they would expect if they were teaching in an all-black school.

Another line of research has implications for desegregation policy. Several studies (Forehand, Ragosta, and Rock, 1976; Coulson et al., 1977; Crain, Mahard, and Narot, 1982) show that black achievement is higher in schools where the racial attitudes of the staff and the overall racial climate of the classroom are more positive. This implies that certain kinds of desegregation plans produce enhanced achievement by creating more favorable racial situations. Thus, it seems that existing theory suggests that there should be differences in the effectiveness of different kinds of desegregation plans. It is the purpose of this chapter to begin searching for evidence that this is the case.

SAMPLE OF STUDIES

The small-scale studies of minority achievement after desegreation constitute a fugitive literature. Very few of the studies are published in journals or books. Many are unpublished doctoral dissertations, obtained through University Microfilms; others are reports of school system evaluations or papers read at the American Educational Research Association meetings, identified by the ERIC retrieval system. After a lengthy search, we located ninety-three studies that measured the impact of desegregation on minority achievement.[1] Nearly all of these studies deal only with black students, so that we had to make a special effort to look at the effects of desegregation on Hispanic students. We excluded a large number of papers. Many of these were studies that compared students in racially segregated and racially mixed schools, but with no indication that a formal desegregation plan had been put in place. We judged that these studies would tell us little that the more sophisticated large-scale studies such as the Coleman Report had not already shown. We also dropped a number of studies in which the research design does not meet a minimum standard of quality. For example, we discarded studies that simply compared the achievement of black students in desegregated schools with black students in segregated schools with no reasonable effort to verify that the two sets of students were of similar background or had similar test scores prior to desegregation.

The 93 studies were a very mixed bag, and their results were equally mixed. Following a procedure suggested by Glass and Smith (1979) for meta-analyses, we divided the 93 studies into 323 samples of students. If a research project studied several samples of students who differed in age or in the research method used to measure the effect of desegregation on them, these were treated as separate samples. Slightly over half of the samples showed an increase in achievement after desegregation, while the remainder were divided between samples that showed no change and samples that lost ground. It is important to keep in mind that the point of all these studies is to measure the effect of desegregation: that is, difference between the achievement of desegregated minority students and the achievement that those same students would have had if they had attended segregated schools. This must necessarily be a hypothetical question, which can be answered only by inference, since no student can possibly be desegregated and segregated simultaneously. The question of how to draw this inference most accurately has plagued desegregation research for the past decade.

The first review of the literature, and the impetus for all the work since then, was provided by St. John (1975). While she found that a majority of the studies showed desegregation improving achievement, she nevertheless concluded that the quality of the studies was too uncertain, and the results too mixed, to allow a definitive conclusion. Weinberg (1977), reviewing nearly the same set of studies, was less cautious and concluded that desegregation did raise achievement. Bradley and Bradley (1977) reviewed a small number of these same studies and concluded that there were so many methodological problems that it was impossible to draw any conclusion about the effects of desegregation. More recently, Krol (1978) conducted a meta-analysis patterned after the work of Glass and Smith, and found a general positive effect of desegregation. In an earlier paper, we reviewed 41 studies and came to the same general conclusion—that desegregation tended to raise achievement test scores. All of these papers, however, have been forced to dwell at length on various problems created by the different kinds of methodologies used.

In assessing the methodology of a study we must ask two general questions: First, are the desegregated students typical of students experiencing desegregation? Second, how best can one estimate what their achievement performance would have been in the absence of desegregation? Many of the studies we reviewed had problems with both of these issues. Most studies of desegregation were conducted almost immediately after the desegregation plan studied was put into effect. This meant that the students were not representative of graduates of desegregated schools—they were still in school in nearly every case and, in a number of cases, they began desegregation not at kindergarten or first grade but after they had already attended segregated schools. Thus, their experience is not representative of a future cohort of students who would experience 12 or 13 years of desegregation by the end of high school. Many critics have commented about the unfairness of evaluating desegregation prematurely, when the students have only experienced one or two years in desegregated schools. However, critics have not paid attention to the other side of that issue—the fact that many of these students began desegregated schooling only after first attending segregated schools.

Choosing a comparison group is sometimes very difficult. In many communities every school is desegregated, so that no minority students remain in segregated schools to serve as a comparison group for the desegregated students. In this circumstance there are a variety of makeshift solutions, none of them completely satisfactory. Even when some segregated schools remain, the problem of deciding whether the segregated and desegregated minority students are truly similar is a difficult one. If one of the two groups comes from a more affluent background, the test scores of that group's members will normally be higher. Statistical procedures to correct for this bias are inadequate.

Our first task was to attempt to deal with these two general issues by separating the genuine effects of desegregation from the false effects created by the methodological decisions made.[2] To determine the bias introduced by incomplete treatments, we recorded a variety of dates—when the students were desegregated, when they were posttested, and (if the design was longitudinal) when they were pretested. From this we could determine the number of years they had spent in segregated schools before beginning desegregation and the duration of desegregation at the time achievement effects were estimated. We found that we could separate the studies into seven general categories according to the type of methodology used to create a comparison between desegregated and segregated black students. We then ranked the seven strategies according to our best judgment about their relative effectiveness.

Group 1

The best design is a randomized experiment—when desegregated and segregated students are selected by a flip of the coin, guaranteeing that there could be no differences between the two groups (other than that which might occur by a statistical fluke analogous to having a coin come up heads many times in a row).

Groups 2 and 3

The next best designs use a group of segregated black students as a control group, but do not randomly assign some students to desegregated and others to segregated schools. All of these studies pretested the desegregated and segregated students before or simultaneously with desegregation in order to show that they began with roughly equal achievement levels (or to statistically correct for differences if they were present). We divided control group studies into two categories because some of them went one step further and described the desegregation plan in such a way that the reader could conclude that the desegregated students were not chosen because they wanted to be reassigned, or because they appeared to be better candidates for desegregation, but because of an arbitrary geographic pattern that seemed to preclude much chance of a strong difference between these students and those left out of the plan. (Another example: some volunteers for desegregation were compared with students who volunteered for desegregation too late to be accepted, on the assumption that these students were similar in their motivation.) The studies that did not explain why some students were desegregated rather than others were placed in a third category.

Group 4

This group contained cross-sectional studies with segregated black student control groups. In a very small number of studies, a black control group was used without a pretest to demonstrate that their scores were similar to those of desegregated students before the plan took effect. Most of these latter studies were dropped from our analysis, but a few were kept when there was some evidence of similarity between the two groups.

A randomized experiment provides the best estimate of the effects of desegregation; the inferior designs used in groups 2 to 4 provide estimates that have more error, either overestimating or underestimating the effects of desegregation. This is a serious problem, but the problems that arise if there are no segregated black students to use as a control are even more serious. The next three designs not only introduce error into our estimate of the effects of desegregation, but they introduce a systematic negative bias—all three designs tend to underestimate the effects of desegregation.

Group 5

This group is made up of studies using cohort designs. In cases where all black students are desegregated, the best option is simply to compare the performance of desegregated black students to the performance of black students in the same grade a few years earlier. Unless there has been a drastic population shift in the community, these students should come from the same sort of family backgrounds. Until recently, however, there has been a steady decline in achievement test scores in the United States. This decline, if it occurred in a desegregated community, would make desegregation appear to have a negative effect.

Group 6

When all black students are desegregated, one option is to compare the performance of black students to the performance of white students in the same community. The achievement of white students is, of course, an inadequate proxy for the performance of blacks. Worse yet, during the later elementary school years, when many of these studies were done, there normally is an increase in the "gap" between white and black scores. Thus, a study of desegregated black students might find that the gap between black and white students had increased from a lower grade (predesegregation) to a higher grade (postdesegregation). This normal increase would thus be misread as evidence that desegregation had lowered achievement.

Group 7

Finally, the researcher may choose simply to compare the performance of black students to the national norms on the achievement test being used. But, again, black students in later elementary school years can be expected to fall further behind the test norms, making it appear that desegregation has lowered achievement.

For each of the 323 samples under study, we recorded the age of the students at desegregation and the dates of pretesting and posttesting, as well as the type of control group design used. Multiple regression equations were then constructed in order to estimate the effects of these factors. We found that the duration of desegregation made no difference. Students who had experienced four years of desegregation did not show a stronger effect of desegregation than those desegregated only one or two years. This was a very surprising conclusion. We also discovered that the age at which desegregation began made a very important difference. We found 11 samples of students who were desegregated at kindergarten and found the effects of desegregation to be positive in every case. At the other extreme, when students were desegregated for the first time in secondary school, less than half of the samples showed positive effects of desegregation.

It appears that the beneficial effects of desegregation take place during the very earliest primary school grades, and students who are desegregated after that time inadequately represent the true effects of desegregation. Thus, when grade of desegregation was entered into a regression equation in an effort to predict the effect of desegregation on achievement, we found that the lower the grade of first desegregation, the higher the achievement effect. We also found, as expected, that the type of study design was significantly related to outcome. Those studies that used white students or test norms as a proxy for segregated black student achievement found much weaker effects of desegregation. At the other extreme, desegregation plans that were studied using a randomized experiment showed stronger effects of desegregation. Both grade at initial desegregation and type of design were significantly related to the outcome.

Table 4-1 shows the percentage of studies that yielded positive results at each grade of initial desegregation and with each type of design. (The total number of studies is in parentheses.) To simplify the table we have collapsed the two nonrandom longitudinal designs with black control groups, combined the small number of cross-sectional studies with the cohort designs, and collapsed studies that used white student achievement as a control group with those that used test norms. All 11 studies of students desegregated at kindergarten show positive effects of desegregation. Similarly, a high percentage of the studies of students desegregated in first grade show favorable results. In general, the studies that used randomized experiments were somewhat more likely to find positive results in the upper elementary school grades, and the norm-referenced studies were least likely to find positive results. At the extreme, of the eight studies of students desegregated in secondary school that use white or test norm controls, none show positive desegregation effects.

Having established that the methodology used affected the chances of obtaining a positive effect of desegregation, our next task was to attempt to estimate what the magnitude of the effect of desegregation on black achievement would be if the strongest methodological design was used. In order to do this, we had to create a common unit of measurement to describe the effects of desegregation. Some studies reported results in grade equivalents, others in raw test score points, some in changes in IQ, and others with more elaborate statistics. Following Glass, we converted all these into standard deviation units. (In the upper elementary school grades, a standard deviation unit is equal to about three grade levels; in the lower primary grades, a standard deviation is a smaller number of grades. A typical student of below-

TABLE 4-1
Percentage of Studies Showing Positive Desegregation
Outcomes, by Grade at Which Students Were Desegregated
and Type of Research Design

Type of Design	Grade of Desegregation					Raw Average
	K	1	2-3	4-6	7+	
Random experimental	100 (1)	100 (8)	71 (7)	60 (5)	—	81 (21)
Longitudinal	100 (2)	73 (11)	46 (46)	62 (39)	69 (29)	59 (127)
Cohort comparison	100 (5)	78 (23)	56 (25)	40 (37)	45 (11)	56 (101)
Norm-referenced	100 (3)	0 (2)	43 (14)	37 (19)	0 (8)	35 (46)
Average	100 (11)	77 (44)	50 (92)	49 (100)	52 (48)	56 (295)

Note
The total number of studies is in parentheses.

average performance who moved up one standard deviation would move from the 17th percentile to the 50th, and his or her IQ would change from 90 to 105.) We used the reference tables for the Comprehensive Test of Basic Skills (CTBS) to convert scores given in grade equivalents to standard deviation units—a somewhat dangerous practice, since several different tests were used and each had its own statistical characteristics. The CTBS is the most commonly used test, however, and if tests are properly normed, the grade equivalent/standard deviation conversion should be the same for all tests. After these conversions were made, our statistical estimates of the effect of desegregation research designs and of using different grades at initial desegregation were used to estimate how much each study's result would be raised or lowered if that study had been, in fact, a study of students desegregated at first grade, using a randomized experimental design. We found that our best estimate of the achievement gain was about one-third of a standard deviation. This would raise a student's achievement in the first grade by a fraction of a year; if that student held on to this advantage throughout school, however, he or she would be approximately one grade level higher than if he or she had been in a segregated school.

In the course of doing this analysis we were able to identify those studies that were methodologically strongest. We found 23 studies that were made of students desegregated at either kindergarten or first grade and that used black students in a segregated school as a control group or compared scores to those of previous cohorts. As Table 4-2 shows, the authors of these studies analyzed 45 samples of students involved in 19 desegregation plans in 18 cities (two desegregation plans, a decade apart, were studied in Nashville). Where there is more than one sample in a grade, the effects of each are listed. Of the 45 samples, 40 show positive effects and, of those for which a size of effect could be estimated, desegregation raised achievement by a quarter of a standard deviation, or 0.3 of a grade year or more.

Apparently, St. John (1975) and Bradley and Bradley (1977) were correct in arguing that methodological factors made an important difference in the study of desegregation. This analysis satisfies us that desegregation has consistently positive effects for black students. Very little work has been done on the achievement effects of desegregation for Hispanic students, but what research there is shows a similar pattern. The Coleman Report (Coleman et al. 1966, p. 310) found that Hispanics showed higher achievement test scores in schools with more white students. Mahard and Crain (1980) made a second study using data from the National Longitudinal Study (NLS) of the high school graduating class of 1972, and found a positive correlation between attending predominantly white schools and achievement for Mexican-Americans, Puerto Ricans, and Cubans. We also found one technically adequate study of a specific desegregation plan (Morrison 1972) to show Anglo-American achievement to be higher in desegregated schools. A group of Hispanic children who were desegregated in third grade, initially had lower test scores

TABLE 4-2
Results of Studies of Students Desegregated at Kindergarten
or First Grade, Where Adequate Research Design Was Used

State, City[a]	Grade at Deseg.	Design	Effects[b]	Source
Northeast				
Conn., Hartford (met)	K	Random	0.37s	Mahan and Mahan (1971)
	1	Random	0.12s 0.32s	Mahan and Mahan (1971)
New Haven	1	Random	0.35s	Wood (1968)
New Haven (met)	1	Random	0.24s	J. Samuels (1971)
N.J., Newark (met)	1	Random	1.60s	Zdep (1971)
N.Y., New Rochelle	K	Longitudinal	(+)	Wolman (1964)
Rochester (met)	1	Longitudinal	0.70s 0.75s	Bowman (1973)
	1	Random	0.2y 0.7y 0.1y	Rock et al. (1968)
	K	Longitudinal	0.93s	Rentsch (1967)
	1	Longitudinal	0.03s	Rentsch (1967)
Midwest				
Ill., Evanston	1	Cohort	−0.01s −0.05s	Hsia (1971)
Peoria	1	Longitudinal	0.07s −0.06s	Lemke (1979)
Mich., Ann Arbor	1	Cohort	0.05s	Carrigan (1969)
Grand Rapids	K	Longitudinal	0.1y	Scott (1970)
	1	Longitudinal	0.1y 0.3y	Scott (1970)
Minn., Minneapolis	1	Longitudinal	(+) (+)	Danahy (1971)
South				
Ga., Dekalb Co.	1	Longitudinal	−0.2y	Moore (1971)
Miss., anon. (northeast)			0.26s 0.53s	Moorehead (1972)
Gulfport	1	Longitudinal	0.7y	Frary & Goolsby (1970)
S.C., Beaufort Co.	K	Cohort	0.3y	Chenault (1976)
Tenn., Nashville	1	Longitudinal	0.05s 0.43s	Anderson (1966)
Nashville[c] (met)	1	Cohort	0.28s 0.19s 0.36s	Nashville-Davidson County
			0.24s 0.19s 0.41s	Public Schools (1979)
West				
Calif., Berkeley	1	Cohort	(0)	Dambacher (1971)
	1	Cohort	0.18s	Lunemann (1973)
Pasadena	K	Cohort	0.49s 0.49s 0.60s	Kurtz (1975)
	1	Cohort	0.20s 0.02s	Kurtz (1975)
Nev., Las Vegas	1	Cohort	0.1y	Clark County School District (1975)

Notes

[a]"met" indicates metropolitan plan.

[b]"s" indicates effect in standard deviation units; "y" indicates effect in grade level years. Where there is more than one sample in a grade, the effect of each is shown.

[c]Two separate desegregation plans were studied in Nashville.

than Hispanics in segregated schools; by the eighth grade they were slightly over one year ahead. The effects of desegregation were stronger, however, for Hispanics than for blacks (see Morrison 1972, pp. viii, 120).

An accurate estimate of the overall effect of desegregation on achievement has implications for policy as well as research methodology. The finding that strong effects of desegregation occur in the earliest primary grades is a strong argument against delaying desegregation past grade one. Only a few school systems leave the early primary grades segregated; the most significant is Dallas. Our analysis indicates that this is a very unfortunate policy. Many school systems leave kindergarten students segregated. This analysis suggests that it would be academically very beneficial to include minority kindergarten students in a desegregation plan. All 11 studies recorded in Table 4-1 show positive effects—even those with severely biased methodologies. In Table 4-2, the five samples in the three studies that measure the effect of desegregation at kindergarten in standard deviation units show a mean gain of 0.57 standard deviations. If such gains persist into upper elementary school, this would represent a gain of nearly two grade levels in achievement.

This analysis also had implications for an understanding of how desegregation works. Our analysis did not find the duration of desegregation to affect achievement. One study in particular makes this point very well. Iwanicki and Gable (1978) evaluated the Hartford desegregation project in middle elementary school. These students had been desegregated at early grades. The study found that the rate of growth in achievements measured over one-year periods in mid-elementary grades, was no greater for desegregated students than for students who remained in the segregated schools. When we contrast this to the highly favorable findings in this same district for desegregation at kindergarten and first grade (see Table 4-2), we are led to conclude that desegregation creates a sudden burst of achievement growth lasting through the early grades of elementary school, but that this higher level of achievement is merely maintained by the students and does not increase through the later years of elementary school. None of our present theories of the way desegregation works would explain this pattern. More research that follows students over a long period in several districts is needed in order to determine if this is indeed the typical pattern. If it is, we will have to rethink the impact of desegregation, viewing it as a kind of early childhood intervention. Research on desegregated Head Start programs would also be helpful.

READING AND LANGUAGE ARTS SKILLS

In order to further understand the effect of desegregation, we looked at achievement test performance on each subtest of the achievement batteries administered in the 93 studies. In the many cases where separate subtest gains were reported, we found an interesting pattern. Averaging all the samples of desegregated students together, we found that desegregation increases each subtest about equally. (There is a slight tendency for mathematics gains to be greater than reading gains but the difference is small and not significant.) However, when we looked separately at those samples of students who showed the smallest gains in achievement after desegregation, we found that their scores in the reading comprehension subtest lagged behind their scores in mathematics, spelling, or vocabulary. In school districts where students experienced greater gains than normal, reading subtest scores outpace scores in the other subtests.

This finding can be interpreted in two ways. One is that it is a statistical artifact—since reading comprehension is a critical element in achievement test performance, it may be simply that a good score in achievement requires a high level of reading performance. The second interpretation is a substantive one: minority students come into desegregated schools with difficulties in reading comprehension. Schools that are unable to provide help to these students will not find their performance helped by desegregation; those that are able to make a special effort to deal with reading problems will find students benefiting from the entire curriculum and scoring well on all parts of the test. The language arts subtest shows the same pattern—very low scores in schools where students do not benefit from desegregation very much, very high scores where they do. This suggests that a desegregated school must make special efforts to work with language problems, which are perhaps related to the need to learn standard English grammar. This would seem to imply that teachers in desegregated schools should make special efforts to assist their black students in reading comprehension. We are reluctant to make such a policy recommendation on the basis of a single piece of research, but we do believe that additional research on the relationship of desegregation to various areas of achievement is likely to be valuable.

There are very few studies of desegregation in secondary school. Among these, the studies that reported performance on tests in subject matter areas showed an interesting pattern, however. In secondary schools where minority students benefited little from desegregation, their performance in subject matter tests—science, history, and so on—lagged well behind their performance in reading and mathematics. In schools where achievement gains were large, they were largest in these subject matter tests. Although this result must be considered tentative because of the very small number of studies involved, it seems consistent with the findings of the National Opinion Research Center (1973) study, which argued that the overall social climate of the secondary school is of critical importance to minority student performance. If a bad racial climate inhibits the academic motivation of black students, this effect should appear most strongly in those tests that measure material specifically taught in secondary school classes. Overall reading and math performance, much of which is carried forward from earlier grades, would not be hindered as much by the negative social climate that inhibits learning. Put more simply, a negative secondary school racial climate does not make black students stupid, but it does prevent them from learning in the courses they take.

When all studies, of both successful and unsuccessful desegregation plans, are considered, tests in all areas of achievement show approximately equal gains as a result of desegregation. There is one exception. The largest gains appear consistently on tests of general intelligence. Increases in IQ scores after desegregation generally outrun performance on all subareas of standard achievement tests. In 29 cases where a comparison was possible, IQ scores were greater than the average of the other subtests in 16 cases and less than the average in only five.

Table 4-3 reports the IQ gains following desegregation for 38 samples of students studied by 12 authors. We have divided the studies into three categories based on the overall quality of the methodology used. Standing alone is the Wood (1968) study, a randomized experiment conducted in Hartford, Connecticut. It shows gains of four or more IQ points during the first year of desegregation and is a technically excellent study. In the second group we list six studies where the IQ growth of desegregated students is compared to that of segregated students—our next best design to randomization. Of the 18 studies in this category, 13 show IQ gains resulting from desegregation, with half the studies showing gains of three IQ points or more. In the last grouping we include five studies that we think should not be taken as seriously as the others because of technical problems, even though these studies also show IQ gains resulting from desegregation. The last four of these studies are of technically weaker design, having no segregated black control group for comparison. The first study, done in Hartford, is of technically excellent design, but the students used in it are, to a large degree, the same students studied by Wood; we have discounted this study in order to avoid being overly influenced by a single desegregation plan.

From these studies we estimate that desegregation tends to raise black achievement by approximately four IQ points on average. This figure, if correct, represents a significant increase in performance on these tests. The average pretest scores in this collection of studies is around 91—a four-point increase would erase nearly half of the gap between that and the norm of 100.

At one time it was believed that IQ tests measured an ability to learn that was physiological, unaffected by school environment. This view is no longer held, and some research has shown that certain kinds of school curricula have a greater impact on IQ than others. For example, the Stanford Research Institute study of the Follow-Through experiment (Stallings, 1978) found that students in "traditional" Follow-Through compensatory programs showed gains in basic skill scores but little gain on a nonverbal IQ test (the Ravens test). Conversely, students in more self-directed learning environments showed less increase in basic skills but more gain in IQ. It seems reasonable to argue

TABLE 4-3
Results of 13 Studies of Desegregation and Black IQ Gains

State, City	Grade	Method	Effect on IQ (points)	Source
Conn., Hartford	K–1	Randomized	4.5[a]	Wood (1968)
	2–3		5.5[a]	
	4–5		4.0[a]	
Fla., Brevard Co.	10	Longitudinal	10.7[a]	Williams (1968)
Ky., (unnamed)	5–6	Longitudinal	− 4.5	Meketon (1966)
	5–6		7.3	
Mich., Flint	5	Longitudinal	2.0	Van Every (1969)
N.Y., Rochester	1	Longitudinal	1.2	Rentsch (1967)
	2		0.0	
	3		6.6	
	4		0.4	
	5		− 2.5	
N.Y., Syracuse	1	Longitudinal	− 1.1	Beker (1967)
	2		− 0.6	
	3		3.7	
	1		1.6	
	2		5.9	
	3		5.0	
Okla., Tulsa	3	Longitudinal	7.2[a]	Griffin (1969)
			7.2[a]	
			6.2[a]	
Conn., Hartford	K	Randomized	6.0[a]	Mahan and Mahan (1971)
	1		1.3	
	2		4.7	
	3		7.6[a]	
	4		− 1.2	
	5		0.4	
Fla., Hillsborough County	4	Norms	6.5[a]	Taylor (1974)
Mich., Ann Arbor	K	Cohort	5.2	Carrigan (1969)
	1		3.4	
	2		2.4	
	3		− 3.9	
	4		− 4.2	
	5		− 1.6	
Miss., (unnamed—northeast)	1	Cohort	5.0	Moorehead (1972)
	1		7.0[a]	
N.Y., White Plains	2	Cohort	− 1.0	Bondarin (1970)
	5		1.0	

Notes
[a] $p < .05$

that the desegregated classroom is a cognitively more stimulating environment, if for no other reason than that the student is confronted with a variety of stimuli and behaviors that he or she would not experience in the more homogeneous environment of his or her neighborhood school.

FINDINGS RELEVANT TO DESEGREGATION POLICY

We now come to the heart of this exercise—having removed the extraneous effects of differences in methodology from the results of these 93 studies, we are in a position to inquire whether certain kinds of desegregation plans seem to have stronger effects on desegregation than others. One important conclusion is a negative one—issues related to voluntary versus mandatory desegregation and one-way versus two-way busing seem irrelevant. Mandatory plans and voluntary plans show approximatley equal achievement gains.[3] We also can find no evidence of difference between the effects of desegregation on achievement scores in formerly black schools and its effects in formerly white schools.

Metropolitan Plans

One important finding is that the metropolitan desegregation plans analyzed show stronger achievement effects than the plans examined in other studies. Recall that in Table 4-2 there were several northeastern studies of metropolitan plans. These plans, in Hartford and New Haven, Connecticut; Newark, New Jersey; and Rochester, New York, all involved the voluntary transfer of black students from inner-city schools to suburban schools and were all evaluated with experimental designs. In these cases, the number of students who would be willing to attend suburban schools far exceeded the number of spaces available to them, so that students were chosen by lottery. When those students selected for the plan were compared to those who were not, in every case sizable achievement gains were reported.

The other type of metropolitan plan is the result of the merger of suburban and central-city school districts. In this data set we have only one example— the Nashville and Davidson County public schools, which were merged and desegregated shortly thereafter. This, the second Nashville study recorded in Table 4-2, shows sizable achievement gains for black students. Another study, which was located too late to be entered into our computer file of studies, comes from Louisville, Kentucky, where consolidation of the city and suburban districts took place in 1975. The newly formed Jefferson County school system compared the performance of fifth-grade black students in 1978 to those in the fifth grade in 1975, when desegregation began, and found black students' overall performance rising from the 25th percentile nationally to the 33rd percentile. At the same time, white students rose from the 50th percentile to the 54th (Raymond, 1980). These striking gains do not appear for older students, who were desegregated after starting school in segregated classes. The other major metropolitan desegregation plan is Newcastle County, Delaware, the result of the merger of several suburban systems with the Wilmington public schools. We have not received any achievement data for minority students there.

Table 4-4 shows the expected achievement gain for students in metropolitan desegregation plans and in other types of communities. We were able to identify 235 samples of students where the setline could be determined. These expected scores are statistically adjusted to eliminate differences in methodological quality and the effects of desegregation at later grades. The estimates of effect are computed by assuming that the studies in each case were randomized experimental evaluations of students desegregated at first grade. Since we estimate that the average gain is 0.3 of a standard deviation, we show in Table 4-4 effects of desegregation varying on both sides of this 0.3 value. The importance of the data in the table lies not in the magnitude of the four values, but their relationship. What we find is that metropolitan studies show the strongest effect of desegregation, while studies in suburbs and in central cities show weaker effects. Lying between the two are the results of studies made in countywide school systems, which are common in the South. A countywide system is a kind of metropolitan desegregation plan, but different in that desegregation does not involve the reassignment of black students into schools that were traditionally administered by a school district serving only suburban students. Thus, it is a different form of metropolitan desegregation but shows results similar to the plans that are normally referred to as metropolitan in nature.

Why should metropolitan desegregation plans show stronger desegregation effects? There are two plausible explanations, although neither of them can be tested with these data. The first is that metropolitan desegregation represents the most complete form of socioeconomic desegregation. Minority students from low-income central-city neighborhoods are reassigned to suburban schools in affluent areas. If the plan was limited only to the central city, the number of middle-class white students available would be sharply reduced. By the same argument, desegregation within suburban schools might

TABLE 4-4
Effect of Desegregation on Achievement Scores by Type
of School District

School District Type	Mean Effect (std. dev.)	Number of Samples
Central-city	0.285	97
Suburban	0.241	76
County	0.339	31
Metropolitan	0.364	30

be relatively ineffective because the minority children living in suburban ghettos would not be as poor as those living in central cities—thus improvement to the same level of achievement in desegregated schools would not be as marked a gain for them, since their performance in segregated schools would already be fairly high. This hypothesis would explain why countywide plans would be as effective as other kinds of metropolitan plans, since both would involve the full range of socioeconomic differences in the area.

There is a second explanation as well, having to do with the administration of school districts. This hypothesis argues that suburban school districts, spared the conflict and tension that surround the operation of many central-city school districts, have been able to recruit stronger teaching staffs and better principals and provide a more effective administrative environment for their schools. Once a metropolitan school district is created or minority students are reassigned to suburban schools, these schools are able to maintain their stronger academic traditions. However, this hypothesis is not borne out by one study; Natkin (1980) found that black students bused to suburban schools did no better on achievement tests than those who remained in the newly desegregated inner-city schools. Had there been a large difference in the quality of teaching or administration in the two kinds of schools, one would have expected the bused students to do better. The suburban Louisville schools were affected by staff desegregation as well as student desegregation. Intuitively, we would expect this to have both negative and positive effects on black students in suburban schools. They would be harmed by the dislocation of teaching staffs and the high turnover of staff in these schools. At the same time, they would probably benefit from the presence of more black teachers in the suburban schools. In this way we would expect formal metropolitan desegregation plans involving the merger of suburban and central-city districts to be more effective in the long run than voluntary plans, which sometimes leave virtually all-white teaching staffs in the suburban schools serving the inner-city minority transfer students.

The Racial Composition of Desegregated Schools

We also looked at the effectiveness of desegregation in schools of varying racial compositions on student achievement in desegregated schools. We were guided by two findings from the literature. The first is that the various large-scale studies of schools have found black achievement directly related to percentage white in the school—the whiter the school, the higher the minority achievement. The second, from the National Opinion Research Center, was that there was an optimal point in percentage white—that when percentage white exceeded 80 percent, achievement began falling. In Table 4-5, we have plotted the expected achievement gain in 150 northern and 90 southern samples of students once the effects of differences in methodology and grade of desegregation have been removed. We find similar patterns in the North and the South. In the South the pattern is quite clear and is statistically significant.[4] Achievement reaches a peak for schools between 19 and 29 percent black and drops off on either side in a reasonably steady manner. In the North the pattern is more complex. There is, again, a high point in the 9 to 18 percent range with a decline in both directions, although the decline is not completely even and the overall pattern is not statistically significant. The differences are not small. In the North a school with a relatively small black population (9 to 18 percent) has achievement scores that are 0.1 to 0.2 of a standard deviation higher than schools with larger black populations. In the South, the difference may also be as much as 0.2 of a standard deviation.

The finding that schools with smaller black populations have higher achievement can be explained in two ways. First, if the main effect of desegregation is to place students from low-income families into schools with affluent students, the more white students there are, the greater will be the average income level in the school. (We cannot test this directly, since none of the 93 studies reported the actual social class of either black or white students.) Secondly, a smaller black population makes it more difficult to resegregate the school by creating an all-minority class of supposedly low-ability students. Presumably, such a segregated classroom would be detrimental to achievement.

The finding that achievement is lower in the schools with the smallest percentage black population is also consistent with theory as well as with the National Opinion Research Center study (1973). The argument is simply that the overwhelmingly white school is a hostile environment for black students: there are not enough black students and not enough black teachers to provide minority students with the sense of being integrated into the school.

TABLE 4-5
Desegregation Effect on Achievement Scores by Percentage
Black of Desegregated School

	Region			
	North		South	
% Black	Std. dev.	No. of sample	St. dev.	No. of sample
1– 8	.304	(19)	.319	(12)
9– 18	.430	(29)	.398	(8)
19– 29	.243	(29)	.494	(7)
30– 37	.274	(27)	.364	(20)
38– 44	.188	(26)	.274	(10)
44–100	.303	(20)	.278	(33)
Total	.270	(150)	.331	(90)

The argument is that they continue to feel like outsiders, not really a part of the school situation, and inhibited in their learning because of this. (See Crain et al. 1982, for an elaboration of this argument.)

Civil rights advocates have frequently argued for the establishment of a "critical mass" of black students, insisting that desegregation plans now spread black students so thinly that they make up less than 15 to 20 percent of the school. These achievement results seem consistent with that request. At the same time, these data provide additional support for the metropolitan desegregation argument. For it is only with metropolitan desegregation that one can be guaranteed a large enough population of white students to provide for predominantly (but not overwhelmingly) white student bodies.

Why Might Desegregation Improve Minority Achievement?

It seems reasonably clear that minority children who attend desegregated schools perform better on standardized achievement tests than do similar students who attend segregated schools. Why this is the case is considerably less clear.

A number of explanations for the finding of improved minority achievement have been offered, among them the salutary influence of middle-class peers, improved teacher behavior toward minority students, and more equitable distribution of resources. Research on these topics varies considerably in both amount and persuasiveness, and we will not attempt to review it here. What we will do is examine two recurrent (and, we will argue, misleading) themes in this work and suggest a new way of thinking about the connection between desegregation and minority student achievement.

All of these earlier explanations deal with forces that are presumed to act upon minority students more or less independently of the meanings these students attach to such forces. In part, this reflects the tendency of desegregation research to conceive of minority students as passive recipients of their schooling experience rather than as active participants in and interpreters of that experience. In part, it is due to the all-too-common assumption that the "curriculum" is limited to what is formally taught, untouched by our complex and troubled history of race relations and, thus, that students confront the identical "curriculum" in segregated and desegregated schools alike.

In our view, both these assumptions are false. While desegregation itself may be an important force that is external to the student, it is a force heavily imbued with social meanings. Further, it is the students themselves who both interpret these meanings and orient their achievement behavior in a manner consistent with that interpretation. In short, we ought not to be so quick to assume that the student is a vessel both empty and isolated.

Our argument is that segregated and desegregated schools convey different messages to minority students, messages that shape their expectations about what the future holds. These generalized expectations then either lead or fail to lead to purposive behavior directed at the realization of specific, culturally valued goals.

We begin with a rarely cited analysis from the Coleman report (Coleman et al., 1966) that suggests that there are group differences in the nature of the link between expectations and achievement and that desegregation influences the strength of this link for minority students. Coleman et al. found that locus of control (internal versus external), interest in learning, and academic self-concept were the best predictors of student achievement at all grade levels, outstripping all family background variables and all school factors. For minority students, locus of control was most important of these, while for majority students, academic self-concept was. According to Coleman et al., ". . . it appears that children from advantaged groups assume that the environment will respond if they are able enough to affect it; children from disadvantaged groups do not make this assumption, but in many cases assume that nothing they will do can affect the environment—it will give benefits or withhold them but not as a consequence of their own action" (p.321). In other words, disadvantaged groups tend to have an external locus of control. Coleman et al., note further than an increase in school percentage white was associated with an increase in the internality of control for black students.

If segregated schooling conveys a "symbolic message" (St. John, 1975) about what such a student can reasonably expect from life, then lower expectations of success are not surprising. Conversely, desegregation may convey a different message, the message that many things are now possible and that there is a connection between one's behavior and its consequences.

The concept of locus of control (Rotter, Seeman, and Liverant, 1962) appears in many guises in diverse literatures. In the sociological literature on alienation, for example, it closely resembles what Seeman (1959, 1975) has called "powerlessness" and what Olsen (1969) had referred to as "attitudes of incapability." Gamson (1968) has used a similar concept, which he has termed "efficacy." All of these treatments have in common the conceptualization of a greater or lesser belief in one's ability to influence events.

Paige (1971), in his study of riot participation, has argued that information is a precondition for efficacy. We would suggest that the "information" gained from the experience of desegregation itself and the exposure to its symbolic messages may set the stage for change in one's beliefs about personal efficacy, or control.

Our argument continues with the idea that increased internality of control will lead to higher minority achievement in the desegregated school by encouraging purposive, achievement-related behavior. There is considerable evidence that the generalized attitude of control over one's environment leads to purposive behavior, both in specific settings and in contexts that transcend those settings. Seeman and Evans (1962), for example, found that "high internal control" tuberculosis patients were more likely to educate themselves about their disease. Seeman (1964, p. 284) has noted that high-internal prisoners were more apt to learn about parole and that this learning influenced behavior outside of prison. He writes: "The effect of alienation is reflected in the inmate's behavior both within the reformatory and on the outside, as is shown by the fact that his parole learning is related to the merit earnings he gets within the institution and to his achievement record on the outside . . ." (Of course, it does not do to push the analogy too far. While the relationship between control and purposive behavior may well be similar for students, prisoners, and hospital patients, there are probably important differences between these groups. Unfortunately, there is little research on this topic.) Crain and Weisman (1972) found that high-internal black students were more likely to commit themselves to more personal and demanding civil rights activity.

There is also a considerable amount of research documenting the connection between nonpurposive behavior and perceptions of low control. Kanter (1977), for example, has argued persuasively that perceptions of low power and blocked opportunity lead to withdrawal and defeatism. Merton (1957) has made a similar argument, suggesting that cultural goals come to be devalued to the extent that societal emphasis on such goals is not matched by a corresponding emphasis on institutional means of achieving them. In our society, both within the context of the school and without, students are encouraged to believe that education is the gateway to the cultural goal of mobility. We would argue that the meaning of this message differs for segregated and for desegregated blacks, a difference that has consequences for their achievement behavior. Quite simply, we would suggest that segregated blacks tend to behave as if they believe this to be true when, in fact, they do not. That is, that segregated blacks engage in what Merton terms "ritualism," behavioral conformity which masks private disbelief. (For evidence that low internal control and conformity are related, see Lefcourt, 1966.) This helps to explain why so much research has failed to uncover the expected differences between segregated and desegregated blacks and between blacks and whites on academic values, academic self-concept, effort, and educational and occupational aspirations (Crain et al., 1982; Patchen, 1982; Proshansky and Newton, 1968). Schuman (1972), in his study of antiwar sentiment, has shown that groups may hold similar attitudes for very different reasons. If our analysis is correct, segregated and desegregated students are differentially motivated in their endorsement of the value of education, and this has important consequences for their academic achievement.

Our discussion is not meant to imply that previous explanations for the finding of improved minority performance in desegregated schools are wrong. It seems quite likely, for example, that prejudiced teachers can undermine the most able and determined of minority students. It also seems reasonable to argue that an equitable distribution of educational resources may enhance achievement, and that exposure to middle-class, achievement-oriented peers may do likewise. Clearly, many factors are involved. Rather, our discussion is meant to suggest that in a search for the single, "true" explanation, we sociologists have overlooked two important points that ought to have been obvious all along: that desegregation is invested with social meanings and that minority students may draw inferences from those meanings.

CONCLUSION

It is often said that science is a cumulative process—that each research paper makes a small contribution as it is built upon by others. Certainly, the many students who wrote doctoral dissertations about school desegregation over the past 20 years were not able to anticipate that the advent of high-speed computers and the development of meta-analysis would enable their work to make a contribution of this kind. But this is exactly what has happened. The overall pattern of results of these studies has been obscured by methodological errors that are nearly unavoidable in many cases. Because of this, it was impossible from a quick reading of them even to say whether or not desegregation was beneficial for minority achievement. But once reasonable estimates have been derived for the correction factors needed to compensate for inadequate methodology, a clear pattern emerges.

We can see from this analysis that desegregation is indeed beneficial, although it must begin in the earliest grades. We have also seen what research has led us to suspect for some time—that desegregation in a predominantly white society requires predominantly white schools, and desegregation in a society where whites have run to the suburbs to establish a "white noose" around decaying, predominantely minority central cities requires metropolitan desegregation. We have also learned some things that were not expected. The discovery that a school can have too many white students and thus harm black achievement confirms what up to now had been a largely speculative argument for a "critical mass" of black students in desegregated schools.

There is a great deal more work to be done. Our finding that desegregation enhances IQ test scores as much or more than it does achievement test scores calls into question a lot of our assumptions about the meaning of intelligence and invites us to think more about why desegregation is beneficial. Similarly, the finding that desegregation's success seems peculiarly dependent on scores in reading comprehension and language arts invites researchers to think further about this issue. Finally, and most important, the discovery that effects of desegregation are almost completely restricted to the early primary grades— that desegregation is successful as an early childhood intervention—means that we must begin rethinking what desegregation is doing for black students.

Some policy implications are clear—this study demonstrates the usefulness of early desegregation, metropolitan desegregation, and desegregation in predominantly white schools with a critical mass of black students. In terms of the policy options available to officials in federal and local administrations, the success of voluntary one-way transfer programs to suburbs is particularly relevant. Some states have enabling legislation to permit programs of this kind. While there is a great deal of opposition to these programs from central-city administrations, central-city teachers' unions, and some central-city black political leaders, there is also a good deal of support—from suburban school administrators with declining enrollments, from integrationist groups in the suburbs, and from black parents themselves. While this kind of program is hardly a substitute for court-ordered metropolitan desegregation, it is a reasonable first step that can be taken without waiting for the courts. Since it is a policy that has little opposition from the traditional antibusing groups that have frightened so many school boards, some school systems may wish to utilize it in order to demonstrate their willingness to take at least some steps toward desegregation.

NOTES

1. For brevity, references to all 93 studies are omitted. They appear in Crain and Mahard (1981b).

2. The analysis of the effect of methodology on the estimate of the effect of desegregation is described in much more detail in Crain and Mahard (1981a).

3. In an earlier paper (Crain and Mahard, 1978), we noted that mandatory plans seemed to show higher achievement gains. We were reluctant at that time to accept this as a firm finding, and we were apparently correct, since with the larger sample we cannot find any difference between the two types of plans.

4. The significance tests reported here are based on the number of authors rather than on the total number of samples, since multiple samples from the same author do not constitute independent populations.

Portions of this chapter are reprinted from Robert L. Crain and Rita E. Mahard, Minority Achievement: Policy Implications of Research," pp. 55–84 in Willis D. Hawley, Ed., Effective School Desegregation: Equity, Quality, and Feasibility, © 1981 Sage Publications, Inc., with permission.

5

Resegregation:
Segregation Within Desegregated Schools

Janet Eyler, Valerie J. Cook, and *Leslie E. Ward*

Because school desegregation is often preceded by years of litigation and controversy about the creation of racially or ethnically mixed schools, it is all too easy to think of desegregation in its narrowest sense and to assume that once racially mixed schools have been set up the desegregation process is complete. However, it is crucial to recognize that it is precisely at this point in the desegregation process that interracial schooling *begins* for the students and that the nature of the students' experiences is crucial to their academic and social development. (Hawley et al., 1981, p. 81.)

*T*his report focuses on what happens within schools after the school bus has arrived. Specifically, this study examines how the resegregation of students within desegregated schools occurs, identifies currently available alternatives to minimize it, and suggests directions for future research and development to meet this problem.

Within-school resegregation refers to the separation of children by race or ethnicity within the walls of the desegregated school. Resegregation is a major threat to desegregation in that it reestablishes racial isolation that the reassignment of students from school to school was intended to eliminate. Among its consequences, resegregation undermines the possibility for interracial or interethnic contact and equal-status interactions, and denies students exposure to similar educational expectations and experiences. Resegregation thus impedes the basic goals of school desegregation: it hinders the elimination of racial stereotypes and prejudice; it delays advances in minority achievement; and it perhaps damages the chances of minorities for economic success later in life.

The problem of resegregation is extensive and pervasive. In an analysis of 1976 Office of Civil Rights (OCR) data, Morgan and McPartland (1981) found that while racial segregation was primarily due to segregated schools, resegregation played an important role in contributing to racial isolation in education. They noted that

> majority white desegregated schools—which comprise about three-quarters of all desegregated schools and enroll about half of all black students attending desegregated schools—seem especially prone to extreme classroom resegregation. For example, at the high school level, predominantly black and entirely white classes are found in majority white schools at several times the rate that would be expected by chance. These patterns are most pronounced in the South and at the secondary school level where school desegregation has been reported to be better accomplished than other regions or levels. In other words, when black students find a greater chance of school desegregation they are also likely to find a somewhat greater chance of classroom resegregation. [pp. 12–13]

There are several reasons why resegregation occurs in schools. The first, and most important, is the traditional response of schools to student diversity. Students are sorted and categorized, and programs are matched to their apparent needs. Behavioral standards are adopted to reduce diversity, and students who do not conform are excluded. To the extent that race and ethnicity are associated with criteria used to sort or exclude students, these processes will result in racial imbalance of classes and racial disproportionality in exclusion.

This process will probably be allowed to continue as long as school officials perceive a conflict between the goal of integration and the educational goals of the school. They choose to resegregate because they think resegregation is necessary in order for each child to attain the highest possible levels of achievement. The traditional practice of sorting students into apparently homogeneous groups may also continue because of a lack of administrative and instructional resources for effectively organizing schools in a different way for instruction.

The paradox of desegregation may be that it reinforces or revives the traditional resegregating responses of schools to diversity. The comprehensive changes required by desegregation increase in complexity and uncertainty the situations with which school personnel must cope. The resulting demands frequently overload the professional capabilities and the tolerance for ambiguity of teachers and administrators. The need to reduce that overload typically leads to a search for clarity and simplification that manifests itself in classifications, programs, and routines that are resegregative.

A second reason resegregation occurs is that the fragmented nature of public policy making results in policies that are at cross purposes. Just as the government supports both tobacco crops and warnings on cigarette packages, public policy about education is made in a variety of decision-making arenas. Decisions are made in response to pressures from different groups and interests that ultimately may conflict. At the same time that courts and some agencies are making policies that mandate or facilitate integration, other agencies may develop programs that seem to undercut it. For example, categorical aid programs that require or allow disadvantaged students to be removed from the classroom for compensatory services will have a resegregative effect. Bilingual programs may be difficult to staff and run if students with limited English proficiency are scattered through a district as the result of a desegregation plan. Consequently, such students may be clustered into certain schools and receive most of their instruction in segregated settings.

A third reason for resegregative practices may be racism or the inability of individuals within the school system to deal with cultural differences in a sensitive way. In its harshest form, this inability may result in blatant attempts to segregate minority students into particular classrooms or tracks. School personnel may have preconceptions about the abilities of minority students that increase the likelihood that these students will be classified into lower tracks. Or they may sort students into bilingual classes by ethnicity rather than language facility. Such insensitivity may extend to misperceptions of cultural behavior that cause students to be punished or suspended.

Traditional responses to diversity that have collided with desegregation policies include: ability grouping and tracking; compensatory educational services; special education; bilingual education; and discipline practices. These will be discussed in the next section.

RESEGREGATION AS A RESULT OF ASSIGNMENT TO ACADEMIC PROGRAMS

Schools typically sort students into homogeneous groups for instruction, and these instructional groupings often entail different educational goals. Selection is made on the basis of a mix of objective and subjective criteria including standardized testing, recommendations of teachers, counselors, and other school personnel, and parent and student choice. The reasons for a student being placed in a particular program are complex and the research limited, but the result clearly is resegregation. Student diversity takes many forms, and in the attempt to address these differences, a variety of grouping practices are used. These practices include several forms of tracking, ability grouping, and remedial programs for students thought to be in the normal range of ability; a variety of special education programs for handicapped students; and several ways of organizing instruction in bilingual education programs for students with limited English proficiency (LEP).

Ability Grouping and Tracking

Resegregation Through Ability Grouping and Tracking

Ability grouping and tracking are the primary methods for separating students into homogeneous groups and are, thus, a major force for resegregation. Ability grouping may refer to the practice of assigning students to separate classrooms on the basis of some assessment of their "abilities" or to similar groupings of students within classes. The term "tracking" has been used to refer to two phenomena. It sometimes describes rigid ability grouping where students take all of their classes in a high- or low-ability group. Here, however, it will be used in the second, more narrow sense to refer to differentiated curricula for secondary students. College preparatory, vocational, and general tracks are typical. In some high schools, the practices of ability grouping and tracking may be combined, resulting in honors, regular, and remedial sections within a track. Courses that are required of students in all tracks, which might allow integration of students in different tracks, may also be ability grouped according to the already established tracks.

Elementary schools. The practice of ability grouping by class or within classes is pervasive in public schools. Studies from across the country report anywhere from 46 to 77 percent of schools assigning elementary students to classrooms by assessment of ability (U.S. Commission on Civil Rights, 1974; Findley and Bryan, 1975; Mills and Bryan, 1976; Tompkins, 1978; Epstein, 1980). Within classrooms, assessments of reading ability are the usual basis for grouping, which may extend to other classroom activities (Haller, 1981). In one study, 84 percent of the 886 elementary teachers questioned used ability grouping within their classrooms, and those few teachers who chose not to use it had classes that they perceived to be relatively homogeneous (Epstein, 1980).

Ability grouping tends to segregate children by race and social class with disproportionately more poor and minority children in lower levels (Findley and Bryan, 1971; Esposito, 1971; Goldberg, Passow, and Justman, 1966; U.S. Commission on Civil Rights, 1974; Green and Griffore, 1978). As long as the well-documented relationship between typically used measures of ability and race continues, any desegregated school system that uses ability grouping extensively is likely to have high levels of resegregation.

The resegregation that occurs through ability grouping is exacerbated by the apparent rigidity of these group assignments. Once students have been assigned to a level, they have little chance of promotion (Epstein, 1980; Green and Griffore, 1978). Decisions, sometimes made as early as kindergarten, (Rist, 1970) may channel students through their entire elementary and secondary school career.

The scope of the educational program for the slow group may prevent a student whose initial placement results from academic inexperience or misperception by the teacher from catching up with peers. Teachers appear to spend less time and attention on students that they perceive to be less able (Rist, 1970; Oakes, 1980), and a poorer curriculum may be provided for low-ability groups (Green and Griffore, 1978). Moreover, there is little evidence that instruction is tailored to help students in slow groups meet the instructional goals of the schools (Froman, 1981). Indeed, the differences in achievement that result from these elementary groupings will be used to track students into high school programs with explicitly different educational goals.

Secondary schools. American comprehensive high schools generally offer students a differentiated curriculum. Track assignment, usually made in grades 9 or 10, is based upon achievement, the preferences of students (and perhaps parents), the recommendations of counselors, or teachers, and the availability of programs. Tracking is related to ability grouping practices in that children in high-ability groups generally choose or are assigned to a college preparatory curriculum, and children in low-ability groups typically choose or are assigned to vocational and general tracks.

Rigid tracking practices lead to extensive resegregation, with black students disproportionately overrepresented in vocational or general tracks and underrepresented in college preparatory tracks (Harnischfeger and Wiley, 1980; Larkins and Oldham, 1976). Hispanic students are also overrepresented in low-ability tracks (U.S. Commission on Civil Rights, 1974), and this appears to be more prevalent in schools with a substantial Hispanic population (Carter and Segura, 1979). There is also some evidence that resegregation occurs within the vocational track. Black females are likely to be highly concentrated in homemaking and consumer programs (Wulfsberg, 1980; Green and Cohen, 1979). Minority students are also more likely than whites to be enrolled in vocational programs that center around specific training for low-level occupations (Oakes, 1982).

Tracking has also been found to have spillover effects on the scheduling of common courses and electives and on noncurriculum aspects of the school program, so that resegregation occurs even where it is not necessitated by track placement. This further limits opportunities for interracial contact (Larkins and Oldham, 1976; Green and Cohen, 1979).

The Relationship of Tracking and Ability Grouping to Desegregation

There is no evidence specifically linking the introduction of new tracking and ability grouping practices to desegregation plans. It is not known if the use of tracking or the assignment of minorities to vocational and general tracks has increased, decreased, or stayed the same in districts where desegregation has been carried out. Intensive interviews of professionals in 18 school districts undergoing court-ordered desegregation suggest, however, that resegregation has occurred within most schools undergoing desegregation, with ability grouping and tracking generally noted as the cause (Trent, 1981).

There is also evidence to suggest that the use of rigid grouping or tracking practices is related to the racial composition and perceived heterogeneity of the student body and to teacher attitudes about integration. The greatest amount of resegregation occurs in schools that are racially balanced (Morgan and McPartland, 1980) and use of tracking increases as the proportion of black students rises (Epstein, 1980).

Low teacher support for integration has been associated with tracking and the use of rigid ability grouping within classes, and with the selection of compensatory programs that isolate low-achieving students from their peers. Low teacher prejudice is associated with use of classroom techniques that facilitate interracial contact (Epstein, 1980; Gerard and Miller, 1975).

There is no direct empirical evidence that racial or ethnic bias contributes to the disproportionate low placement of minorities, but there is some evidence that social-class cues are used in such placements (Rist, 1970; Findley and Bryan, 1971; Lunn, 1970; Haller and Davis, 1980). To the extent that teachers make placement decisions based on their impressions of students, one would expect minority students to suffer some displacement into lower groups or tracks. There is evidence that educators view both Chicano students (Brischetto and Arciniega, 1973) and black students as less promising and more troublesome than majority students (Henderson, Goffeney, Butler, and Clarkson, 1971; Rajpal, 1972; St. John, 1975; Gerard and Miller, 1975; Weinberg, 1977). The high visibility of race and ethnicity compared to social class makes these students vulnerable to decisions based on prejudice.

The Persistence of Ability Grouping and Tracking

In spite of the evidence that tracking and grouping resegregates students there is considerable professional resistance to relinquishing the practice. Historically, it has dominated school organization in the United States and elsewhere. The practice enjoys tremendous support from school professionals (National Education Association, 1968), who believe it is the best choice for meeting the learning needs of students of diverse academic backgrounds because it is administratively convenient, consistent with the value of maximizing individual achievement, and necessary for the group instructional methods commonly in use in the schools.

The view that students are best taught in homogeneous groups is not supported by several decades of research on ability grouping. This is particularly clear when the criteria used for evaluation are cognitive achievement, affective outcomes, and equity.

Froman (1981) conducted an extensive review of the literature on ability grouping and drew a number of conclusions that are consistent with the views of others who have surveyed this field (for example, Esposito, 1971; Findley and Bryan, 1975; Goldberg et al., 1966). There is some evidence that high-ability students benefit in cognitive achievement from tracking or grouping but none that middle-ability groups benefit. Moreover, low-ability groups tend to fall behind when they are tracked and, conversely, to make cognitive gains in heterogeneous classes (Froman, 1981; Marascuilo and McSweeny, 1972). Interestingly, the positive effect of tracking on high-ability students tends to be found in earlier studies and not in later, better controlled ones (Froman, 1981).

Tracking has a negative effect on the self-esteem of lower-ability groups and may inflate the self-regard of high-ability groups (Froman, 1981). While the association between self-esteem and achievement is not well understood, a system that leaves many students with low self-regard and does not clearly promote achievement can be questioned. Low expectations, reinforced by low-ability group placement, may perpetuate low achievement. Several studies of achievement among minority students demonstrate that they do better with teachers who have high expectations and positive attitudes (Narot, 1973; Forehand, Ragosta, and Rock, 1976). This is, of course, consistent with the findings of a considerable body of research on teacher expectancies.

The persistence of tracking and ability grouping in spite of evidence that they are not educationally effective and have clear resegregatory effects in desegregated schools may result partly from the difficulty of working with a diverse class, particularly when school personnel lack skills and resources. Teachers have few resources for instructing heterogeneous groups of students; and there is evidence that they may be less successful when they face highly diverse student bodies equipped with traditional instructional techniques (Evertson, Sanford, and Emmer, 1981). Furthermore, it is administratively simpler to divide a school or classroom into groups and deliver all services to students in those groups. Homogeneous grouping that may be appropriate for one learning task is then extended to experiences where heterogeneous groups could be as effective. At the school level, administrative ease sometimes leads to tracking based on compensatory program delivery (Kimbrough and Hill, 1981).

Compensatory Education Programs

Resegregation Through Compensatory Education Programs

Numerous federal and state education programs have been enacted in the past two decades with the intention of decreasing the inequality of educational benefit for various populations. By both judicial and legislative action, provision of remedial or compensatory educational services has been required for poor and low-achieving children and children in minority-isolated and recently desegregated schools. Two significant programs were Title I of the Elementary and Secondary Education Act (ESEA), which distributes funds to school districts for the provision of compensatory services to economically and educationally disadvantaged children (now Chapter I of the ECIA Block Grant), and the Emergency School Aid Act (ESAA), which provided assistance to school districts for purposes related to implementing desegregation and overcoming minority group isolation and has now been supplanted by Chapter II of the Block Grant. In addition to their major focus, the federal programs have had special provisions for particular groups of disadvantaged children. ESEA, for example, funds separate programs for children of migrant workers. In addition to these federally mandated programs, at least 12 states operate their own compensatory education (CE) programs.

There is disproportionate minority student participation in compensatory education programs. Blacks, Hispanics, and other minority students are represented more heavily than whites in the low-income and low-achieving categories, and consequently are overrepresented among Title I beneficiaries. This overrepresentation, however, is not solely the result of disproportionate poverty and low achievement. Within categories of economic status and educational performance, greater percentages of minority students than of whites are selected for Title I services (Breglio, Hinkley, and Beal, 1978).

Student "pullout" from the regular classroom is the dominant method of delivering Title I services. It has been estimated that 75 percent of compensatory aid programs entail removing the child from the regular classroom. For about one-third of those involved in pullout programs, all instruction takes place in settings with other CE students (Poynor, 1977). There is also evidence of substantial use of pullout in ESAA (Wellisch, 1979) and state-funded CE programs (Brookover, Brady, and Warfield, 1981).

The average student receiving compensatory education spends about one-fourth of total available learning time in the program. Students in pullout programs miss regular instruction in a variety of subject areas—not infrequently in those that are targeted for remediation, such as reading or math, so that compensatory education has not meant additional instruction for many eligible students (National Institute of Education [NIE], 1976; Brookover et al., 1981; Kimbrough and Hill, 1981). It is, of course, common sense that since students receiving compensatory education spend the same number of hours in school as others, this resource is not "additional" education, but a substitute for what normally goes on.

Pullout results in resegregation. Minority students receive an above-average amount of compensatory reading and math instruction delivered in small groups by special teachers. Students are typically pulled out from less to more segregated settings (Hinkley, Beal, and Breglio, 1978; Kimbrough and Hill, 1981; Brookover et al., 1981).

The Relationship of Compensatory Programs to Desegregation

Several authors have noted an inherent tension between compensatory education and integrated education as strategies for increasing equality of educational opportunity. Compensation is seen as requiring the concentration of disadvantaged students for intensive remedial treatment, while integration relies on the dispersion of minority students among their more advantaged peers and in schools of better quality (Levin, 1978; Radin, 1978). This conflict has been observed especially in the operation of Title I programs in desegregating school systems, where school may lose services because desegregation reassignment changes their socioeconomic status (Berke and Demarest, 1978; Thiemann and Deflaminis, 1978). This problem was ameliorated in 1978 by changes in Title I eligibility criteria for students affected by desegregation and by the use of ESAA funds for compensatory education for schools and students who lose their Title I eligibility because of desegregation (NIE, 1977b; Hawley and Barry, 1980).

The fact remains, however, that where desegregation is in progress, direct service compensatory programs may be difficult to implement without concomitant resegregation. This potential for resegregation is exacerbated in schools that operate several categorical programs and have substantial numbers of students who are eligible for more than one type of service. Typically, these schools place multiply eligible children in every program for which they qualify. This results in numerous pullouts or, in some cases, the establishment of a separate track based on participation in compensatory programs (Kimbrough and Hill, 1981).

The Persistence of Compensatory Education as an Instructional Approach

Why do school systems rely on pullout, a resegregative technique, to deliver compensatory services? Whether or not the trade-off between compensation and integration is justified depends to no small extent on the educational efficacy of pullout programs. The most appropriate conclusion to draw from the relevant research is that pullout has not been supported on achievement grounds, but that mainstream approaches to compensatory education have not been adequately evaluated (Rossi, McLaughlin, Campbell, and Everett, 1977; Poynor, 1977). In any event, the effect of pullout on achievement does not appear to offset its resegregative effects.

If the educational efficacy of pullout does not provide an adequate rationale for its widespread use, what accounts for its predominance in Title I and other categorical programs? While neither the legislation nor the regulations stipulate the setting in which services are to be delivered, there are several requirements that make pullout seem the obvious way to achieve compliance:

1. Title I funds must not be commingled with other revenue sources, but rather spent on identifiable services.
2. The services must be provided only to the identified, eligible students within a school (usually not all eligible students are served because of the requirement that funds go to schools where eligible students are concentrated rather than to the students themselves).
3. The services must "supplement, not supplant" the regular services provided to all students.

These provisions require that Title I provide a recognizable program for targeted students that is an addition to the regular school program. The easiest way for schools to do this has been to separate Title I students from others for the compensatory services (Glass and Smith, 1977; Brookover et al., 1981).

Special Education

Resegregation Through Special Education

The provision of special education is based on the right of all American children, including the handicapped, to an education. It has been assumed that handicapped children need special materials, instructional methods, and teachers. These special services have generally been provided by grouping students according to their handicapping condition. Assignment to a special education class is usually based on a combination of standardized test results, subjective evaluations by school personnel, and parental consent. Because minority children are likely to perform at a lower level than white children on standardized tests and are likely, as a group, to be regarded less favorably, they tend to be overrepresented in special classrooms, especially those for the mildly retarded.

Passage of Public Law 94-142, the Education for all Handicapped Children Act of 1975, was the culmination of a decade of court decisions and laws designed to establish the right of handicapped children to an appropriate education. Provisions requiring nondiscriminatory assessment and placement in the least restrictive environment (LRE) are the most important of the components of the law affecting racial and ethnic segregation in special education. The legislative history of P.L. 94-142 indicates that the issues affecting minority group children were not the major concern of the dominant advocate groups. Rather, emphasis was on the inclusion in public schools of the more severely handicapped children who had historically been barred.

The more severe handicapping conditions are fairly easily discernible. They include severe emotional disturbance, trainable and severe mental retardation (TMR and SMR), and speech and physical handicaps. It is in the determination of the mildly handicapping conditions—educable mental retardation (EMR) and learning disability (LD)—a process that relies heavily on the judgments of school personnel, that questions of resegregation arise.

While the regular curriculum is organized in ways that lead to resegregation, the tendency for special education programs to become ghettos for black children is even more dramatic. The great disproportionality of black youngsters in special education classes, and particularly in the more stigmatizing EMR classes, has been amply documented (Children's Defense Fund, 1974; Cook, 1980; Columbus Public Schools, 1980; Center for National Policy Review, 1980). The resegregative impact of this pattern is mitigated only by the comparatively small percentages of youngsters involved. Whereas most children will be affected by school policies related to ability grouping and tracking, nationally about 5.9 percent of white students, 5.8

percent of Hispanics, and about 8.4 percent of black students are assigned to all categories of special education. The figures for EMR assignment are about 1 percent of whites, 1 percent of Hispanics, and 3.5 percent of blacks. There are also substantial regional variations, with the greatest disproportion of black children in EMR settings found in the South (Center for National Policy Review, 1980).

There is a good deal of evidence to suggest a dramatic decline during the past decade in the overrepresentation of Hispanic students in EMR classes. Early 1970s data on Hispanic enrollment in EMR classes showed substantial disproportionality; this was most dramatic in districts serving large numbers of Hispanic students (Carter, 1970; U.S. Commission on Civil Rights, 1974). More recent reports show Hispanic enrollments in EMR classes approximmating those of Caucasian students, although there is still a tendency towards overrepresentation in districts with substantial Hispanic enrollment (Aspira, 1979b; Carter and Segura, 1979; Center for National Policy Review, 1980).

The disproportion in the representation of minorities in learning disability (LD) classes is not nearly as great as in EMR classes. Nationally, black students were slightly less likely to be categorized as LD than as EMR and dramatically less so in the Northeast and Midwest. By contrast, Hispanics tend to be slightly overrepresented nationally in classes for LD (Aspira, 1979b; Center for National Policy Review, 1980).

Since the classification "LD" refers to children of normal intelligence with some specific impediment to learning, it is generally believed that children find it less stigmatizing to be labeled "LD" than "EMR." The disproportionate number of black students assigned to the more stigmatizing program raises some serious questions about the evaluation and assignment of black children in special education classes. The decline in the proportion of Hispanic children in EMR classes may reflect a change in assessment procedures that eliminates the obviously unfair technique of testing a Spanish-speaking child with an English IQ test. Their slight overrepresentation in LD classes may reflect ambiguity in the definition of LD, especially as it relates to the understanding of the effect of having Spanish as a first language in a predominantly English-speaking educational system.

The extent to which categorizing minority children as EMR or LD will result in resegregation depends on how special service delivery is organized. Although P.L. 94–142, the Education for all Handicapped Children Act, mandates placement in the least restrictive environment appropriate to the child's development, in the early years of implementation of P.L. 94–142, state education departments and local school districts were primarily concerned with the identification of eligible children and the establishment of limited-English-proficiency (LEP) and due process procedures (Hargrove, Graham, Ward, Abernethy, Cunningham, and Vaughn, 1981; Stearns, Green, and David, 1980). Less attention has been paid to implementing the LRE provision, and professionals have not received the technical support necessary to achieve this goal. In practice, the placement options generally available in schools are (in order of increasing restrictiveness): resource room service, parttime special class, fulltime special class, and special day school. Resource room services are often limited in scope; for example, some school districts allow a maximum of one hour per day of resource help. These services are designed to offer specialized help to special students who are mainstreamed into regular classes. Children classified as EMR are generally placed in full-time special classes. Children classified as LD may receive resource help or fulltime placement, depending on the perceived severity of the learning disability.

The Relationship of Special Education Programs to Desegregation

For a number of reasons, it is difficult to determine whether special education assignments for black children have increased with desegregation, and if such assignments are systematically being used to resegregate. One problem is that data on special education by race were not gathered nationally before 1973. In the past decade increased attention has been given to special education programs and to the provision of additional resources for special education, and this has in many cases coincided with the process of desegregation. In school districts where an increase in special education placement occurred simultaneously with desegregation, it is difficult to determine how much it did so in response to desegregation and how much in response to an increased focus on special education assignment. This is especially true when there are no racial data preceding desegregation.

There is some evidence that special education assignment for black children may increase immediately after the establishment of busing to integrate and that this may be a specific response to desegregation. Some school districts have experienced an immediate increase in referrals for special education evaluation when black children have been bused to previously white schools (Galusha, 1980; Watkins, 1980; Columbus Public Schools, 1979, 1980, 1981).

The Persistence of Special Education as an Approach to Service Delivery

Because full-time placement of minority children in special education classes (especially EMR) tends to resegregate them, it is important to examine the educational effectiveness of this organizational practice. Researchers studying the effectiveness of the different ways of organizing service delivery in special education have generally compared the effectiveness of special classes for EMR children to mainstreaming. Several excellent reviews conclude that researchers have failed to show a difference in achievement between students placed in full-time EMR classes and those who have been mainstreamed (Abramson, 1980; Corman and Gottlieb, 1978; Semmel, Gottlieb, and Robinson, 1979).

If special classes are not academically effective, then why do schools persist in using this format? There are educationally important differences between the child with an IQ of 60 (EMR range) and the child with an IQ of 140 (gifted range). An ordinary teacher may not have the knowledge, technical facilities or assistance to support an appropriate educational program for the range of diversity that exists when EMR students are mainstreamed. Furthermore, special classes are administratively the easiest way to provide services to groups of children who had not been routinely served by the school.

Bilingual Education

Resegregation Through Bilingual Education

Bilingual education programs are based on the concept of students having the right to equal benefit from educational opportunities. Given equal access to English-based instruction, the limited-English proficient (LEP) students do not have the same opportunity for learning as English-proficient students. The magnitude of the need for bilingual education is difficult to gauge, since there are no accurate counts of the number of LEP children (Thernstrom, 1980), and LEP children have varying degrees of language proficiency in both languages (Alexander and Nana, 1977). Most of the students in need of bilingual education are Hispanic, though a significant proportion of Hispanic children who need special language services are not enrolled in such programs (Aspira, 1979b; Department of Education, 1980; Fernandez and Guskin, 1981). According to Fernandez and Guskin (1981), "among the 12 states where the need for bilingual programs is the greatest, only one-third to two-thirds of the Hispanic children are being served. Though bilingual programs are not reaching all those who need them, children who do participate tend to find the programs segregative (Kimbrough and Hill, 1981).

There are very few reliable data on characteristics of students in bilingual education programs or on the ways in which programs are organized and services delivered. Thus, the conclusion that bilingual education is resegregative can only be tentative.

The resegregative impact of a bilingual program will depend on the goals of the program and its instructional focus. Transitional programs are designed to facilitate rapid development of competence in English. Advocates see this not only as the key to preparing LEP students to perform well in the regular school curriculum but as the best approach to enhancing their opportunities in an English-speaking society. Many proponents of bilingual education are equally concerned with developing the students' facility in their mother language. They support maintenance programs to develop competence in both languages and foster a bicultural identity. The resegregative impact of such programs might be softened if English-speaking students were active participants and developed proficiency in the second language as well; this would create a two-way rather than a one-way program. In such programs, which would be viewed as alternative rather than remedial, children who were initially monolingual English would acquire bilingual competency. Few two-way programs exist, however.

Programs with the goal of transition are generally one-way and use a strategy of teaching English as a second language (ESL). English is taught as a foreign langauge (U.S. Commission on Civil Rights, 1972) to assist the LEP child in gaining the English language proficiency he or she needs in order to have a successful education. While ESL classes are segregated, they may separate the children from their English-speaking peer for only part of the day. If transition to regular classes is facilitated, they may not, in the long run, be resegregative. About half of all bilingual programs use the ESL model (Aspira, 1979b).

In addition to ESL, other instructional models include bilingual, bilingual-bicultural, or bilingual-bicultural-bicognitive education programs. In contrast to ESL, bilingual education is based on the rationale that students learn best when taught in their native language and that LEP students should have the opportunity to keep pace, in their native language, with their English-speaking peers in other subjects.

Programs that include the study of the history and culture associated with a student's mother tongue are termed bilingual-bicultural programs. A few proponents of comprehensive bilingual programs argue that LEP students have developed different cognitive styles as a result of their socialization experiences and thus should be taught using teaching styles and strategies different from those used with their English-proficient peers. This is termed bilingual-bicultural-bicognitive education, and has obvious implications for resegregation (Lopez, 1978; Ramirez, 1973; Ramirez and Castaneda, 1974).

Bilingual programs, when they are established as one-way maintenance programs for Hispanics only, are equivalent to the establishment of a dual educational system. Two-way programs are, by definition, integrated.

While the resegregative impact of bilingual programs for the LEP child depends on the extent to which they are organized to minimize pullout from regular classes and on their success at developing English proficiency, there is some evidence that they may have a resegregative effect on children from ethnic minority backgrounds who are not seriously deficient in English. Children are sometimes assigned to bilingual classrooms and programs because of their ethnicity rather than a lack of English proficiency (Epstein, 1977; Carter, 1979; American Institutes for Research, 1977–78; Orfield, 1977). Where bilingual programs require inclusion of non-LEP students, those included may be English-proficient Hispanics, which contributes to ethnic resegregation (Carter, 1979). Another reason that English-speaking Hispanics are heavily represented in bilingual transitional programs is that transfer out is rare in many of these programs, which creates Hispanic tracks within the school (American Institutes for Research, 1977–1978).

Because students receiving bilingual education are frequently also eligible for other compensatory services based on poverty or low achievement, they are at special risk of being resegregated through frequent pullouts for programs in different categories. When large numbers of children are multiply eligible, some school districts organize them into classes, which, again, result in a segregated track within the school (Kimbrough and Hill, 1981).

The Relationship of Bilingual Education to Desegregation

The relationship between bilingual education and desegregation can be described as mutually antagonistic. While bilingual education may be a resegregative threat to desegregation, desegregation can be a threat to the integrity of bilingual education programs.

"In several cases since 1974, the very existence of ongoing bilingual bicultural programs has been seriously threatened by the imminence of a school desegregation decree" (Cohen, 1975). This threat is usually manifested in the proposed application of strict ratios in the student assignment plan (Fernandez and Guskin, 1981). Thus, Hispanic involvement in recent desegregation cases has been at the remedy stage of the court hearings in attempts to preserve the integrity of bilingual programs within a desegregation remedy (Fernandez and Guskin, 1981). This was the case in Milwaukee (Baez, Fernandez, and Guskin, 1980) and Boston (Aspira, 1980; Brisk, 1975).

There is some indication that students who need bilingual education or ESL are more likely to participate in these programs in highly segregated school systems. "It appears that segregation highlights the need for special language programs, serves as an incentive for implementing these programs, and facilitates provision of the programs" (Aspira, 1979a). Desegregation has resulted in dispersion of LEP students throughout a district, in fragmentation of bilingual teaching teams, and in individual pullout of students for bilingual services that had been provided in organized group programs prior to desegregation. Furthermore, the dispersion of LEP students exacerbates tensions between those who want transition programs and those in the Hispanic community who favor maintenance programs (Aspira, 1979a; Fernandez and Guskin, 1978).

Carter (1979) suggested that desegregation need not become a threat to bilingual education. He noted the increasingly popular movement away from an emphasis on the racial balance of schools and toward considering ethnic/racial isolation, an approach that would allow a critical mass of LEP students to be assigned to particular schools rather than evenly dispersed throughout a district. This would facilitate provision of needed special services as well as integration. Theoretically, a variety of goals and organizational characteristics could be combined in bilingual education programs. In fact, very little is known about how these programs are now implemented and their consequences for resegregation.

Summary

We have reviewed the practices that schools use to address the academic heterogeneity of the student population. The resegregative effects of ability grouping and tracking, compensatory education, special education, and bilingual education have been documented. Resegregation occurs because of characteristics of the student assignment process and of program organization. Student assignment involves a complex decision-making process with potential for bias in testing, school personnel judgments, and student and parent choices. Student assignment practices tend to result in the overrepresentation of minority children in the lower academic groupings and their underrepresentation in the higher academic groupings.

Program organization will vary according to the type of practice schools use to address the academic heterogeneity of the study population. Ability grouping and tracking too often become rigid organizational structures in which it is difficult to advance once placed in a low group. Compensatory education is generally offered on a pullout basis, whereas special education and bilingual education vary along a continuum from pullout to full-time separate classes. The degree to which these grouping practices result in resegregation depends on the extent to which minorities are overrepresented in enrollment and the extent to which the children are segregated from the regular classroom. The problems that school districts face in attempting to deliver educational services are exacerbated by the multiple program eligibility that results from fragmented public policymaking. It seems that while public policy has encouraged and financed school efforts to provide programs for identified groups of children, not enough attention has been devoted to the problems that arise when individual children belong to several groups.

THE IMPACT OF DISCIPLINARY PRACTICES ON RESEGREGATION

The practices evidenced in its policy on discipline are the school's attempt to deal with the diversity of the student population while maintaining the stability and order necessary to the business of teaching and learning. Since 1973, when the Southern Regional Council published *The Student Pushout: Victims of Continued Resistance to Desegregation*, there has been concern about the exclusion of minority children from desegregated schools for disciplinary reasons. The council suggested that newly desegregated districts suspended and expelled disproportionate numbers of black youngsters, starting them on a cycle that resulted ultimately in their dropping out of school. This pushout phenomenon is thus thought to contribute to resegregation.

In this section we will document the racial disproportionality in suspension and dropouts in American schools, examine its relationship to school desegregation, and explore some possible reasons for this disproportionality.

Resegregation Through Suspensions

Suspensions are a widely used disciplinary technique. Basing its assessment on the OCR fall 1973 survey of 2,917 school districts, the Children's Defense Fund (1974) estimated that one out of every 20 school-age children was suspended in the 1972–73 school year.

Suspension is overwhelmingly a secondary school practice; the figure was 8 percent for secondary students in 1972–73 (Kaeser, 1979b) with many districts far exceeding this. Minority students, however, are suspended at younger ages than whites (Children's Defense Fund, 1974).

A clear pattern of racial disporportion in suspension has been extensively documented in school districts across the country. Black students were from two to five times as likely to be suspended as white students in all regions of the country (National Public Radio, 1974; Children's Defense Fund, 1974; Arnez, 1976, 1978; Kaeser, 1979b). They also received lengthier suspensions (Hall, 1978) and were more likely to be repeatedly suspended (Children's Defense Fund, 1974).

The data for Hispanics was mixed, with few regions showing large disparities between the percent Hispanic in a school system and the percent suspended who are Hispanic. Those regions with the largest Hispanic enrollments report a slightly smaller proportion of Hispanics suspended than whites (Carter 1981; Aspira, 1979b).

The Relationship of Suspension to Desegregation

In order to determine the resegregative impact of the disparity in suspensions of minority students, it would be useful to have racial data on suspensions before desegregation so that rates before and after desegregation could be compared. Although most school districts did not analyze discipline data prior to desegregation, there is some direct evidence of an increase in disproportionate suspensions and a good deal of suggestive related material.

A number of districts show an overall increase in the number of suspensions during the first year of desegregation (Columbus Public Schools, 1980; Project Student Concerns, 1977; Foster, 1977; Southern Regional Council, 1979). Several cities report an increase in the disparity between black and white suspensions as well as an increase in overall suspension rates subsequent to desegregation (Southern Regional Council, 1979). Some note, however, that this was a transient phenomenon in their district and that it declined after the first postdesegregation year (Trent, 1981).

Adding to the concern that disproportionate suspensions are acting to resegregate students is growing evidence that postdesegregation suspension rates may be related to the racial composition of the school. In a number of districts, suspensions of black students were most pronounced in racially balanced schools that had recently undergone desegregation; previously integrated schools that experienced little change in black enrollment underwent little change in suspensions (Larken, 1979; Hall, 1978; Southern Regional Council, 1979). Thus, it is the schools with the greatest potential for interracial contact that are most likely to use disciplinary techniques that substantially resegregate students within the school.

Resegregation Through Dropout Patterns

While children are removed from school only temporarily by disciplinary suspension, the dropout leaves permanently. Moreover, just as there is racial and ethnic disparity in suspension practices, there is such disproportionality in dropout rates. The national dropout rate for fourteen- to seventeen-year-olds was 10 percent; the rate was 15 percent for blacks, 20 percent for Hispanics, and 22 percent for American Indians (National Center for Education Statistics, 1981). This national pattern is reflected in most of the more focused studies of black dropout rates (Grantham, 1981; Bennett, 1981; Bennett and Harris, 1981; Green and Cohen, 1979). Hispanics tend to complete fewer years of schooling than blacks and drop out at a younger age (U.S. Commission on Civil Rights, 1974; Aspira, 1979b; Haro, 1977; Carter, 1970).

Although there is surprisingly little evidence that a student who is repeatedly suspended eventually drops out of school, districts with high suspension rates also have high dropout rates (Grantham, 1981). Schools that had high rates of black suspensions also had disproportionate numbers of black students dropping out of school (Bennett and Harris, 1981; Grantham, 1981). This suggests that the fear that disproportionate suspensions leads to "pushout" of minority students is warranted. There is some evidence linking segregation with higher dropout rates for Hispanics and blacks (Aspira, 1979b).

In the only study directly linking dropout rate to desegregation, Felice and Richardson concluded that the dropout rate for minority students is dependent upon the social climate of the schools into which they are placed. Their major finding was that minority students in higher socioeconomic (SES) school environments with more favorable teacher expectations had lower dropout rates (Felice and Richardson, 1977).

Reasons Resegregation Occurs Through Disciplinary Procedures

A number of reasons have been advanced to account for the racial and ethnic disparity in disciplinary actions. Some suggest that the disproportion stems from greater misbehavior on the part of minority students. Others point to differential application of school behavior standards. Still others note that problems will arise if rules developed for one group are rigidly applied to students of different backgrounds without any attempt to adapt discipline policy to reflect plural cultural norms. The increase in suspensions that occurs when minority students attend previously all-white schools suggests that a combination of factors may be at work.

Students who are not successful in school and who find it a hostile place to be are more likely to have disciplinary problems and to be suspended.

Powerful predictors of suspension include low grade-point average, low IQ scores, low test scores as well as being male or black (Cotton, 1978). Although students with these characteristics are more likely to present disciplinary problems, there is a good deal of evidence to suggest that part of the problem of disproportionate suspension rates lies with school practice.

Many schools and districts with high minority enrollments do not suspend minority students at a high rate (Children's Defense Fund, 1975; Van Fleet, 1977). Within districts that suspend a disproportionate number of minority students, enormous differences in racial disparity exist among individual schools (Kaeser, 1979b; Larkin, 1979; Project Student Concerns, 1977). Even where minority students integrating several high schools were drawn from the same area of the city, large differences in racial disproportionality related to school characteristics have been found (Bennett and Harris, 1981).

School officials have a great deal of discretion in the use of suspension as a disciplinary practice. Some educators do not use suspension at all; others use it infrequently; still others use it frequently for a wide range of offenses. It is in school districts that use it frequently that the disproportate suspension of minorities is also high.

In general, suspensions tend to be given for behavior that is not violent or dangerous to persons or property and thus might be dealt with by means less drastic than removing the student from school. Attendance violations such as cutting classes, truancy, and tardiness were by far the most frequent suspendable offenses, followed by smoking, nonviolent disruptive acts, and violation of school rules on such areas as bus and cafeteria conduct. Physical violence or threat of it, and other major offenses such as theft and drug abuse were much less frequent (Project Student Concerns, 1977; Children's Defense Fund, 1974; Arnez, 1978).

Although not all studies have shown differences in the types of offenses leading to suspension, where there are differences blacks are more likely to be suspended for "subjective" or "discretionary" offenses. Subjective offenses are those requiring a personal judgment and include disobedience, insubordination, disruptive or disrespectful behavior, profanity, and dress code violations. Objective offenses are more clearly measured and include truancy, use of alcohol or drugs, assault, possession of weapons, and the like (Foster, 1977; Arnez, 1978; Bennett and Harris, 1981). There is also some evidence that black students are punished for offenses allowed white students (Foster, 1977; Green and Cohen, 1979) or given heavier penalties for similar offenses (Southern Regional Council, 1973).

School climate and teacher attitudes are also associated with disciplinary problems generally. Desegregation results in a socially heterogeneous population of students within the school. Many teachers are confronted with students whose behavior they do not understand, and they feel ill equipped to respond to or cope with such behavior. Hispanic students come from a culture in which norms of appropriate behavior differ from Anglo norms. Teachers confronted with Hispanic-appropriate behavior may tend to interpret that behavior from their own Anglo-normative base, thus misinterpreting the student's behavior, intentions, or needs. Black students may adopt styles of dress and behavior that are in conflict with school professionals' sense of propriety. Given these tendencies, one might expect to find the increase in disciplinary problems and suspensions that has, in fact, occurred. Moreover, there is some evidence that teachers in desegregated schools recognize that a lack of effective communication with students from cultures different from their own contributes to disciplinary problems (Trent, 1981; Wynn, 1971).

Just as positive teacher attitudes about integration contribute to the selection of instructional strategies that facilitate integration (Epstein, 1980), they are also associated with fewer disciplinary problems. Teachers who support busing for desegregation perceive a smaller increase in disciplinary problems than teachers who oppose it (Peretti, 1976). Student and staff perceptions of disciplinary practices in schools with high disproportionality in suspensions and dropouts differ from those in schools with low disproportionality. Students perceive punishment to be unfair in schools where disproportionality is high (Bennett and Harris, 1981).

While teacher attitudes and expectations can help prevent disciplinary problems, teachers like students, are part of a larger system. If the student feels alienated from the school, if there is not an effective instructional program for students with academic difficulties, if attempts are not made to develop rules and disciplinary practices that are seen as fair by all students, then individual teachers, regardless of their attitudes about desegregation or minority students, may be confronted by behavior that leads ultimately to suspension.

In summary, there is evidence that disciplinary practices contribute to resegregation within desegregated schools. Suspensions are a common disciplinary technique, and black students are much more likely to be suspended than other students. This phenomenon of racial disparity is thought to be acute in recently desegregated schools, particularly in those in which the proportion of black students is above 15 percent. Racial disparity in dropout patterns has also been observed, and there is an association between suspension patterns and dropout patterns in schools.

ALTERNATIVES TO RESEGREGATIVE PRACTICES

In order to reduce or eliminate within-school resegregation, schools must implement fundamental changes in the organization of instruction, in the assessment of student performance, and in their ways of dealing with student behavior. Student assessment should incorporate a wide range of information from a variety of sources and should be interpreted by well-informed consumers of testing information. Instruction should be organized so that heterogeneous groups of students have the opportunity for educational interaction; special support services should be provided with as much integration with the regular school program as possible. Disciplinary policy should emphasize keeping students in school and dealing with the sources of behavior problems, including the influence of school climate on behavior. Policy should be developed and enforced in a racially and ethnically equitable manner.

The perpetuation of traditional instructional and organizational practices may be due to ignorance of the universe of alternatives. Solutions to the problem of resegregation are much more complicated than simply ending ability grouping and tracking, adding alternative discipline systems, or sensitizing teachers. There are differences in children's ability to do schoolwork that must be accommodated by differences in instruction and curriculum. The task is to find methods of assignment, instruction, and organization that are responsive to differences and yet encourage equal-status interracial contact.

Alternative Assessment Strategies

Ability and achievement tests are the major tools for assigning students to homogeneous groups (Findley and Bryan, 1971). Minority children are "at risk" in the assessment stage of service delivery because of their substantially lower scores on standardized tests of intelligence and achievement (Shuey, 1966; Samuda, 1975; Joseph, 1977).

Though the fact that cultural factors create distortions in test results has been known for years, the debate on this has only recently been forcefully brought to public attention through litigation (Oakland and Ferginbaum, 1980). Cook (1979b) has criticized some court decisions (for example, *Diana* v. *State Board of Education* [1970], *Larry P.* v. *Wilson Riles* [1979] and *Parents and Action for Special Education* v. *Hannon* [1979]) for their narrow focus on the tests used in the assessment process. She explained that there are three sources of bias in assessment: the tests themselves, the assessment process or examiner-examinee transaction, and the decision-making process. Cook (1979a, 1981) has proposed a conceptual framework for nondiscriminatory assessment, proposing five models: (1) psychometric, (2) alternative, (3) transactional (4) ecological, and (5) interdisciplinary. These five models are described and offered here as strategies to avoid or reduce resegregation at the assessment stage.

The *psychometric model* attempts to control for bias that results from the characteristics of the testing instruments used in assessment. The first approach within the psychometric model is to develop tests with attention to minority representation throughout all phases of the development. The second approach requires that existing tests be used and interpreted with respect to their psychometric properties. One example is Kaufman's (1979) interpretation guidelines for the WISC-R test, which are based on the research regarding the WISC-R in addition to knowledge of the psychometric basis of the test and test administration. The development and publication of multiple norms, so that individual children can be compared to the norm for their own group as well as that of other groups, will also help in the interpretation of results. A third approach, which has generally been regarded as a failure (Sattler, 1974), has been the development of tests that are designed to either reduce cultural influences or be culture free or culture fair. The fourth, and opposite, approach of developing culturally specific tests (for example, Williams, 1975) has been found equally unacceptable (Bennett, 1970). The psychometric model calls for the development of tests based on sound technology and the interpretation of all tests with respect to their psychometric properties. The psychometric model is necessary but not sufficient for a nondiscriminatory assessment.

The *alternative assessment model* attempts to control for bias by using nontraditional assessment techniques that are potentially culture fair. The first of these alternatives is criterion-referenced assessment, a measurement approach in which a level of mastery of the tested material is obtained as a "score" (Popham and Husek, 1969). At first impression, criterion-referenced assessment appears to be "culture fair." However, the objectives chosen for learning and social behavior and the nature of the test items will, by definition, reflect the culture of the school. The second alternative model is that of Piagetian assessment, which, it was hoped, would be culture free. However, Boehm (1966) and Hunt and Kirk (1974) demonstrated marked differences in the attainment of concepts by children in different socioeconomic groups. The third alternative, learning-potential assessment, uses a test-teach-retest paradigm where actual learning ability and strategy is observed. Such an approach is used by Feuerstein (1979) in his *Learning Potential Assessment Device* and by Budoff and his associates in research (Budoff, 1967; Budoff, 1972; Budoff and Friedman, 1964). Both Feuerstein and Budoff conclude that a large number of IQ-defined retardates show learning potential, and are not mentally retarded but educationally retarded. Learning-potential assessment procedures show promise for predicting the ability to learn.

The *transactional assessment model* attempts to control for bias resulting from transactions among examiners, students, and environment. In the large sense, this bias results from the examiner's unfamiliarity with the cultural background of the student. Transactional assessment is a process approach to assessment that fully involves the examiner (Cook and Plas, 1980; Fischer and Brodsky, 1978), the student (Byrnes, 1979; Cook, 1979b; Cook and Lundberg, 1978; Fischer and Brodsky, 1978), and perhaps the student's family (Coles, 1977; Martinez-Morales and Cook, 1981; Ramirez and Castaneda, 1974) in order to maximize student performance. A second aspect of transactional assessment is the evaluation of the way the child approaches the task (rather than the score that he or she achieves) by expert clinical observation during the testing session (Meyers, Sunstrom, and Yoshida, 1974) or by "testing the limits"; that is, going back to the item after standardized administration and varying the directions, time, guidance, and so on given to the child completing the task (Sattler, 1974). Transactional assessment procedures rely on the expertise of individual examiners and their awareness of the cultural influences on their own observations and conclusions.

The *ecological assessment model* attempts to control for bias by examining the child in the context of his or her ecologies, comparing competencies across settings. Wallace and Larsen (1978) describe the diagnostic tools used in ecological assessment: systematic observation, teacher-child interaction system, checklists and rating scales, and sociometric techniques. Because ecological assessment should include assessment of the child in ecologies other than school, adaptive behavior is also assessed in this model. The inclusion of adaptive behavior assessment is an extremely potent nondiscriminatory assessment procedure (see Mercer, 1973). Adaptive behavior assessment is essential for a nondiscriminatory assessment, and its consideration in the diagnosis of mental retardation is required under P. L. 94–142.

The *interdisciplinary assessment model* attempts to control for bias that results from a human decision-making process. This approach brings together a variety of professionals who have worked with the child with their discipline's techniques, approaches, frameworks. The interdisciplinary team is to include the child's teacher as the professional educator with whom the child has most contact. Furthermore, the child's parents are essential members of the team, and the child, too, may be included. The interdisciplinary approach alone does not constitute a nondiscriminatory assessment; furthermore this approach appears to be poorly implemented in that parents are functionally excluded and team decisions are influenced by bureaucratic factors rather than by the needs of the child (Weatherly, 1979).

Because each of the models of nondiscriminatory assessment described above addresses different sources of bias in the assessment process, it is obvious that no one model can stand alone in the nondiscriminatory assessment of children. Rather, these models need to be integrated into an approach to service delivery. One attempt at an integrated approach is that of the *System of Multicultural Pluralistic Assessment* (SOMPA) (Mercer and Lewis, 1978). Although the SOMPA is the best organized approach to nondiscriminatory assessment, it has not gone without criticism (see Oakland, 1979; Brown, 1979; Goodman, 1979). Furthermore, the SOMPA is only one attempt at integrating some of the components of the five models of nondiscriminatory model of service delivery by well-trained professionals in an interdisciplinary team. These professionals should have an understanding and respect for cultural diversity; a wide knowledge of child development and pathology, and of education; the ability to go beyond traditional psychometric procedures using alternative assessment; and the ability to work well with other professionals, regular classroom teachers, parents, and children.

Alternatives to the Traditional Organization of Categorical Programs

The degree to which compensatory education, special education, and bilingual education result in resegregation is very much a function of their organization. Alternatives to the traditional ways of organizing categorical programs have in common a focus on reducing reliance on pullout and integrating special services into the regular educational program of the school.

Compensatory Education

A reliance on pullout has been almost universal in compensatory education programs. Since a primary cause for this reliance lies in the federal guidelines governing these programs, alternative allocative and regulatory mechanisms may reduce the practice and, concomitantly, its resegregative effects. The new amendments to Title I, which allow simplified record keeping and reporting, provide an opportunity to address this issue in the regulations.

There have been several demonstration projects where Title I regulations governing the targeting of services and combining of funds across compensatory programs have been relaxed. One of these programs allows services to be provided to all students in a school where 75 percent of them are eligible. These changes have resulted in the reduction or elimination of pullout and the instituting of in-class compensatory programs. Reductions in compensatory services were more than offset by the additional instruction in the regular classroom (Milne, 1977; Rubin and David, 1981). Schools with fewer students eligible for compensatory aid, however, may continue to find pullout the most practical way to deliver services.

Another method for avoiding pullout is to provide Title I services in the regular classroom by defining the Title I specialist as a consultant and resource person rather than simply as a subject matter specialist. Instead of working with groups of students, the resource teachers act as consultants to regular classroom teachers and other school personnel. They assist teachers in assessing specific learning problems and preparing individual learning plans, train classroom aides and parent volunteers, and help the principal plan the schoolwide instructional program (Tobin and Bonner, 1977). This approach resolves the frequently encountered problem of a loss of coordination between the students' regular and compensatory instructional program.

The success of compensatory education depends on the coordination and joint planning of regular and compensatory programs (Glass and Smith, 1977; Frechtling and Hammond, 1978) and on the school climate (Rossi et al.,

1977; Coulson et al., 1977). Pullout wreaks havoc with the ability of classroom teachers to plan and schedule instruction in the core curriculum (Kimbrough and Hill, 1981), but problems in coordination and planning are difficult to overcome even where regulations are relaxed.

Special Education

In special education, mainstreaming (at least part-time placement in a regular classroom) is the major alternative to special class placement. Concerns about how civil rights were affected by the disproportionate placement of black and Hispanic children in EMR classes were among the major motivations of the mainstreaming movement (Dunn, 1968). Most research comparing the effects of mainstreaming and special classes on academic achievement of EMR children has failed to show significant differences between the two (Abramson, 1980; Corman and Gottlieb, 1978; Semmel et al., 1979).

There is also little evidence that mainstreamed EMR children have more positive self-concepts or higher rates of acceptance by their nonretarded peers (Corman and Gottlieb, 1978; Semmel et al., 1979). However, little attention has been paid to the variety of possible mainstreaming conditions. The amount of time spent in regular classrooms, the availability of resource room and other support services, and the organization and curricula of regular and special classes are variables that have seldom been examined in research on mainstreaming. Neither is there much information about the effects of mainstreaming on minority children. Available data suggest, however, that mainstreamed minority students from EMR classes may be placed in low-track classes that are as racially isolated as the special education classes (Kaufman, Agard, and Semmel, 1978). Thus, the effectiveness of mainstreaming in reducing resegregation depends on the extent to which regular classrooms are integrated and organized heterogeneously.

At this time, no particular special education program, mainstreamed or segregated, has strong empirical support in either the cognitive or the affective domain. The strongest arguments in favor of mainstreaming remain legal and moral ones: "The argument (is) not advanced that retarded children will perform better in mainstreamed settings, only that they will not perform worse. The data support the latter assertion" (Semmel et al., 1979, p. 269).

Bilingual Education

The relationship of models of bilingual education to resegregation is primarily found in the characteristics of the students participating in each model. English as a Second Language (ESL) is by definition segregative, since the only participants in ESL programs are limited-Engligh-proficiency (LEP) students. However, the children are likely to participate in ESL classes for only a portion of the day and for only a relatively short time within their educational career. This may offset the segregative nature of the program. All other models (bilingual education, bilingual-bicultural education, bilingual-bicultural-bicognitive education) may be segregative or integrative depending on goals (transmition or maintenance), student participation (one-way or two-way), and organizational structure.

When the effects of resegregation are being considered, decisions about whether a transition or a maintenance program is chosen must be influenced to a great extent by who is expected to participate in the program (one-way or two-way). Transition programs are generally associated with remedial or compensatory education; they will not attract white or black students (Carter, 1979; Epstein, 1977; Fernandez and Guskin, 1981; Vazquez, 1976). Thus, participants in a transition program are likely to be Hispanics or members of other linguistic minorities. The segregation by ethnicity may be offset by the temporary nature of the program if transition is, in fact, effected. Should a district choose to implement a transitional program, emphasis must be placed on the organizational structure of the program if resegregation is to be minimized. LEP students may join their English-proficient peers for coursework and activities that do not rely on English proficiency. Time spent in the bilingual program may also decrease with the age of the child so that eventually the child is involved in the program only for formal study of the mother language.

Two-way maintenance programs are by definition integrative. Such programs are most appropraite for communities having a relatively large proportion of Hispanics. The involvement of non-Hispanic students is most likely to occur under local circumstances where Spanish proficiency has economic and political relevance. An example is Dade County, Florida (Cohen, 1975; Gaarder, 1975; Mackey and Beebe, 1977). These programs tend to be "fragile"; that is, their continued existence depends upon the commitment of school personnel and the community to the program (Carter and Segura, 1979).

Where the major concern is not rapid integration into the English-speaking classroom and society but the development of competence in the language spoken in the child's home, as well as instruction in the child's ethnic heritage, then one-way maintenance programs will be chosen, and these are resegregative. An approach that offers a compromise between respect for the child's ethnic heritage and development of competence in English has been tested by Lily Wong Fillmore with children from Chinese-speaking homes. She found that students who were taught in English by bilingual teachers excelled in achievement. These teachers were sensitive to and respectful of the children's cultural heritage and able to help them over rough spots with quick personal guidance in their primary language (Fillmore, 1980). Such a program need not segregate the students from their English-speaking peers.

There is very little evidence on the extent of different types of bilingual education programs or on their consequences. In theory, alternatives that emphasize transition into the mainstream, or programs that involve two-way language acquisition and include English-proficient students, should be the least resegregative.

Alternative Instructional and Organizational Practices

More "mainstreamed" delivery of categorical services and the reduction of ability grouping in regular classes require the use of ororganizational and instructional techniques that accommodate student diversity. Schools have traditionally responded to diversity in the regular education program by creating homogeneous instructional groups. Given the evidence on racial and ethnic segregation in tracked and ability-grouped classrooms, the potential value of flexible and heterogeneous grouping in avoiding resegregation is clear. A variety of instructional practices have been developed for use in classrooms that encompass a wide range of individual differences in ability and achievement. These alternatives differ in their approach to heterogeneity. Some emphasize individualized instruction, while others use small groups. Classroom and staff organization may also increase flexibility and thus enhance capacity for handling student diversity. While there is a very great need for further research and development on this topic, there are a few organizational and instructional alternatives that have been shown to have positive effects on interracial contact and educational attainment.

Cooperative Learning Techniques

The most promising approach to classroom organization is the family of techniques called cooperative learning or student team learning. These instructional methods involve students working together in small, heterogeneous groups to learn academic materials and may include intergroup competition. Some relevant research reports are Johnson and Johnson (1974); Weigel, Wiser, and Cook (1975); Lucker et al., (1976); Hamblin, Hathaway, and Wodarski (1971); and Slavin (1977a, 1977b, 1977c, 1977d, 1977e, 1977f, 1978a, 1978b, 1979a, 1979b, 1979c, 1979d, 1980a, 1980b).

These techniques usually involve the creation of teams of students. Each team of roughly four to six students represents the full rage of ethnic groups, ability, and gender in the classroom. Academic work is structured so that the children on each team are dependent on each other, but also so that disparity in achievement levels does not lead automatically to disparity in contributions to group goal attainment. For example, one team learning technique (Jigsaw) is structured so that each child is given information that all group members need to complete their work. Another technique, Student Teams-Achievement Division (STAD) gives rewards for improvement in academic performance, so that students with weak academic backgrounds have the potential to contribute as much to the success of the team as the best students.

There is a considerable body of evidence suggesting that these approaches lead to higher than usual academic achievement gains for low-achieving students and almost always improve relations between majority and minority group children (Slavin, 1980a; Sharan, 1980). Compared to individualized instruction, the cooperative learning method produced higher achievement on a test of the materials studied and a slightly more positive effect on students' self-concept, especially regarding peer relationships (DeVries, Lucasse, and Shackman, 1979). Genova and Walberg (1979) note in their study of school integration that "racial mixing" is the key to success and that the use of interracial learning teams is the most effective strategy for fostering interracial interaction within classrooms.

The work of Elizabeth Cohen and others on the Multi-Ability Classroom (MAC) has also shown promising results in fostering equal participant influence in cooperative learning groups. This approach is based on the premise that students need special preparation for participation in cooperative mixed-ability groups in order to counter the effects of status generalization often found in heterogeneous and racially integrated classrooms. Rosenholtz (1977), for example, found that children seen as high in reading ability and high in status in group reading tasks also have high status in task groups that do not require reading.

Mixed-ability groups are assigned cooperative learning tasks that require a number of abilities and do not exclusively rely on reading, writing, and computation skills. In addition, students are prepared for the task by discussing the range of abilities it requires and are instructed that while no group member will possess all of the necessary skills, every member will be able to contribute at least one. The multiple-ability assignments may be preceded by Expectation Training, in which low-status students are prepared for special tasks that they then teach to other students (Cohen, 1980).

Multiple-ability intervention helps to equalize status and participation in cooperative learning groups of both single-race and multiracial composition (Stulac, 1975; Cohen, 1969; Rosenholtz, 1980) and to ensure group success (Blanchard, Adelman, and Cook, 1975). In addtion, low-achieving minority students have been found to exhibit more active learning behavior in classrooms that approximate the MAC model (Cohen, 1980; Ahmadjian-Baer, 1981).

Evidence on the effects of interracial academic cooperation that does not employ a specific team technique is less clear but suggests that the effects are positive (U.S. Commission on Civil Rights, 1976; Slavin and Madden, 1979). This suggests that at the very least, teachers should not allow groupings created for specific purposes, such as reading instruction, to spill over into other instruction, especially if these specialized groupings prove to be racially segregative.

Individualized Instruction

Numerous approaches to and definitions of individualized instruction, as well as a professional consensus regarding its importance, have been developed over the past two decades. The elements of individualization usually include: (1) clearly stated academic objectives, (2) attention to individual needs, including individual diagnoses and prescription, and (3) structured sequential instruction (Archambault and St. Pierre, 1978). These characteristics have been emphasized in compensatory education and in special education (in the Individual Education Program requirements in P.L. 94–142, for example) as well as in individualized instruction techniques intended for general use.

A potential danger in individualized instruction is that students, especially those who are low achieving and somewhat discouraged to begin with, will set a pace that allows them to fall further and further behind over time. This approach, to be effective, needs firm management, continuous evaluation and feedback, and remediation for students with difficulties (Brodbelt, 1980). Teachers need to be sure that high expectations for achievement are communicated to students.

Some educators have also cautioned that individualized education programs may lead, ironically, to homogeneous grouping practices (Bailey, 1981). Students who are working at similar levels may be grouped together, and because of the self-paced nature of classroom work, interaction among students may be limited. Thus, well-intentioned efforts to deal with individual differences may conflict with the goals of integrated education if they contribute to the racial and social stratification of students. Perhaps as a result of these concerns, proponents of various individualization techniques specify ways that they can be used in combination with flexible grouping practices (Bailey, 1981; Wang, 1979a). Examples include phasing of instruction and student self-scheduling.

Phasing describes a set of characteristics usually found in nongraded individualized programs, including the following: (1) instructional groups are temporary and student mobility among them is high, (2) groups are separate for each subject area, (3) group assignment standards and instructional objectives are clearly specified, and (4) evaluation is based on individual progress. Bailey (1981) describes a high school science course based on the phasing model in which students are randomly assigned to sections of a large class with a team of several teachers. Within this format students attend voluntarily selected lecture-discussions differentiated by level of cognitive difficulty, laboratory sessions based on sequential mastery of specific skills, heterogeneous discussion groups and field trips, and independent study or tutorial sessions. Thus, students receive instruction in a variety of group settings. Similar programs have been implemented in multi-age classrooms, incorporating a combination of instructional groupings. In one program, for example, heterogeneous groups of students are scheduled for work in learning stations. While they work, the teachers select students with similar skill needs for small group instruction. An evaluation of this project reported achievement gains above the national norms, with an average gain of two years in reading and one and a half years in arithmetic in one school year (District of Columbia Public Schools, 1980).

Self-scheduling is designed to increase students' sense of responsibility for their own learning and use of time and to achieve a better "fit" between students' rate of learning and available learning time. The self-schedule system differs from other individualized instruction systems in that students work on assignments in the order they choose for the amount of time they need and record their own scheduling. A concomitant effect of self-scheduling is to increase the instructional time available to the teacher, both by reducing classroom management activities and by ensuring that fewer students will need attention at any one time (Wang, 1979a, 1979b).

Students using self-scheduling in an inner-city elementary school have been found to complete more tasks in less time than students using the same individualized program but with block scheduling (Wang, 1979b). A self-scheduling system needs to be used with other classroom practices such as multi-age grouping and team teaching in order to provide opportunities for peer interaction in small groups.

Peer Tutoring

Cross-age tutoring, in which older low-achieving children teach younger low-achieving children, is based on the rationale that the children being taught will benefit from additional individual help while the tutor will also learn through teaching and preparing to teach. Numerous peer tutoring programs were developed in the 1960s in inner-city schools with large black and Hispanic populations and were seen as a way to capitalize on classroom heterogeneity and to improve race relations (Gartner, Kohler, and Riessman, 1971). English-speaking and Spanish-speaking students, for example, can tutor each other in language skills and also gain cultural exposure and understanding.

Considerable evidence exists of cognitive and affective gains for older low-achieving tutors. Evidence of comparable effects for those being taught is less consistent. Some studies show positive academic and attitudinal changes for both tutor and student, while others have found that the benefits for the former do not also accrue to the latter (Devin-Sheehan, Feldman, and Allen, 1976).

While positive results have been found for both black and white same-race tutoring pairs, very few studies have examined mixed-race pairs. One study that did so found that cross-race tutoring produced greater interracial interaction and acceptance for both tutor and student, although there were no significant gains in achievement (Devin-Sheehan, Feldman, and Allen, 1976).

Team Organization

Team-organized schools group students in teamhouses or minischools with an interdisciplinary group of teachers. Students are randomly assigned to minischools and typically stay in the same unit through several grade levels. The team organization is especially advocated for middle schools and is designed to increase classroom heterogeneity, increase student interactions across grade levels, and increase student-teacher interaction. A main effect of the team-organized or minischool system is effectively to reduce the size of the school for the student in order to reduce the anonymity and personal distance in the large setting. This system is also thought to foster teachers' sense of professionalism, since it requires professional cooperation among teachers and responsibility for a common group of students (Walline, 1976). In a study comparing such schools with more traditionally organized ones, students in the team-organized schools had significantly more other-race friends and perceived their school's interracial climate more favorably (Damico, Green, and Bell-Nathaniel, 1981).

Alternatives to Suspension

Alternatives to out-of-school suspension encompass both specific programs designed to reduce suspension and behavior problems and subsequent dropping out, and school characteristics and practices that have been associated with low suspension rates. Here, examples of the range of in-school suspension (ISS) and related programs will be described, and available evidence on their effectiveness in reducing overall suspension rates and minority suspension rates will be summarized. Some common characteristics of low-suspension schools will also be noted.

In-School Suspension Programs

In-school alternatives to suspension can be divided into three categories: guidance and counseling programs, time-out rooms, and in-school suspension centers. The last category is a broad one in which the length of time, the degree of isolation, and the comprehensiveness of services vary a great deal. In fact, many programs are hybrids that include elements of all three types. In addition, there are alternative schools for students who have severe behavior problems or who have already dropped out or been expelled from regular schools (Garibaldi, 1979).

Counseling programs. These programs provide individual, peer, or group counseling sessions for students, usually on a referral basis. Typically the objectives emphasize the improvement of self-concept, motivation, and attitude toward school. A variety of methods are used, employing such techniques as Glasser's reality therapy, values clarification, conflict resolution, and training in decision-making skills (Bader, 1978; NIE, 1979). Some programs concentrate on helping students with problems to set academic and behavioral objectives (McNab, 1978). Others focus on providing services on a schoolwide basis as a prevention effort. Some schoolwide programs provide, for example, "desegregation aides" who conduct discussion sessions and conflict resolution activities (Higgins, 1974) or regular classroom instruction in human relations, basic encounter groups for students and staff, parent training, and school and home "survival courses" for students with behavior problems (Bailey, 1978).

Time-out rooms. Students are simply sent to a vacant room to "cool off" after a classroom disruption or conflict with a teacher. No examples were found of school programs that rely exclusively on this device. Frequently it is one of a range of interventions or a first step that is followed by counseling or in-school suspension (NIE, 1979; Bailey, 1978).

In-school suspension centers and alternative schools. ISS centers are special classrooms where students are sent in lieu of an out-of-school suspension. Students usually work on regular classroom assignments under the guidance of a supervising teacher; frequently additional academic services are also provided such as tutoring and study skills instruction (NIE, 1979). Counseling sessions and parent conferences are usually a part of the ISS program (NIE, 1979; Cotton, 1978). Students spend an average of three days in ISS (Garibaldi, 1979) on referral of teachers or administrators. They may be largely isolated from the rest of the school, eating lunch at separate times and remaining in one classroom all day. Some schools provide a continuum of ISS-type alternatives, ranging from only part-day and very short-term centers, to centers that are totally self-contained (schools within a school) with separate instructional programs, to alternative schools at separate locations (NIE, 1979; Cotton, 1978).

Effectiveness of programs. Published evaluation data on suspension alternatives tend to be impressionistic and not very specific or complete. There is some evidence that these programs result in fewer out-of-school suspensions and lowered recidivism rates (NIE, 1979; Bader, 1978). Indications of reduced minority disproportion in suspension rates are few, even though this disproportion was a major factor in the establishment of many alternative programs (Garibaldi, 1979). Frequently, racial data is not available. Some success in reducing minority disproportions has been reported by programs in Dallas, Louisiana, and Florida (Cotton, 1978; NIE, 1979; Bailey, 1978).

Even without a reduction in racial disproportionality, a significant reduction in the use of out-of-school suspension may reduce its resegregative impact. This benefit will be lost if the in-school suspension programs used are not effective in helping students remain in the classroom and become simply another way to isolate large numbers of minority students from their peers. ISS program administrators and observers continue to express concern about the degree of racial isolation and disproportion in alternative programs (Arnez, 1978; Arnove and Strout, 1980; NIE, 1979). These programs can become identified as "minority programs," especially when they involve a voluntary transfer to an alternative school, and a number of highly segregated alternative schools have been noted (Williams, in NIE, 1979). Mizell (in NIE, 1979) has urged that particular attention be paid to this issue, including careful collection of data on the racial composition of programs and on referrals of minority students by teachers and principals.

School Differences in Suspension

Clearly, one cannot account for the disproportionate suspension rates for minority students by focusing on disciplinary practices alone. A pattern of repeated suspensions and dropping out is a clear-cut manifestation of the lack of fit between the needs of the student and the culture of the school. The climate of the school, including the level of acceptance of minority students as well as the success of the instructional program in promoting achievement for all students, will influence both the tendency of minority students to act out and the treatment of those who do misbehave.

The importance of the total school environment has been borne out in studies of schools with a low incidence of disciplinary problems and low use of suspension. These studies have identified features of organization and school climate that appear to be related to the school's orderliness. The scope of this essay does not allow an extensive summary of the literature on the organizational climate of schools, but it is worth noting some of the findings related to school suspension rates.

Most authors agree that the leadership of the school principal is an important element in dealing with student behavior (Brodbelt, 1980; Kaeser, 1979a). In one study conducted in Louisville, principals in low-suspension schools gave higher priority to fostering mutual respect between students and staff, were visible around the school, and felt that they had greater discretion in making disciplinary decisions than did high-suspension principals. Teachers reacted positively to this leadership and indicated more positive perceptions of student respect for teachers, of the honesty and sincerity of people in the school, of students' enjoyment of school, of students' feelings of acceptance in school, and of the school's learning environment (Bickel and Qualls, 1979).

Other studies of effective schools with relatively few disciplinary problems have identified successful schools as being "child centered" rather than "subject centered" with a commitment to serving all students, high expectations for both teachers and students, and an approach to student behavior that uses a wide range of disciplinary techniques with an emphasis on self-discipline and problem solving rather than punishment (Kaeser, 1979a). Teachers are able to establish and enforce a clear set of classroom rules and spend more time on teaching and less on discipline regardless of the racial and socioeconomic composition of the school (Brodbelt, 1980).

Many of the instructional strategies identified as potentially effective ways to avoid tracking and rigid ability grouping have been found to be effective in building a more positive organizational climate and reducing disciplinary problems. Effective schools were those that paid attention to each student's progress. Brodbelt (1980) noted that in studies of successful schools the curriculum was characterized by structure and firm management with continuous evaluation, remediation, and individualized instruction. These schools were also more likely to use flexible scheduling and grouping (Kaeser, 1979a).

Effective schools were also structured to increase contact between students and faculty. In the larger schools, this often means dividing students among minischools to allow students and faculty to get to know each other better. Some researchers view the reduction in size to be a key element in the success of many alternative schools in reducing disciplinary problems and suspensions (Arnove and Strout, 1980; Duke and Perry, 1978).

While the Louisville study identified climate and leadership differences in schools with low overall suspension rates, the disproportionate suspension of black students was *not* related to these characteristics (Bickel and Qualls, 1979). However, a case study of two school districts that examined schools with low minority disproportion in suspension found that what distinguished these from schools with a greater racial disparity were perceptions of a favorable interracial climate and staff support for integration (Bennett and Harris, 1981).

Leadership that facilitates development of a positive organizational climate and an effective instructional program is important but probably not sufficient to correct racial disparity in the enforcement of school discipline. School leaders must be committed to creating a school climate that reflects an explicit concern with race relations in general and with interracial fairness in administering discipline. School administrators can manifest this concern in at least two ways. First, rules governing behavior and establishing disciplinary offenses should be developed with broad participation, including staff, students and parents. The common expectations for behavior in school that result from this process should be widely disseminated throughout the school. In addition, tardiness and other attendance-related offenses probably should not be punishable by suspension, and vague prohibitions that allow a great deal of discretion in enforcement, such as "insubordination," should probably be eliminated altogether.

Second, administrators should analyze carefully the reasons for minority suspensions and other disciplinary actions. Schools should keep records of suspensions including the reason for the suspension, the teacher or staff person involved, and the race and sex of the student involved. This allows the school principal, parents, and others to analyze the reasons for suspension by race and sex, and to determine if particular teachers or staff members have problems needing attention. It also allows particular patterns of student misbehavior to be identified so that targeted interventions can be planned. Until the leadership in a school understands the causes of disproportionate minority suspension in that school at that time, solutions are impossible.

In-service training for teachers and administrators can facilitate the implementation of effective assessment and discipline practices. Teachers frequently request in-service training in classroom management immediately after desegregation begins, and such programs have been found to reduce disciplinary problems in recently desegregated schools. Administrators can also benefit from in-service training in developing and administering rules of conduct and in establishing a positive interracial climate (Smylie and Hawley, 1982).

Summary and Recommendations for Research and Development

The problem of resegregation usually grows out of schools' responses to externally imposed change. While desegregation within schools yields increasing academic and behavioral diversity, the schools rely on traditional assessment, instructional, and disciplinary practices that are aimed at producing homogeneous groups of students that also tend to be racially and ethnically more homogeneous than the school population at large. These practices may be well-intentioned and based on the dominant educational philosophy of meeting individual educational needs. Nevertheless, the means for achieving this goal, which are typically part of the school culture and manifested in its organizational routines, conflict with the institution of educational processes that are intended to bring about integrated education in desegregated schools. This creates a paradox for students. At the same time as diversity increases at the school level, the diversity of contacts experienced by each student may actually decrease as homogeneous grouping practices are more extensively used to manage this diversity.

Academic grouping practices that are commonly used to manage diversity include ability grouping and tracking, compensatory education, special education, and bilingual education. Resegregation results from the pupil assignment practices and organization of these programs. Factors associated with resegregation include the use of standardized testing, cultural insensitivity among school personnel, and student and parent choice. Traditional student assignment practices invariably result in the disproportionate channeling of minority students into low-ability groups and other programs addressing academic deficiencies. The organization of the programs thus becomes crucial, for it is the organization that determines the degree to which the programs become resegregative.

Program organization determines the degree to which minority students have an opportunity for equal-status interaction with their majority peers. Any ability grouping or tracking system will tend to resegregate as long as race and class are associated with measures of achievement. Flexible programs that group for particular goals will provide more opportunities for interracial contact than rigid programs that track students for all academic experiences on the basis of a particular achievement such as reading level. Full-time programs for special and bilingual education result in obvious resegregation. Pullout programs may be potentially less segregative since less time is usually spent out of the regular classroom. Many minority children, however, are involved in numerous compensatory programs on a daily basis as a result of their eligibility for multiple programs. The fragmented nature of the public policies mandating such programs and the concomitant fragmentation of the services provided at the school level serve to exacerbate the problem of resegregation.

The school's response to the social diversity of the student population is also reflected in its disciplinary procedures. Black students, rather than Hispanics, are disproportionately suspended. Both blacks and Hispanics drop out of school at disproportionate rates, but Hispanics tend to have a higher dropout rate than blacks and to drop out at an earlier age. Teacher attitudes and school climate are associated with resegregation through disciplinary policies. Alternatives to suspension, while potentially promising, have not been shown to eliminate racial disproportionality in suspensions.

Schools, to reduce or eliminate within-school resegregation, must implement fundamental changes in the organization of instruction, in the assessment of student performance, and in their ways of dealing with student misbehavior. Student assessment should be interpreted by well-informed consumers of testing information. Instruction should be organized so that heterogeneous groups of students have the opportunity for educational interaction; special support services should be integrated into the regular school program as much as possible. The emphasis in student discipline should be on keeping students in school, on dealing with the sources of behavior problems, including the influence of school climate on behavior, and on the development and enforcement of disciplinary policy in a racially and ethnically equitable manner.

Part of the reason for the persistence of traditional school practices that are resegregative may be that teachers and administrators are overwhelmed by the changes required. For many, this means change in attitudes and behavior as well as changes in instructional methods and strategies for social control and classroom management. Some of these changes are a part of adapting to any innovation but in school desegregation, all these problems—each of which is a source of personal stress—must be confronted simultaneously.

As noted previously, there are available alternatives to traditional methods of assignment, instruction, and organization that are responsive to differences and yet encourage equal status contact. These alternatives however, fall far short of an adequate technology for avoiding or eliminating resegregative practices.

In the course of gathering and analyzing information for this essay, we have become acutely aware of specific research needs in several areas related to resegregation. Almost every topic we investigated is characterized by gaps in data and analysis on the sources of the problem, or by a paucity of alternative models by which to understand and solve the problem, or both. Frequently, the assertion that resegregation occurs is built on fragmented pieces of collateral evidence, because much of the research on educational practices either is not conducted in a desegregated setting, or the race of the students affected is not mentioned.

The most important topics for further research, development, evaluation, and dissemination are:

1. *Instructional techniques for teaching heterogeneous groups of students.* Only cooperative learning techniques among the flexible and heterogeneous grouping practices are backed by empirical evidence that provides considerable confidence in their effectiveness.
2. *Scheduling, grouping and instructional practices to facilitate interaction among heterogeneous high school students.* Resegregation is particularly acute in high schools where differentiation of the curriculum is most pronounced; there is almost no information about strategies to mitigate the separation that occurs.
3. *Disciplinary techniques, including alternative forms of in-school suspension, that reduce the disproportionality of suspensions or exclusions of minority group children.* The literature is replete with examples of techniques, but there is an absence of comparison among programs that would allow identification of program characteristics that are linked to desirable outcomes in different settings. Data on the impact of different techniques on disproportionate minority suspensions are also sparse.
4. *Further development and evaluation of psychological assessment techniques for evaluating minority children fairly.* There is little evidence to suggest how currently developed experimental techniques affect assessment and placement of minority group children.
5. *Development and assessment of alternative approaches to the delivery of categorical services.* There has been little sustained analysis of the effects of alternatives to pullout programs.

Traditional practices, though resegregative, have survived because they are thought to be necessary to achieve the two basic goals of the school: academic achievement for individual students and order. Until educators have techniques for effectively dealing with the educational needs of a diverse student body in an integrated setting, desegregation will not be seen as a viable educational strategy. Resegregation is a manifestation of the failure of desegregation to prove itself to educators and parents as a strategy that benefits children.

6

Directions for Future Research

Willis D. Hawley, Christine H. Rossell, and *Robert L. Crain*

The essays in this book document how much more is known today about the effects of desegregation on students and communities than was known only a few years ago. Still, many of the things we "know," we only know in a tentative and partial sense; many important questions about why things happen and what consequences they have remain unanswered. Indeed, some important issues remain virtually unstudied.

In this chapter we (1) identify some of the reasons school desegregation research has yielded less knowledge than one might expect from the level of energy that has been expended, (2) delineate some of the issues that seem most important to pursue in order to improve the effectiveness of desegregation and related policies and broaden the knowledge base we have about education, and (3) propose some general strategies for improving the quality and productivity of desegregation research.

SOME SOURCES OF CONFUSION AND INADEQUACY IN THE EXISTING RESEARCH

Efforts to synthesize the research findings on the effects of desegregation have led some to conclude that the evidence is so mixed or contradictory that one can draw no reliable conclusions from it. Others have concluded that desegregation has no consistent benefit and as a result have withdrawn or withheld support from it.

The research synthesized in this volume clarifies the available evidence and provides a greater sense of confidence that desegregation can be effective in a number of ways. Still, there are many questions that need more definitive answers. One explanation for the apparent ambiguity of much of the research is that the effects of desegregation vary enormously from community to community and from school to school. To say this is but to suggest that research has not captured the complexity of the process and the factors that affect different types of outcomes.

Most of the shortcomings of desegregation research can be traced to four characteristics of the existing studies: (1) the virutal absence of relatively comprehensive conceptual and theoretical frameworks; (2) methodological weaknesses, including inappropriate measures of the dependent variables; (3) inadequate specification and operationalization of potential causal and explanatory factors; and (4) the relative isolation of desegregation research from other inquiries about school effectiveness.

The key to enhancing the productivity of desegregation research lies in the development of theory to guide research design and analysis. Without theory, efforts to design research and to interpret data will be less fruitful than they might be, and research findings will have limited effects on the cumulative development of knowledge.

One of the most serious dangers posed by the absence of theory is that we may misunderstand or misinterpret relationships between variables. This is particularly true for desegregation research because the issues examined often involve conflicting values and ideological meanings. A good example is the interpretation of the findings of the so-called Coleman Report (Coleman et al., 1966). That study was frequently construed as deemphasizing the importance of school resources (including teachers) and emphasizing the importance of peers, especially those of a middle-class background, in shaping achievement. This resulted in all manner of mischief, including the presumptions that schools do not matter much and that black children can learn best when in the presence of whites. Neither presumption, however, makes much theoretical sense. More recent analyses suggest that peers do count, but primarily because of how teachers behave in more heterogeneous environments. This difference in emphasis is crucial. Where the earlier assumption suggested the educational policy was largely unimportant, the later interpretation suggests that schools can and do differ in ways that affect children. When theory is applied to data analysis, the result indicates that relatively low-cost, intuitively sensible policies and practices that will benefit students can be introduced in desegregated schools.

In addition to the absence of theory and the problems of research methodology, there are several other, more specific characteristics of the empirical research on desegregation that account for the inadequacy and apparent inconsistency of the knowledge base from which strategies for more effective desegregation can be developed. First, most studies of the effects of desegregation on children focus on black students to the exclusion of other races and ethnic groups. Although there is some analysis of the effect of desegregation on whites, much of it is a byproduct of comparisons with blacks. There is very little work on Hispanics and seemingly no published research at all on other minorities.

Second, the bulk of the research focuses on the first year or two of desegregation. As several of the chapters in this volume have indicated, this has important consequences, since there is every reason to believe that the benefits of desegregation for children and their community increase after the initial, often unstable and conflictual, period. Because there is little or no research on the impact of desegregation after the period during which the plan is formulated, adopted, and initially implemented, we know almost nothing about organizational adaptation, the politics of parental response to desegregation over time, and how administrators and teachers cope with the complex problems of making desegregation work.

A third shortcoming of the research is that studies of the politics of desegregation emphasize local events and ignore the interaction and effects of state and federal actions (except court action), a notable exception being the work of Orfield (1978a). Moreover, despite the substantial interest in the local politics of desegregation, only a few researchers have sought to relate such efforts to what goes on in schools, much less to what happens in classrooms.

Fourth, as all the authors of this volume have noted, much of the "desegregation" research, even the best known (Coleman et al., 1966; St. John, 1975), is actually about racially mixed schools and provides no information as to whether the racial mix was the consequence of planned desegregation. Indeed, given the pre-1966 time period covered in the Coleman Report, it is likely that almost all of the racial mixing resulted "naturally" rather than from planning. Planned desegregation is an identifiable social process that has a particular starting point and carries with it, in one measure or another, assumptions that change is required or desirable. To consider the experiences that children, teachers, and parents have in such a process to be the same as those they have in schools that are "integrated" because of residential patterns or school district consolidation is a precarious assumption.

Desegregation research has yielded less knowledge than one might hope for in part because it has not been undertaken in the context of research on school effectiveness generally. This may suggest that desegregation has been seen as having little relevance to the processes of teaching and learning. The isolation of research on desegregation from most other educational research has meant that we know too little about how desegregation actually brings about the results it does. It is interesting to note that within the National Institute of Education, the desegration research unit was considered a part of the Institute that focused on law, governance, and organizations rather than a part of the branch that focused on teaching and learning.

What Do We Need Most to Know?

The research reviews in this volume have drawn from the research some conclusions on how to make desegregation more effective. Considering the problems just described, this has not been an easy task. As a result we do not believe that the conclusions and recommendations we make here are the last word on the subject. Let us identify some of the questions to which research aimed at fostering quality integrated education might most profitably be addressed.

Pupil Assignment Strategies

Desegregating a school system involves two tasks: (1) developing a pupil assignment plan and other strategies to eliminate racial isolation and ensure reasonable enrollment stability, and (2) developing and implementing programs and practices that result in equity and educational quality. How these two aspects of the desegregation process are interrelated deserves careful inquiry.

The effectiveness of a pupil reassignment plan seems to depend on:

1. its efficiency in eliminating racial isolation,
2. its stability or "holding power,"
3. its effects on housing patterns, and
4. the extent to which it stimulates and facilitates the implementation of educational policies and practices that benefit students.

In general, these four conditions are interactive. It seems reasonable to assume that attaining positive results with one condition will generally, though not always, enhance the likelihood of attaining positive results with the others. But just how these interact is uncertain.

The Logistical Efficiency of Desegregation Plans

There are many ways to reassign students to achieve racial balance. If the criteria for evaluating the effectiveness of these strategies are financial cost, the time students spend getting to school, and the number of students reassigned, few generalizations about efficacy can be made.

Ensuring Stable Enrollment

In some communities, the reassignment of students for the purposes of desegregation may result in white flight. Black, Hispanic, and Asian flight may also occur in some cities, but each is small by comparison, and we know little about it. By contrast, as Rossell indicates, there is a substantial body of research dealing with white flight.

This research tells us that the extent of white flight from desegregation is primarily a function of three factors: (1) the extent of black reassignments to formerly white schools, (2) the extent of white reassignments to formerly black schools, and (3) the proportion black in the school system. The last two factors are substantially more important than the first. This research also tells us that although whites overwhelmingly oppose busing for school desegregation for whatever reasons, they do not act capriciously, but calculate the costs and benefits of various options available to them. Hence, public policy that changes these costs and benefits may be able to influence the extent of white flight.

Among the more or less specific needs for information on strategies that might reduce white flight, these seem to be the most important:

1. What racial mix produces the greatest net benefit in interracial contact, and under what conditions does this involve trade-offs between white flight and racial balance?
2. Do magnet schools in a mandatory desegregation plan reduce white flight in both the short and the long run and facilitate community acceptance, and ultimately improve interracial contact in comparison to mandatory plans without magnet schools? If so, what types of magnets are most integrative?
3. Is white flight greater from black schools than from Hispanic schools and, if so, under what conditions?
4. What are the effects of the media on white flight and how can policymakers influence this?
5. What are the ways parents define educational quality and how do these definitions influence their behavior?
6. How do various strategies for parental and citizen involvement in the development of the plan affect the willingness of parents to send their children to public schools?
7. How important to parents, other things being equal, is the stability of their child's school assignment?
8. How can the language development needs of students with limited English-speaking ability be accommodated within desegregated plans?
9. What assumptions do parents have about the amount of time a student can spend riding the bus before the "lost " time affects learning and how correct are these assumptions?

School Desegregation and Housing Desegregation

There is evidence that school desegregation fosters racial integration of housing. The reasons for this appear to be that (1) desegregated schools may stabilize racially changing neighborhoods, and thus reduce the incentive to move to (and the availability of) racially isolated neighborhoods, and (2) some plans create incentives for integration (for example, by excluding integrated neighborhood schools from busing). Busing not only is the source and symbol of antagonism toward desegregation, but it limits the flexibility of some educational programs and makes it more difficult (but certainly not impossible) for some parents to participate actively in their children's education.

Specification of the circumstances under which different pupil assignment strategies foster housing desegregation should be a first-order research priority. What is needed, then, is a series of case studies of cities. These cities should have varying socioeconomic characteristics and predesegregation racial patterns in housing. We need to know how and why school desegregation ultimately leads to an increase in residential integration defined not just in terms of racial balance, but also in terms of the net increase in the proportion white in the average minority child's residential block, taking into account white flight.

The theoretical framework for researching white flight outlined in Rossell's article might serve as a way of identifying the types of data and conditions one would want to include in a housing effects study. The inquiry appears to call for an integration of quantitative and qualitative methodologies. Housing records, census information, and surveys lend themselves, of course, to aggregate data anlaysis. It seems important, however, to do enough field work and descriptive investigation to specify the behavior of realtors, the differences among neighborhoods, and the relationship between housing choices, the quality of the housing stock, and the quality of public services and amenities available in each area seemingly affected by desegregation. Knowledge of this sort would also allow one to estimate the likely impact of state and federal policies affecting housing.

Effects of Pupil Assignment Plans on Educational Options

While pupil assignment has the purpose of reducing racial isolation, it also has the consequence of creating structural conditions that affect the character of a student's educational experience. Beyond determining the racial mix of a school, pupil reassignment affects the socioeconomic mix of students in a school, the grade structure, the size of schools, the degree of continuity a student has with teachers and peers, and the availability of different types of educational programs including extracurricular activities. In short, it seems likely that pupil reassignment plans, in themselves, have induced substantial changes in the structure and climate of schools aside from their effect on the racial composition of student bodies and faculties.

There is virtually no research on this. That is, there is no knowledge base upon which to assess the educational constraints and opportunities created by different types of assignment plans. This is especially important since these "secondary" effects of assignment plans may have substantial consequences for the racial stability of the plan and the integration of housing.

The Academic Achievement of Minorities

The Mahard and Crain review indicates that minority children who attend school with white children tend to perform better on standardized achievement tests than do students who attend segregated schools, and the effect is greatest when desegregation begins in early grades. Unfortunately, as Rossell points out, parents are most opposed to desegregation of their children in the early grades, and such desegregation produces the most white flight. As a result, courts and school boards have often excluded from the desegregation plan the very students who can most benefit from it.

There are several theories that might account for the effects of desegregation on the academic performance of minority students. Each theory suggests direction for research.

Peer Influence

Since the Coleman Report (1966), it has been popularly believed that desegregation would enhance the achievement of minorities because it brought them into contact with higher-achieving peers. More recent research (Patchen, Hofmann, and Brown, 1980; Maruyama and Miller, 1979) has called into question this "lateral transmission of values" theory.

Therefore, the first issues we would want to address are whether and how peer achievement influences student performance. If peer influence is significant, is it stronger within than across races? Hawley (1976) found that the academic motivation of black students was more strongly correlated with that of black peers than with that of white peers. Whites were unaffected by black motivation.

Peers might also influence achievement indirectly by affecting teacher behavior. Teachers may use the achievement levels of some students to establish norms for others. In that case, the average level of motivation would be less important than the extent of heterogeneity in the classroom. An important question that warrants research is: how wide can the achievement gap be before the potential benefits of heterogeneous classrooms are undermined? The answer to this question may depend, in turn, on factors such as the lowest level of student achievement, class size, teacher preparation, subject taught and the instructional strategy used (for example, team learning).

Desegregation May Be a Catalyst for Programmatic Change

The assumption that underlies this theory as to why desegregation affects the academic achievement of minorities is that the specific changes and difficulties a school must face when it desegregates leads to new and better programs, a greater capacity for change, and a search for new answers to problems that transcend desegregation itself. This theory is an intriguing one that enjoys some anecdotal support, but there has been no systematic research bearing on it. Some research questions that might be addressed are:

1. What types of programs and processes do desegregating school systems adopt that might, at least hypothetically, improve the overall quality of schools?
2. What other changes, if any, are adopted that have no necessary relationship to desegregation?
3. Do adoptions of either kind persist over time?

Desegregation May Increase the Equity with Which Educational Resources Are Allocated

This theory rests on several assumptions, all of which merit further research. The first assumption is that the physical facilities and quality of teaching in a school make a difference in the quality of education and opportunities for minority students. The second is that economic resources and their allocation are in the hands of whites even where communities are politically "controlled" by minorities. The third assumption is that these resources derive from an economic system that is white-dominated and from state and federal agencies dominated by whites. The last two assumptions are based, in turn, on an assumption that whites will discriminate against racially isolated schools in the allocation of resources.

The central issue, in our view, concerns the effects of resource allocation on teaching. It is relatively easy to demonstrate that teaching is related to student outcomes. But why do teachers teach where they do, and why do they teach the way they do?

1. Does salary matter? This is presumably relevant across, but not within, school systems.
2. Do working conditions and physical facilities make a difference?
3. Does the quality of instructional resources affect the quality of teaching?

Desegregation May Improve the Behavior of Teachers Toward Minorities

This theory holds that desegregation results in more heterogeneous classrooms that produce situations where teachers demand higher performance and self-discipline from minority students. It is thought that this occurs because teachers' expectations for achievement and behavior may be greater as higher-achieving students are held up implicitly or explicitly as the standard to which low-achieving students should aspire. In addition, parents may make demands on schools for better teaching for lower-achieving students as they seek to ensure a good education for their own children. The question that needs to be addressed, obviously, is whether all this occurs and under what conditions?

Segregated or Racially Isolated Schools Are Inherently Inferior

This theory is articulated in *Brown* v. *Board of Education* (1954), but it is not clear that this is true; neither is it clear how desegregation may change a student's self-esteem. Epps (1978) reviews the literature and concludes that desegregation does not negatively affect the self-esteem of minorities. But this issue is not closed by any means, for different dimensions of self-concept or self-image may be affected by desegregation and by teacher behavior, and these may vary for boys and girls and for students of different ages.

Recently, however, the relevance of studying self-esteem, at least as it has been studied in the past, has come into question. There is little evidence that general self-esteem, however measured, is causally related to achievement (Gerard and Miller, 1975; Pugh, 1976; Kerckhoff and Campbell, 1977). If, in fact, it is not—and more evidence is needed before the case is closed— one reason may be that minorities learn not to look to school as a source of self-esteem. It seems very important to know whether this hypothesis is correct, and if so, what can be done to change that orientation.

Changing Contexts and Assumptions

Mahard and Crain suggest that the gains minorities make in desegregated schools are the result of their being freed from the assumptions of inferiority and low expectations that are inherent in segregated schooling. The Mahard and Crain theory seems to encompass aspects of other potential explanations for the relationship between desegregation and minority achievement.

Effects of Desegregation on White Children

The available evidence indicates that the rate of white achievement seldom declines when desegregation occurs. But this evidence is derived from studies that almost always focus on minority children, so the data are seldom fully developed. Moreover, most people do not believe it. Therefore, it seems important to determine with greater certainty whether desegregation leads to a reallocation of resources and a direction of teacher attention away from white students that affects their achievement.

Effects of Desegregation on High Achievers

The available evidence also indicates that high-achieving students seldom decline in academic achievement. If school desegregation encourages teachers to be more responsive to differences in student learning needs and if new resources result in new programs, it may be that all students benefit. For example, in some cases where cooperative learning techniques have been adopted, it appears that high-ability students improve their performance (compared to control groups), though low-achieving students benefit proportionately more (Slavin, 1980a).

Much more speculative is the hypothesis that, other things being equal, the diversity of the student environment in desegregated schools enhances cognitive development. The theory is that just as learning calculus has benefits for problem-solving capacities that go beyond the applications of the substantive knowledge one learns in calculus, it may be that seeking to understand social diversity, resolve value conflicts, and meet other challenges that are part of functioning effectively in socially and culturally diverse settings enhances cognitive development.

Desegregation and the "Average Student"

One of the things one hears parents of all races say during desegregation controversies is that it is the "average student" who gets hurt in the process. The argument is that schools will focus on the needs of lower achievers and those who have more visible difficulty adapting to new school environments and that high achievers will get attention because teachers need them or because they will demand it. This would result in the needs of the average student being given less attention. We know of no research that explicitly examines this intuitively reasonable thesis.

Dealing with Diversity

While desegregation-induced diversity among students and faculty is a source of learning opportunities, it also results in increased differences in values, behavior, and academic achievement. As a result, some desegregated schools may decline in effectiveness, at least in the short run. If we could learn more about the conditions under which the problems that result from the complexity and diversity of desegregated schools are effectively managed, the net benefit of desegregation could be enhanced. Three important questions are:

1. Are there some mixes of ability and social background among students that pose fewer problems for teaching and interpersonal conflict than others?
2. Do teachers in desegregated schools experience exceptional psychological stress and, if so, what are its consequences and how might it be dealt with?
3. What are the most effective instructional practices and classroom structures for coping with diversity?

The research on cooperative learning (Sharon, 1980; Slavin, 1980a) suggests some answers to these questions. As Schofield and Sager, and Eyler et al. point out in their essays, team learning is an alternative to rigid forms of ability grouping that invariably lead to resegregation. This resegregation has deleterious effects on positive interracial contact and the school climate, as well as on academic achievement.

While various forms of cooperative learning represent promising ways to avoid tracking and to alter the educational climate of heterogeneous schools, certain other approaches to ability grouping may also be conducive to learning (see for example, Cohen, 1980; Findley and Bryan, 1975; Klausmeier, Rossmiller, and Saily, 1977). How these might vary in effectiveness by the age of students involved and what their effects are on the attainment of other values are issues worthy of systematic inquiry.

Desegregation and Race Relations

The basic theoretical framework within which much research on race relations has been conducted is the equal-status-contact theory of Allport (1954). A considerable amount of research has aimed at augmenting and refining this theory. We will try to summarize some of the key points of contention and identify some of the most important issues that need further research.

What Does Equal Status Mean?

The question here has two related dimensions. First, does the equal-status requirement apply to the immediate interaction context or does it apply to the status students bring with them to the school situation? Second, given that whites are dominant in the society, are student expectations such that minorities must be given status advantage to equalize contact, as Cohen (1975) suggests? Related to these considerations is the question of how differencs in the social-class composition of schools affect race relations.

What Is the Nature of the Contact That Is Required?

Must the contact needed for desegregation be interpersonal and intimate (Amir, 1976), or may it involve role and position interaction (Pettigrew, 1969)? Must there be, as the limited research suggests, a "critical mass" of students of any given race or ethnic group before interracial interaction can take place? Is the critical mass different in numbers or proportions for different-size schools, different racial groups, or in biracial schools as compared to "multiethnic" ones?

Do Patterns of Race Relations Vary by Gender?

Do black girls, for example, have less status in desegregated settings than black boys? What can be done about this?

Does the Age of the Student Affect Race Relations?

It is clear that the younger children are, the greater the impact desegregation has not only on achievement, but on positive racial attitudes and behavior (Katz, 1976). It is important, however, to determine if strategies for improving race relations vary in their effectiveness by the age of the student. For example, does the stress many students seem to experience at junior high school age mean that race relations programs and academic programs should be diffcrent for this age group?

How Can Principals Affect Race Relations?

As Schofield indicates, principals can have an important impact on school race relations. But what, exactly, can principals do that makes a difference?

Teacher Attitudes.

There is enough reason to believe that teacher behavior of various sorts facilitates good race relations. But we don't know exactly how attitudes and behavior are related. Can teachers behave in positive ways without having positive attitudes? Does positive behavior influence these attitudes and beliefs? The answers to these questions have significant implications for teacher training programs and recruitment to the profession.

The Race of the Teacher

Almost all observers urge that desegregated schools have teachers of different races. There is much intuitive widsom to this admonition but little hard evidence to support it. The question we see as important is not whether better race relations are found in schools with interracial faculties. Rather, it seems important to know what it is that such faculties do, or what messages they convey that make a difference.

Measurement Problems

The way researchers have measured race relations has had important consequences for our images of the effects of desegregation. Much research has been based on inappropriate, invalidated measures. In particular, sociometric measures that force students to pick best friends or people they would like to play or work with understate systematically improvements in race relations. As Schofield point out, these measures are usually treated as if ingroup and outgroup choices are a zero-sum game. That is, if a child can name only three friends, for example, outgroup members can be named only by not naming ingroup friends.

Under the most tranquil of circumstance, new students brought into a school as a group can be expected to arouse both curiosity and suspicion, and it takes time for fears to be allayed and new friendships made. Hence, as Schofield and Sugar point out, research designs that only assess attitudes just before or just after desegregation are inadequate.

Inservice Training

While there is a fair amount of prescriptive writing about inservice training for desegregation and a few descriptive studies, the Eyler, Cook, and Ward review indicates that there is little empirical research that allows one to know which strategies are effective in changing the behavior of educators and in benefiting students. Among the empirical studies available, there exists no consensus about what constitutes effective inservice training. Some studies measure changes in educators' attitudes and behavior; others stress such student outcomes as academic achievement and interpersonal and race relations. Moreover, this research generally fails to measure the long-term effects of training on actual classroom practice (Smylie and Hawley, 1982).

There are three general questions that need answers: (1) what criteria can be developed to determine the effectiveness of inservice training over time, (2) what are the most effective training processes according to these criteria, and (3) what topics should be taught to educators? Until we have an answer to the first and second of these questions, answers to the third will be of little consequence.

Research on School Discipline

School discipline research seems to be important for three reasons. First, as Eyler, Cook, and Ward suggest, disciplinary problems are a major impediment, particularly at the secondary school level, to establishing good race relations and a satisfactory learning climate. Second, school discipline is cited by parents in surveys as the number one school problem. Third, strategies that work to solve disciplinary problems may prove to be the most effective mechanisms for reducing minority "push out" and suspension in desegregated schools.

Additional investment in large-scale victimization research would seem to be a reasonable though expensive first step. More analyses of the data contained in the Safe School Study (National Institute of Education, 1978) should also be useful. On the basis of data from 600 schools, Gottfredson and Daiger (1979) suggest some steps to more orderly schools that can serve as the basis for research hypotheses.

1. Develop schools of smaller size, where teachers have extensive responsibility for and contact with a limited number of students in several aspects of their education, and where steps are taken to ensure adequate resources for instruction.
2. Promote cooperation between teachers and administrators, especially with respect to school policies and sanctions for disruptive behavior.
3. Develop programs—such as team learning, for example—for improving race relations and the learning climate.
4. After having improved the school climate, develop school rules that are fair, clear, and well publicized, and apply the rules in ways that are firm, consistent, and even-handed.

Desegregation and Hispanics

If present trends continue, there will come a time in the not-too-distant future when Hispanic public school students outnumber their black cohorts. Indeed, in many districts, Hispanics already outnumber blacks at the present time. For example, there are more blacks than Hispanics in only seven of the metropolitan areas west of the Mississippi River. Nevertheless, there is very little empirical research on how desegregation affects Hispanic students or how the presence of a sizable Hispanic population will affect the character of the desegregation process in both two-race and three-race districts.

There have been frequent calls for more research, but these admonitions have had little effect. One could seek to develop a full-scale research agenda that replicates the substantial literature on blacks. When one reviews the queries posed as important research questions by reviews of the literature on desegregation and Hispanics (see Uribe and Levinsohn, 1978; National Institute of Education, 1977a), it appears that many of the issues are similar to those raised with respect to blacks. Thus, it may be possible to generate useful knowledge about desegregation and Hispanics by asking why we would expect Hispanics to be affected by or to affect the desegregation process any differently than blacks. Posing the question in this way would allow us to use the existing research on blacks where appropriate and to focus on areas of hypothesized differences.

Is There Life After Desegregated Schooling?

The research assessed in this book has focused on the effects of desegregation on communities and on students. The questions of the long-term consequences of desegregation on the young people who experience it is not addressed in these pages. They are, however, very important to society's acceptance of desegregation in the long run. The available evidence, and it is sketchy, suggests that desegregated schooling encourages people to develop skills and make choices that lead to integration in higher education, employment, housing, and interpersonal relationships (McPartland, 1982). Such conclusions, however, are not certain.

ENHANCING THE PRODUCTIVITY OF DESEGREGATION RESEARCH

We believe that the task of improving the productivity of desegregation research goes beyond the problem of identifying important issues for study. Our comparative ignorance about desegregation is the result not only of the low quality or quantity of research or of misplaced priorities but also of our failure to use the resources available as effectively as we might. This is true of almost all subjects related to education.

In addition to making more use of secondary analysis of data collected by others, it appears desirable to develop a theoretically grounded format for conducting case studies and other inquiries that will facilitate comparative analysis.

As noted in most of the reviews in this volume, the opportunities for comparative analysis of existing studies and for the structuring of new data from existing files are constrained because the studies were undertaken for a variety of purposes and had different initial conceptions of the desegregation process. Indeed, the analytical framework of the research often is not presented.

It is important, therefore, for researchers to agree on a common set of variables that they will report even when some of these variables are not central to their own analysis. The advantage of identifying such variables goes beyond their usefulness to other researchers. Our findings often lead us back to issues that we can only address if we have data not central to our original hypotheses. Moreover, the analytical framework implicit in this array of variables should enrich thinking about alternative explanations of the events being studied.

The list below presents several questions and variables that seem important to many desegregation issues. Whether one can include them in one's design and data gathering obviously depends on available resources, but we believe that they are important regardless of the theoretical or policy questions posed by the study.

Key Variables in the Study of Desegregation Processes and Outcomes

1. Who has been desegregated with whom?
   a. Racial/ethnic mix
   b. Social class of each group
   c. Degree of tracking between and within schools.
2. What was the process by which desegregation initially occurred?
   a. How desegregation came about (court-ordered, board-ordered, mandatory, voluntary, and so on)
   b. Duration of desegregation
   c. Amount and duration of conflict
   d. Amount of community preparation
   e. Amount and type of in-school work with students on racial issues
3. What are the characteristics of the schools and classrooms being studied? (Although the list of school characteristics that might be studied is long, the list of factors that have been linked to student outcomes is much shorter.)
   a. Content and duration of teacher inservice program
   b. Staff attitudes related to race
   c. Racial and ethnic composition of staff
   d. Type of instruction
   e. Time on task for particular topics
   f. Nature of reward systems
   g. Opportunities for interracial interaction
   h. Extent and type of extracurricular activities
   i. Extent and type of remedial programs or special programs
   j. School suspensions and discipline policy
   k. Experience of staff in desegregated settings
   l. School size and staff-student ratio
   m. The leadership role and style of principal
   n. Parental involvement
4. What are the individual characteristics of the students being studied?
   a. Sex
   b. Race
   c. Age
   d. Age of first desegregated experience
   e. Years in desegregated school
   f. Capacity for academic achievement
   g. Interracial contact outside of school
5. When the learning of individuals is part of the research, what is the student's family background?
   a. Learning resources available to the student
   b. Educational background of parents
   c. Level of support for achievement (or other student objectives)
6. What are the characteristics of the community in which school desegregation is taking place?
   a. Racially relevant history (including the history of the region)
   b. Level of information about schools
   c. Racial composition

    d. Role of community leaders

    e. Degree of SES heterogeneity

    f. Economic vitality

  7. What are the consequences for students?

    a. Achievement

    b. Racial attitudes

    c. Racial behavior

    d. Sense of self-confidence, attribution of personal causation

    e. Student victimization

  8. What are the consequences for alumni?

    a. College attendance, field chosen, completion

    b. Job-hunting process

    c. Racial contacts

    d. Housing choices

    e. Political participation

  9. What are the consequences for the school system?

    a. New innovations

    b. Changes in administration

    c. Parent participation and pressure on schools

    d. School board election outcomes

    e. Tax and bond referenda outcomes

 10. What are the consequences for the community?

    a. Racial controversy over school issues

    b. Racial initiatives in nonschool areas

    c. Desegregation in housing

    d. Impact of racial issues in nonschool elections

 11. What characteristics of the school and the school system affect the implementation of desegregation plans and strategies?

    a. School system population size

    b. School system geographic scope

    c. Proportion minority

    d. Fiscal capacity

    e. Housing patterns, etc.

CONCLUSIONS

As all of the reviews in this volume have implied, desegregation is not a laboratory treatment, a sterile and standardized pill whose effect should always be the same. Rather than ask, "Does desegregation work?," it is more appropriate to ask questions like, "Under what conditions does a particular kind of desegregation strategy affect a particular kind of student or adult with respect to a particular outcome?"

While we have focused this concluding chapter on the need for additional research, we want to emphasize that a good deal more is known now about the effects of desegregation than was known only a short time ago. Moreover, much of what is known can provide guidance to policymakers and educators who are concerned with increasing the benefits and minimizing the costs of desegregation. There will always be more that needs to be known about the processes that result in changes in human behavior. But the research summarized in this book, we believe, represents a substantial enlargement of the knowledge base. Moreover, the opportunities for further advancements in understanding are great, especially if desegregation can be seen as an integral part of the teaching/learning process.

As we noted earlier, answers to questions raised by desegregation will not be found only in the desegregation research. Desegregation "specialists" have seldom engaged their generalist colleagues in the issues being studied, and vice versa. More attention to theory would help in the application to our understanding of desegregation of research on teaching and learning, peer influence, ethnicity, social conflict, leadership, social mobility, political participation, organizational behavior, the instruction of handicapped children, and other extensively studied areas of inquiry. Desegregation needs to be seen in more conceptual terms and not only as an area of research that is informed by research on a broad range of topics, but also as one that can provide insight into many enduring questions about education, human development, and social institutions.

References

Abney, G. Legislating morality: Attitude change and desegregation in Mississippi. *Urban Education*, 1976, *11*, 333–338.

Abramson, M. Implications of mainstreaming: A challenge for special education. In L. Mann and D. Sabatino (Eds.), *The fourth review of special education*. New York: Grune & Stratton, 1980.

Acland, H. *Secondary analyses of the Emergency School Assistance Program*. Santa Monica, Calif.: Rand Corporation, 1975. (ERIC Document Reproduction Service no. ED 124 672.)

Ahmadjian-Baer, J. Producing more active learning behavior from poor readers: The multiple ability classroom. Paper presented at the annual meeting of the American Educational Research Association, Los Angeles, April 1981.

Alcxander, D., and Nana, A. *The how, what, where, when, and why of bilingual education: A concise and objective guide for school district planning*. San Francisco: R & E Research Association, 1977.

Allport, G. W. *The nature of prejudice*. Cambridge, Mass.: Addison-Wesley, 1954.

Alvarez, C. M., and Pader, O. F. Cooperative and competitive behavior of Cuban-American and Anglo-American children. *Journal of Psychology* , 1979, *101*, 265–271.

American Institutes for Research. *Evaluation of the impact of ESEA Title VII Spanish/English bilingual education programs*. 4 vols. Palo Alto, Calif.: American Institutes for Research, 1977–1978.

Amir, Y. The role of intergroup contact in change of prejudice and ethnic relations. In P. A. Katz (Ed.), *Towards the elimination of racism*. New York: Pergamon Press, 1976.

Amir, Y., Sharan, S., Bizman, A., Rivner, M., and Ben-Ari, R. Attitude change in desegregated Israeli high schools. *Journal of Educational Psychology*, 1978, *70*(2), 129–136.

Anderson, L. V. The effect of desegregation on the achievement and personality patterns of Negro children. Unpublished doctoral dissertation, George Peabody College for Teachers, 1966. *Dissertation Abstracts*, 1966, *27*, 1529A. (University Microfilms no. 66–11237)

Archambault, F. X., and St. Pierre, R. G. A description of instructional experiences received by Title I and non–Title I students. Paper presented at the annual meeting of the American Educational Research Association, Toronto, March 1978. (ERIC Document Reproduction Service no. ED 152 953.)

Armor, D. J. The evidence on busing. *Public Interest*, Summer 1972, *28*, 90–126.

Armor, D. J. White flight and the future of school desegregation. In W. G. Stephan and J. R. Feagin (Eds.), *Desegregation: Past, present, and future*. New York: Plenum Press, 1980.

Arnez, N. L. Desegregation of public schools: A discriminatory process. *Journal of Afro-American Issues*, 1976, *4*, 274–282.

Arnez, N. L. Implementation of desegregation as a discriminatory process. *Journal of Negro Education*, 1978, *47*, 28–45.

Arnove, R. F., and Strout, T. Alternative schools for disruptive youth. *Educational Forum*, 1980, *44*, 453–471.

Aronson, E., Blaney, N., Stephan, C., Sikes, J., and Snapp, M. *The jigsaw classroom*. Beverly Hills, Calif.: Sage Publications, 1978.

Aronson, E., and Osherow, N. Cooperation, prosocial behavior, and academic performance: Experiments in the desegregated classroom. In L. Bickman (Ed.), *Applied social psychology annual, vol. 50*. Beverly Hills, Calif.: Sage Publications, 1980.

Aspira of America, Inc. *Trends in segregation of Hispanic students in major school districts having large Hispanic enrollment: Analytic report*. Vol. 3A. Washington, D.C.: National Institute of Education, 1979a.

Aspira of America, Inc. *Trends in segregation of Hispanic students in major school districts having large Hispanic enrollment: Ethnographic case studies*. Vol. 2. Washington, D.C.: National Institute of Education, 1979b.

Aspira of America, Inc. *Trends in segregation of Hispanic students in major school districts having large Hispanic enrollment: Desegregation and the Hispano in America*. Vol. 1. Washington, D.C.: National Institute of Education, 1980.

Bader, P. A counseling alternative to suspension: School youth advocacy. In C. D. Moody, J. Williams, and C. B. Vergon (Eds.), *Student rights and discipline*. Ann Arbor: University of Michigan, School of Education, 1978.

Baez, T., Fernandez, R. R., and Guskin, J. T. *Desegregation and Hispanic students: A community perspective*. Rosslyn, Va.: InterAmerican Research Association, 1980.

Bailey, R. Staff, student and parent training as positive alternatives to student suspensions. In C. D. Moody, J. Williams, and C. B. Vergon (Eds.), *Student rights and discipline*. Ann Arbor: University of Michigan, School of Education, 1978.

Bailey, W. Collision: Court ordered desegregation and individualized instructional programs. *Journal of Educational Equity and Leadership*, 1981, *1*, 28–35.

Barber, R. W. The effects of open enrollment on anti-Negro and anti-white prejudices among junior high students in Rochester, New York. Unpublished doctoral dissertation, University of Rochester, 1968.

Becker, H. Non-public schools and desegregation: Racial factors and changes in the share of big-city white pupil enrollment going to non-public schools. Paper presented at the annual meeting of the American Educational Research Association, Toronto, March 1978.

Becker, H. *Racially integrated neighborhoods: Do white families move in?* Report no.

287. Baltimore: Johns Hopkins University, Center for the Social Organization of Schools, 1979.

Begley, T. M., and Alker, H. A. Attitudes and participation in anti-busing protest. Paper presented at the annual meeting of the American Sociological Association, San Francisco, August 1978.

Beker, J. A study of integration in racially imbalanced urban public schools (final report). Unpublished manuscript, 1967. (Available from the Syracuse University Youth Development Center, Syracuse, New York.)

Bennett, C. A study of the causes of disproportionality in suspensions and expulsions of male and black students: Part two—Characteristics of high and low disproportionality schools. Paper presented at the annual meeting of the American Educational Research Association, Los Angeles, April 1981.

Bennett, C., and Harris, J. J., III. A study of the causes of disproportionality on suspensions and expulsions of male and black students: Part one—Characteristics of disruptive and non-disruptive students. Paper presented at the annual meeting of the American Educational Research Association, Los Angeles, April 1981.

Bennett, G. K. Response to Robert Williams. *Counseling Psychologists*, 1970, *2*(2), 88–89.

Berger, J., Cohen, E., and Zelditch, M. Status characteristics and expectation states. In J. Berger, M. Zelditch, and B. Anderson (Eds.), *Sociological theories in progress*. Boston: Houghton Mifflin, 1966.

Berger, J., Cohen, E., and Zelditch, M. Status conceptions and social interaction. *American Sociological Review*, 1972, *37*, 241–255.

Berke, J. S., and Demarest, E. J. Alternatives for future federal programs. In M. F. Williams (Ed.), *Government in the classroom*. New York: Academy of Political Science, 1978.

Bickel, F., and Qualls, R. *Project Student Concerns: A study of minority student suspensions* (interim report). Louisville, Ky.: Jefferson County Educational Consortium, 1979. (ERIC Document Reproduction Service no. ED 178 636.)

Blanchard, F. A., Adelman, L., and Cook, S. W. The effect of group success and failure upon interpersonal attraction in cooperating interracial groups. *Journal of Personality and Social Psychology*, 1975, *31*, 1020–1030.

Blanchard, F. A., and Cook, S. W. The effects of helping a less competitive group member of a cooperating interracial group on the development of interpersonal attraction. Unpublished manuscript, Smith College, 1976.

Blanchard, F. A., Weigel, R., and Cook, S. W. The effect of relative competence of group members upon interpersonal attraction in cooperating interracial groups. *Journal of Personality and Social Psychology*, *32*, 519–530.

Blaney, N. T., Stephan, C., Rosenfield, D., Aronson, E., and Sikes, J. Interdependence in the classroom: A field study. *Journal of Educational Psychology*, 1977, *69*(2), 121–128.

Bloom, B. S. *Human characteristics and school learning*. New York: McGraw-Hill, 1976.

Boehm, A. E. The development of comparative concepts in primary school children. Unpublished doctoral dissertation, Teachers College, Columbia University, 1966.

Bondarin, A. *The racial balance plan of White Plains, New York*. New York: Center for Urban Education, Program References Service, 1970.

Bosco, J., and Robin, S. White flight from court-ordered busing? *Urban Education,* 1974, *9*(4), 87–98.

Bowman, O. H. Scholastic development of disadvantaged Negro pupils: A study of pupils in selected segregated and desegregated elementary classrooms. Unpublished doctoral dissertation, State University of New York at Buffalo, 1973. *Dissertation Abstracts International,* 1973, *34,* 503A. (University Microfilms no. 73–19, 176.)

Bradley, L., and Bradley, G. The academic achievement of black students in desegregated schools. *Review of Educational Research,* 1977, *47,* 399–449.

Breglio, V. J., Hinkley, R. H., and Beal, R. S. *Students' economic and educational status and selection for compensatory education.* Technical Report no. 2 from the Study of Sustaining Effects of Compensatory Education on Basic Skills. Santa Monica, Calif.: System Development Corporation, 1978.

Bridge, G. Judd, C., and Moock, P. *The determinants of educational outcomes: The effects of families, peers, teachers and schools.* New York: Teachers College Press, 1979.

Brischetto, R., and Arciniega, T. Examining the examinees: A look at educators' perspectives on the Chicano student. In R. O. De la Garza, Z. A. Kruszewski, and T. A. Arciniega (Eds.), *Chicanos and native Americans: The territorial minorities.* Englewood Cliffs, N.J.: Prentice-Hall, 1973.

Brisk, M. E. Bilingual education and school desegregation: The case of Boston. Paper presented at the meeting of the International Conference for Bilingual-Bicultural Education, Chicago, May 1975. (ERIC Document Reproduction Service no. ED 126 999.)

Brodbelt, S. Effective discipline: A consideration for improving inner-city schools. *Clearing House,* 1980, *54,* 5–9.

Brookover, W., Beady, C., Flood, P., Schwietzer, J., and Wisenbaker, J. *School social systems and student achievement: Schools can make a difference.* New York: Prager, 1979.

Brookover, W., Brady, N. M., and Warfield, M. Educational policies and equitable education: A report of studies of two desegregated school systems. In *Procedures and pilot research to develop an agenda for desegregation studies.* E. Lansing: Michigan State University, College of Urban Development, Center for Urban Affairs, 1981.

Brown, F. The SOMPA: A system of measuring potential abilities. *School Psychology Digest,* 1979, *8,* 37–46.

Budoff, M. Learning potential among institutionalized young adult retardates. *American Journal of Mental Deficiency,* 1967, *72,* 404–411.

Budoff, M. Learning potential: A supplementary procedure for assessing the ability to reason. *Seminars in Psychiatry,* 1972, *10,* 199–205.

Budoff, M., and Friedman, M. "Learning potential" as an assessment approach to the adolescent mentally retarded. *Journal of Consulting Psychology,* 1964, *28,* 433–439.

Bullock, C. S., III. Compliance with school desegregation laws: Financial inducements and policy performance. Paper presented at the annual meeting of the American Political Science Association, Chicago, 1976a.

Bullock, C. S., III. Interracial contact and student prejudice: The impact of Southern school desegregation. *Youth and Society,* 1976b, *7,* 271–310.

Bullock, C. S., III, and Rodgers, H. R. Coercion to compliance: Southern school districts and school desegregation guidelines. *Journal of Politics*, 1976, *38*, 987–1011.

Burton, N. W., and Jones, L. V. Recent trends in achievement levels of black and white youth. *Educational Researcher*, 1982, *11*(4), 10–14, 17.

Byrne, D. *The attraction paradigm*. New York: Academic Press, 1971.

Byrne, D., and Buehler, J. A. A note on the influence of propinquity upon acquaintanceships. *Journal of Abnormal Social Psychology*, 1955, *51*, 147–148.

Byrnes, M. A. Student participation in educational planning. Paper presented at the Symposium on *Informed involvement of the child in assessment and intervention*. Dallas: Council for Exceptional Children, Dallas, April 1979.

Campbell, A. *White attitudes toward black people*. Ann Arbor, Mich.: Ann Arbor Institute for Social Research, 1971.

Campbell, D. T., and Stanley, J. C. Experimental and quasi-experimental designs for research on teaching. In N. L. Gage (Ed.), *Handbook of research on teaching*. Chicago: Rand McNally, 1963.

Carbonari, J. P., and Birenbaum, V. Evaluation of a panel of American women: Project to reduce prejudicial attitudes in high school students. Paper presented at the annual meeting of the American Educational Research Association, Boston, April 1980.

Carithers, M. W. School desegregation and racial cleavage, 1954–1970: A review of the literature. *Journal of Social Issues*, 1970, *26*(4), 25–47.

Carrigan, P. M. *School desegregation via compulsory pupil transfer: Early effects on elementary school children*. Ann Arbor, Mich.: Ann Arbor Public Schools, 1969.

Carter, D. G. Student discrimination, disproportionality and the law. Paper presented at the annual meeting of the American Educational Research Association, Los Angeles, April 1981.

Carter, T. P. *Mexican Americans in school: A history of educational neglect*. New York: College Entrance Examination Board, 1970.

Carter, T. P. *Interface between bilingual education and desegregation: A study of Arizona and California*. Washington, D.C.: National Institute of Education, 1979.

Carter, T. P., and Segura, R. D. *Mexican Americans in school: A decade of change*. New York: College Entrance Examination Board, 1979.

Cataldo, E. F., Giles, M. W., and Gatlin, D. S. *School desegregation policy: Compliance, avoidance, and metropolitan remedy*. Lexington, Mass.: D. C. Heath, 1978.

Center for National Policy Review. The rights of school children. Unpublished manuscript, Catholic University of America, Center for National Policy Review, 1980.

Chenault, G. S. The impact of court-ordered desegregation on student achievement. Unpublished doctoral dissertation, University of Iowa, 1976. *Dissertation Abstracts International*, 1977, *37*, 7426A. (University Microfilms no. 77-13, 068.)

Children's Defense Fund. *Children out of school in America*. Washington, D.C.: Children's Defense Fund, Washington Research Projects, 1974.

Children's Defense Fund. *School suspensions: Are they helping children?* Washington, D.C.: Children's Defense Fund, 1975.

Clark, E. N. Analysis of the differences between pre- and post-test scores (change scores) on measures of self-concept, academic aptitude, and reading achievement earned by sixth grade students attending segregated and desegregated schools. Unpublished doctoral dissertation, Duke University, 1971. *Dissertation Abstracts International*, 1971, *32*, 2902A. (University Microfilms no. 72-307.)

Clark County School District. *Desegregation report*. Las Vegas, Nev.: Clark County School District, 1975. (ERIC Document Reproduction Service no. ED 106 397.)

Clement, D. C., and Harding, J. R. Social distinctions and emergent student groups in a desegregated school. *Anthropology and Education Quarterly*, 1978, *8–9*, 272–282.

Clotfelter, C. T. The Detroit decision and "white flight." *Journal of Legal Studies*, 1976a, *5*(1), 99–112.

Clotfelter, C. T. School desegregation, "tipping," and private school enrollment. *Journal of Human Resources*, 1976b, *11*, 28–50.

Clotfelter, C. T. Urban school desegregation and declines in white enrollment: A reexamination. *Journal of Urban Economics*, 1979, *6*, 352–370.

Clotfelter, C. and McConahay, J. *Analyses of quantitative measures of desegregation relevant to federal policy and technical assistance*. Durham, N.C.: Duke University, Center for Educational Policy, 1980.

Cohen, E. Interracial interaction disability. *Human Relations*, 1972, *25*(1), 9–24.

Cohen, E. Modifying the effects of social structure. *American Behavioral Scientist*, 1973, *16*(6), 83–101.

Cohen, E. The effects of desegregation on race relations. *Law and Contemporary Problems*, 1975, *39*(2), 271–299.

Cohen, E. The desegregated school: Problems in status, power and interracial climate. Paper presented at the annual meeting of the American Psychological Association, New York, September 1979.

Cohen, E. A multi-ability approach to the integrated classroom. Paper presented at the annual meeting of the American Psychological Association, Montreal, September 1980.

Cohen, E., and Roper, S. Modification of interracial interaction disability: An application of status characteristics theory. *American Sociological Review*, 1972, *36*, 643–657.

Cohen, R. A. Conceptual styles, culture conflict, and nonverbal tests of intelligence. *American Anthropologist*, 1969, *71*, 828–856.

Coleman, J. S. Population stability and equal rights. *Society*, 1977, *14*, 34–36.

Coleman, J. S., Campbell, E. Q., Hobson, C. J., McPartland, J., Mood, A. M., Weinfeld, F. D., and York, R. L. *Equality of educational opportunity*. Washington, D.C.: Government Printing Office, 1966.

Coleman, J. S., Kelly, S. D., and Moore, J. A. Recent trends in school integration. Paper presented at the annual meeting of the American Educational Research Association, Washington, D.C., April 1975a.

Coleman, J.S., Kelly, S. D., and Moore, J. A. *Trends in school segregation, 1968–1973*. Washington, D.C.: Urban Institute, 1975b.

Coles, R. *Eskimos, Chicanos, Indians*. Vol. 4. *Children in crisis*. Boston: Little, Brown, 1977.

Collins, T. W. From courtrooms to classrooms: Managing school desegregation in a deep South high school. In R. C. Rist (Ed.), *Desegregated schools: Appraisals of an American experiment*. New York: Academic Press, 1979.

Columbus Public Schools. Report to the Federal District Court on the status of desegregation, *Penick et al.* v. *Columbus Board of Education et al.*, November 16, 1979.

Columbus Public Schools. Report on the status of desegregation to the Federal District Court, *Penick et al.* v. *Columbus Board of Education et al.*, November 20, 1980.

Columbus Public Schools. Report on the status of desegregation to the Federal District Court, *Penick et al.* v. *Columbus Board of Education et al.*, March 25, 1981.

Cook, S. W. Motives in a conceptual analysis of attitude-related behavior. In W. J. Arnold and D. Levine (Eds.), *Nebraska symposium on motivation*, vol. 17. Lincoln: University of Nebraska Press, 1969.

Cook, S. W. Interpersonal and attitudinal outcomes in cooperating interracial groups. Unpublished paper, University of Colorado at Boulder, n.d.

Cook, V. J. Psychometric critique of school testing litigation. Paper presented at the annual meeting of the American Psychological Association, New York, September 1979a.

Cook, V. J. Results of the child's involvement in the school assessment and intervention process. Paper presented at a symposium on Informed Involvement of the child in assessment and intervention. Dallas: Council for Exceptional Children, 1979b.

Cook, V. J. Influences of home and family in the development of literacy in children. *School Psychology Review*, 1980, *9*, 369–373.

Cook, V. J. Nondiscriminatory assessment: Research integration project. Proposal submitted to the U.S. Department of Education, 1981.

Cook, V. J., and Lundberg, D. D. *The child's right to know.* Presented at the annual meeting of the National Association of School Psychologists, New York, March 1978.

Cook, V. J., and Plas, J. M. Making the relationship primary: Transactional-ecological psychology. Paper presented at the annual meeting of the American Psychological Assocation, Montreal, September 1980.

Cooper, L., Johnson, D. W., Johnson, R., and Wilderson, F. The effects of cooperative, competitive, and individualistic experiences of interpersonal attraction among heterogeneous peers. *Journal of Social Psychology*, 1980, *111*, 243–252.

Cooper, M. Personal communication, March 1980.

Corman, L., and Gottlieb, J. Mainstreaming mentally retarded children: A review of research. In N. R. Ellis (Ed.), *International review of research in mental retardation*, vol. 9. New York: Academic Press, 1978.

Cotton, W. H. Strategies for reducing the disproportionate racial impact on suspensions: The Dallas experience. In C. D. Moody, J. Williams, and C. B. Vergon (Eds.), *Student rights and discipline.* Ann Arbor: University of Michigan, School of Education, 1978.

Coulson, J. E., Ozenne, D. G., Hanes, S. D., Bradford, C., Doherty, W. J., Duck, G. A., and Hemenway, J. A. *The third year of Emergency School Aid Act (ESAA) implementation.* Santa Monica, Calif.: System Development Corporation, 1977.

Crain, R. L. School integration and occupational achievement of Negroes. *American Journal of Sociology*, 1970, *75*, 593–606.

Crain, R. L. Racial tension in high schools: Pushing the survey method closer to reality. *Anthropology and Education Quarterly*, 1977, *8*, 142–151.

Crain, R. L. Report to the Honorable Paul Egly on the Crawford remedy, *Crawford* v. *Board of Education*, City of Los Angeles, Case No. 822-854. Los Angeles County Superior Court, November 14, 1978.

Crain, R. L., and Mahard, R. E. Desegregation and black achievement: A review of the research. *Law and Contemporary Problems*, 1978, *42*(3), 17–56.

Crain, R. L., and Mahard, R. E. *Desegregation plans that raise black achievement: A review of the research*. Report no. N-1210-NIE. Santa Monica, Cal.: Rand Corporation, 1981a.

Crain, R. L. and Mahard, R. E. Minority achievement: Policy implications of research. In W. D. Hawley (Ed.), *Effective school desegregation: Equity, quality, and feasibility*. Beverly Hills, Calif.: Sage Publications, 1981b.

Crain, R. L., Mahard, R. E., and Narot, R. E. *Making desegregation work: How schools create social climates*. Cambridge, Mass.: Ballinger Press, 1982.

Crain, R. L., and Weisman, C. *Discrimination, personality and achievement: A survey of northern blacks*. New York: Seminar Press, 1972.

Cunningham, G. K. Parents who avoid busing: Attitudes and characteristics. Paper presented at the annual meeting of the American Educational Research Association, Boston, April 1980.

Cusick, P., and Ayling, R. Racial interaction in an urban secondary school. Paper presented at the annual meeting of the American Educational Research Association, New Orleans, February 1973.

Cusick, P. A., Gerbing, D. W., and Russell, E. L. The effects of school desegregation and other factors on "white flight" from an urban area. *Educational Administration Quarterly*, 1979. *15*, 35–49.

Dambacher, A. D. *A comparison of achievement test scores made by Berkeley elementary students pre and post integration eras, 1967–1970*. Berkeley, Calif.: Berkeley Unified School District, 1971.

Damico, S. B., Green, C., and Bell-Nathaniel, A. Facilitating interracial contact: Let the structure do it for you. Paper presented at the annual meeting of the American Educational Association, Los Angeles, April 1981.

Danahy, A. H. A study of the effects of busing on the achievement, attendance, attitudes, and social choices of Negro inner city children. Unpublished doctoral dissertation, University of Minnesota, 1971. *Dissertation Abstracts International*, 1972, *32*, 6030A. (University Microfilms no. 72-14, 285.)

Darden, J. T., and Jacob, S. Court-ordered desegregation and extracurricular activities: Impact on racial participation and segregation in high school clubs and organizations. *Urban Education*, 1981, *16*, 37–64.

Davidson, J. D., Hofmann, G., and Brown, W. R. Measuring and explaining high school interracial climate. *Social Problems*, 1978, *26*, 50–71.

Davis, J. Busing. In *Southern schools: An evaluation of the Effects of the Emergency School Assistance Program and of desegregation*. Chicago: National Opinion Research Center, 1973.

Department of Education. Nondiscrimination under programs receiving financial assistance through the Education Department (proposed rules). *Federal Register*, Tuesday, August 5, 1980, *45*(152), 52051–52076.

Devin-Sheehan, L., Feldman, R. S., and Allen, V. L. Research on children tutoring children: A critical review. *Review of Educational Research*, 1976, *46*, 355–385.

DeVries, D. L., Edwards, K. J., and Slavin, R. E. Biracial learning teams and race relations in the classroom: Four field experiments using Teams-Games-Tournament. *Journal of Educational Psychology*, 1978, *70*(3), 356–362.

DeVries, D. L., Lucasse, P. R., and Shackman, S. L. Small groups versus individualized instruction: A field test of their relative effectiveness. Paper presented at the annual meeting of the American Psychological Association, New York, September 1979. (ERIC Document Reproduction Service no. ED 184 006.)

District of Columbia Public Schools. *Meeting students' needs in the multi-age group environment: ESEA Title IV-C* (final evaluation report). Washington, D.C.: District of Columbia Public Schools, 1980. (ERIC Document Reproduction Service no. ED 184 206.)

Duke, D. L., and Perry, C. Can alternative schools succeed where Benjamin Spock, Spiro Agnew, and B. F. Skinner have failed? *Adolescence*, 1978, *13*, 375–392.

Dunn, L. Special education for the mildly retarded: Is much of it justifiable? *Exceptional Children*, 1968, *35*, 5–22.

Edmonds, R. Effective schools for the urban poor. *Educational Leadership*, 1979, *37*, 15–24.

Edwards, K. J., and Devries, D. L. *The effects of Teams-Games-Tournament and two structural variations on classroom process, student attitudes, and student achievement.* Report no. 172. Baltimore: Center for Social Organization of Schools, Johns Hopkins University, 1974.

Epps, E. G. The impact of school desegregation on the self-evaluation and achievement orientation of minority children. *Law and Contemporary Problems*, 1978, *42*(3), 56–76.

Epstein, J. After the bus arrives: Resegregation in desegregated schools. Paper presented at the annual meeting of the American Educational Research Association, Boston, April 1980.

Epstein, N. *Language, ethnicity, and the schools: Policy alternatives for bilingual-bicultural education.* Washington, D.C.: George Washington University, Institute for Educational Leadership, 1977.

Esposito, D. *Homogeneous and heterogeneous ability grouping: Principal findings and implications for evaluating and designing more effective educational environments.* New York: Columbia University, Teachers College, 1971. (ERIC Document Reproduction Service no ED 056 150.)

Estabrook, L. S. The effect of desegregation on parents' evaluations of schools. Unpublished doctoral dissertation, Boston University, 1980. *Dissertation Abstracts International*, 1980, *41*, 6443A. (University Microfilms no. 80-13, 278.)

Evertson, C. M. Sanford, J. P., and Emmer, E. T. Effects of class heterogeneity in junior high school. *American Educational Research Journal*, 1981, *18*, 219–232.

Farley, R. Racial integration in the public schools, 1967–1972: Assessing the effects of governmental policies. *Sociological Focus*, 1975, *8*, 3–26.

Farley, R. Final report. National Institute of Education, Grant G-79-0151. University of Michigan Population Studies Center, 1981.

Farley, R., Richards, T., and Wurdock, C. School desegregation and white flight: An investigation of competing models and their discrepant findings. *Sociology of Education*, 1980, *53*, 123–139.

Felice, L. G., and Richardson, R. L. The effects of desegregation on minority student dropout rates. *Integrated Education*, 1977, *15*(6), 47–50.

Fernandez, R. R., and Guskin, J. T. Bilingual education and desegregation: A new dimension in legal and educational decision-making. In H. Lafontaine, B. Persky, and L. H. Golubchick (Eds.), *Bilingual education.* Wayne, N.J.: Avery Publishing Group, 1978.

Fernandez, R. R., and Guskin, J. T. Hispanic students and school desegregation. In W. D. Hawley (Ed.), *Effective school desegregation*. Beverly Hills, Calif.: Sage Publications, 1981.

Feuerstein, R. *The dynamic assessment of retarded performers*. Baltimore: University Park Press, 1979.

Fillmore, L. W. Learning a second language: Chinese children in the American classroom. In J. Alatis (Ed.), *Current issues in bilingual education*. Georgetown Roundtable on Languages and Linguistics. Washington, D.C.: Georgetown University Press, 1980.

Findley, W. G., and Bryan, M. M. *Ability grouping, 1970: Status, impact, and alternatives*. Athens: University of Georgia, Center for Educational Improvement, 1971.

Findley, W. G., and Bryan, M. M. *The pros and cons of ability grouping*. Fastback no. 66. Bloomington, Ind.: Phi Delta Kappan Educational Foundation, 1975.

Fischer, C. T., and Brodsky, I. L. (Eds.). *Client participation in human services: The PROMETHEUS principle*. New Brunswick, N.J.: Transaction Books, 1978.

Fitzgerald, M. R., and Morgan, D. R. School desegregation and white flight: North and South. *Integrated Education*, 1977, *15*(6), 78–81.

Forbes, R. H. Test score advances among southeastern students: A possible bonus of government intervention? *Phi Delta Kappan*, 1981, *62*, 332–335.

Forehand, G. A., Ragosta, M., and Rock, D. A. *Conditions and processes of effective school desegregation*. Princeton: Educational Testing Service, 1976. (ERIC Document Reproduction Service no. ED 131 155.)

Foster, G. Desegregating urban schools: A review of techniques. *Harvard Educational Review*, 1973, *43*, 5–36.

Foster, G. Discipline practices in the Hillsborough County public schools. Unpublished manuscript, University of Miami at Coral Gables, Florida School Desegregation Consulting Center, 1977.

Foushee, R., and Hamilton, D. *Housing desegregation increases as schools desegregate in Jefferson County*. Louisville, Ky.: Kentucky Commission on Human Rights, 1977.

Francis, W., and Schofield, J. W. The impact of race on interaction in a desegregated school. Paper presented at the annual meeting of the American Sociological Association, Montreal, August 1980.

Frary, R. B., and Goolsby, T. M., Jr. Achievement of integrated and segregated Negro and white first graders in a southern city. *Integrated Education*, 1970, *8*(4), 48–52.

Frechtling, J. A., and Hammond, P. A., III. Policy implications of the instructional dimensions study. Paper presented at the annual meeting of the American Educational Research Association, Los Angeles, April 1978.

Frey, W. H. *Central city white flight: Racial and nonracial causes*. Madison: University of Wisconsin, Institute for Research on Poverty, 1977.

Friedman, P. Racial preferences and identifications of white elementary school children. *Contemporary Educational Psychology*, 1980, *5*, 256–265.

Froman, R. D. Ability grouping: Why do we persist and should we? Paper presented at the annual meeting of the American Educational Research Association, Los Angeles, April 1981.

Gaarder, A. B. Organization of the bilingual school. In E. Ogletree and D. Garcia

(Eds.), *Education of the Spanish-speaking urban child: A book of readings*. Springfield, Ill.: Charles C. Thomas, 1975.

Galusha, R. Director of Psychological Services, Omaha Public Schools. Personal communication, May 1980.

Gamson, W. A. *Power and discontent*. Homewood, Ill.: Dorsey Press, 1968.

Garibaldi, A. In-school alternatives to suspension: The state of the art. In *In-school alternatives to suspension* (conference report). Washington, D.C.: National Institute of Education, 1979.

Gartner, A., Kohler, M. C., and Riessman, F. *Children teach children*. New York: Harper & Row, 1971.

Gay, G. Multicultural preparation and teacher effectiveness in desegregated schools. *Theory Into Practice*, 1978, *17*(2), 149–156.

Geffner, R. A. The effects of interdependent learning on self-esteem, inter-ethnic relations, and intra-ethnic attitudes of elementary school children: A field experiment. Unpublished doctoral dissertation, University of California at Santa Cruz, 1978.

Genova, W. J., and Walberg, H. J. *Promoting student integration in city high schools: A research study and improvement guidelines for practitioners*. Newton, Mass.: TDR Associates, 1979. (ERIC Document Reproduction Service no. ED 181 161.)

Genova, W. J., and Walberg, H. *A practitioner's guide for achieving student integration in city high schools*. Washington, D.C.: National Institute of Education, 1980.

Gerard, H. B., Jackson, D., and Conolley, E. Social contact in the desegregated classroom. In H. Gerard and N. Miller (Eds.), *School desegregation*. New York: Plenum Press, 1975.

Gerard, H. B., and Miller, N. (Eds.). *School desegregation: A long-range study*. New York: Plenum Press, 1975.

Giles, M. W. White enrollment stability and school desegregation: A two-level analysis. *American Sociological Review*, 1978, *43*, 848–864.

Giles, M. W., Cataldo, E. F., and Gatlin, D. S. White flight and percent black: The tipping point re-examined. *Social Science Quarterly*, 1975, *56*, 85–92.

Giles, M. W., and Gatlin, D. S. Mass-level compliance with public policy: The case of school desegregation. *Journal of Politics*, 1980, *42*, 722–746.

Giles, M. W., Gatlin, D. S., and Cataldo, E. F. The impact of busing on white flight. *Social Science Quarterly*, 1974, *55*, 493–501.

Giles, M. W., Gatlin, D. S., and Cataldo, E. F. *Determinants of resegregation: Compliance/rejection behavior and policy alternatives*. Washington, D.C.: National Science Foundation, 1976a.

Giles, M. W., Gatlin, D. S., and Cataldo, E. F. Racial and class prejudice: Their relative effects on protests against school desegregation. *American Sociological Review*, 1976b, *41*, 280–288.

Glass, G. V., and Smith, M. L. *"Pull-out" in compensatory education*. Boulder: University of Colorado, Laboratory of Educational Research, 1977.

Glass, G. V., and Smith, M. L. Meta-analysis of research on class size and achievement. *Educational Evaluation and Policy Analysis*, 1979, *1*(1), 2–16.

Goldberg, M. L., Passow, A. H., and Justman, J. *The effects of ability grouping*. New York: Teachers College, Columbia University, 1966.

Goldman, P. *Report from black America*. New York: Simon & Schuster, 1970.

Gonzales, A. Classroom cooperation and ethnic balance. Paper presented at the annual meeting of the American Psychological Association, New York, September 1979.

Gonzales, A. An approach to interdependent/cooperative bilingual education and measures related to social motives. Unpublished paper. Fresno: California State University, Department of Psychology, 1981.

Goodman, J. F. Is tissue the issue? A critique of SOMPA's models and tests. *School Psychology Digest*, 1979, *8*, 48–62.

Gordon, L. An acculturation analysis of Negro and white high school students. Unpublished doctoral dissertation, Wayne State University, 1967.

Gore, P. M., and Rotter, J. B. A personality correlate of social action. *Journal of Personality*, 1963, *31*, 58–64.

Gottfredson, G. D., and Daiger, D. C. *Disruption in 600 schools*. Technical Report no. 289. Baltimore: Johns Hopkins University, Center for Social Organization of Schools, 1979.

Gottlieb, D., and TenHouten, W. Racial composition and the social system of three high schools. *Journal of Marriage and the Family*, 1965, *27*, 204–212.

Grantham, G. Student discipline issues before and after court-ordered desegregation in New Castle County, Delaware. Paper presented at the annual meeting of the American Educational Research Association, Los Angeles, April 1981.

Green, J. A., and Gerard, H. B. School desegregation and ethnic attitudes. In H. Fromkin and I. Sherwood (Eds.), *Integrating the organization*. New York: Free Press, 1974.

Green, R. L., and Cohen, W. J. An evaluation of the results of the school desegregation order in *Michelle Oliver, et al. Plaintiffs* v. *Kalamazoo Board of Education, et al. Defendants*. Report to the Honorable Noel P. Fox, Chief Judge of the United States District Court, Western District of Michigan, Southern Division (368 F. Supp. 143 W. D. Mich. S. D. 1973), 1979.

Green, R. L., and Griffore, R. School desegregation, testing, and the urgent need for equity in education. *Education*, 1978, *99*(1), 16–19.

Greenwood, N. School desegregation—successes, failures, surprises. *Los Angeles Times*, May 21, 1972.

Griffin, J. L. The effects of integration on academic aptitude, classroom achievement, self-concept and attitudes toward the school environment of a selected group of Negro students in Tulsa, Oklahoma. Unpublished doctoral dissertation, University of Tulsa, 1969. (University Microfilms no. 69-17, 923.

Hall, L. Race and suspension: A second generation desegregation problem. In C. D. Moody, J. Williams, and C. B. Vergon (Eds.), *Student rights and discipline*. Ann Arbor: University of Michigan, School of Education, 1978.

Haller, E. J. Decisions at the margins: Toward an explanation of the relation between ability group placement and pupil SES. Paper presented at the annual meeting of the American Educational Research Association, Los Angeles, April 1981.

Haller, E. J., and Davis, S. Does socioeconomic status bias the assignment of elementary school students to reading groups? *American Educational Research Journal*, 1980, *17*, 409–418.

Hamblin, R., Hathaway, L. C., and Wodarski, J. S. Group contingencies, peer tutoring, and accelerating academic achievement. In E. Ramp and W. Hopkins (Eds.), *A new direction for education: Behavior analysis*. Lawrence: University of Kansas, Department of Human Development, 1971.

Hansell, S., and Slavin, R. E. Cooperative learning and the structure of interracial friendships. *Sociology of Education*, 1981, *54*, 98–106.

Hargrove, E., Graham, S., Ward, L., Abernethy, V., Cunningham, J., and Vaughn, W. *Regulations and schools: The implementation of the Education for All Handicapped Children Act.* Nashville, Tenn.: Vanderbilt University, Institute for Public Policy Studies, 1981.

Harnischfeger, A., and Wiley, D. E. A merit assessment of vocational education programs in secondary schools. Statement to the Subcommittee on Elementary, Secondary, and Vocational Education, of the Committee on Education and Labor of the House of Representatives. September 1980.

Haro, C. M. *Mexicano/Chicano concerns and school desegregation in Los Angeles.* Los Angeles: University of California, Chicano Studies Center, 1977.

Harris, L. Harris polls. Press release. July 8, 1976.

Harris, L. *Attitudes toward busing.* New York: Louis Harris and Associates, 1977.

Harris, L. Majority of parents report school busing has been satisfactory experience. Chicago: Chicago Tribune–N.Y. News Syndicate, March 26, 1981.

Hawley, W. D. Horses before carts: Developing adaptive schools and the limits of innovation. In S. Gove and F. Wirt (Eds.), *Political science and school politics.* Lexington, Mass.: D. C. Heath, 1976.

Hawley, W. D. Increasing the effectiveness of desegregated schools: Lessons from the research. Unpublished manuscript. Duke University, 1980.

Hawley, W. D., and Barry, J. Toward a theoretical understanding of the problems of evaluating and implementing the Emergency School Assistance Act. Unpublished manuscript, Vanderbilt University, Institute for Public Policy Studies, 1980.

Hawley, W. D., Crain, R., Rossell, C., Fernandez, R., Schofield, J., Smylie, M., Tompkins, R., Trent, W., and Zlotnik, M. Strategies for effective desegregation: A synthesis of findings (vol. 1). In W. D. Hawley (Ed.), *Assessment of current knowledge about the effectiveness of school desegregation strategies* (final report). Nashville, Tenn.: Vanderbilt University, Institute for Public Policy Studies, Center for Education and Human Development Policy, 1981.

Hayes, J. G. Anti-busing protest. Paper presented at the annual meeting of the North Carolina Educational Research Association, Charlotte, November 1977.

Henderson, N. B., Goffeney, B. A., Butler, B. V., and Clarkson, Q. D. Differential rates of school promotion from first grade for white and Negro, male and female 7-year-olds. *Psychology in the Schools*, 1971, *8*, 101–109.

Higgins, P. S. *The conflict resolution desegregation aides component of the Minneapolis Schools' 1973–74 Emergency School Aid Act project: An evaluation.* Minneapolis, Minn.: Minneapolis Public Schools, Department of Research and Evaluation, 1974. (ERIC Document Reproduction Service no. ED 117 141.)

Hinkley, R. H., Beal, R. S., and Breglio, V. J. *Student economic and educational status and receipt of educational services.* Technical Report no. 3 from the Study of the Sustaining Effects of Compensatory Education on Basic Skills. Santa Ana, Calif.: Decima Research, 1978.

Hirschman, A. O. *Exit, voice and loyalty.* Cambridge, Mass.: Harvard University Press, 1970.

Hollenbach is defeated by McConnell. *Louisville Courier Journal*, November 7, 1977.

Hsia, J. J. *Integration in Evanston, 1967–1971: A longitudinal evaluation.* Evanston,

Ill.: Educational Testing Service, Midwestern Office, 1971. (ERIC Document Reproduction Service no. ED 054 292.)

Hunt, J. M., and Kirk, G. E. Criterion-referenced tests of school readiness: A paradigm with illustrations. *Genetic Psychology Monographs*, 1974, *90*, 143–182.

Husk, W. L. School desegregation in Jefferson County, Kentucky, five years later: Where are the students? Paper presented at the annual meeting of the American Educational Research Association, Boston, April 1980.

It's no to Hicks, Kerrigan, Palladino, Galvin plan. *Boston Globe*, November 9, 1977.

Iwanicki, E. F., and Gable, R. A quasi-experimental evaluation of the effects of a voluntary urban/suburban busing program on student achievement. Paper presented at the annual meeting of the American Educational Research Association, Toronto, March 1978.

Iwanicki, E. F., and Gable, R. *Final evaluation report 1978–79 Hartford Project Concern programs.* Hartford Conn.: Hartford Public Schools, 1979.

Jackson, G. Reanalysis of Coleman's "Recent trends in school integration." *Educational Researcher*, 1975, *10*, 21–25.

Jacobson, C. Separatism, integrationism, and avoidance among black, white, and Latin adolescents. *Social Forces*, 1977, *55*(4), 1011–1027.

Jacobson, C. K. Desegregation rulings and public attitude changes: White resistance or resignation? *American Journal of Sociology*, 1978, *84*, 698–705.

Jansen, V. G., and Gallagher, J. J. The social choices of students in racially integrated classes for the culturally disadvantaged talented. *Exceptional Children*, 1966, *33*, 222–226.

Jencks, C., Smith, M., Acland, H., Bane, M. J., Cohen, D., Gintis, H., Heyns, B., and Michelson, S. *Inequality.* New York: Basic Books, 1972.

Johnson, D. W., and Johnson, R. T. Instructional goal structure: Cooperative or individualistic. *Review of Educational Research*, 1974, *44*, 213–240.

Johnson, D. W., and Johnson, R. T. Effects of cooperative and individualistic learning experiences on interethnic interaction. *Journal of Educational Psychology*, 1981, *73*(3), 444–449.

Johnson, E., Gerard, H., and Miller, N. Teacher influences in the desegregated classroom. In H. Gerard and N. Miller (Eds.), *School desegregation.* New York: Plenum Press, 1975.

Joseph, A. *Intelligence, IQ and race: When, how and why they became associated.* San Francisco: R & R Research Associates, 1977.

Kaeser, S. C. *Orderly schools that serve all children: A review of successful schools in Ohio.* Cleveland: Citizens' Council for Ohio Schools, 1979a. (ERIC Document Reproduction Service no. ED 181 150.)

Kaeser, S.C. Suspensions in school discipline. *Education and Urban Society*, 1979b, *11*, 465–486.

Kagan, S. Social motives and behaviors of Mexican-American and Anglo-American children. In Joe L. Martinez, Jr., (Ed.), *Chicano Psychology.* New York: Academic Press, 1977.

Kagan, S. Cooperation in the classroom: Cultural and situational sources of variance. In S. Sharan, P. Hare, C. Webb, and R. Lazarowitz (Eds.), *Cooperation in education: Interdisciplinary perspectives.* Salt Lake City: Brigham Young University Press, 1980.

Kagan, S., and Madsen, M. C. Cooperation and competition of Mexican, Mexican-

American, and Anglo-American children of two ages under four instructional sets. *Developmental Psychology*, 1971, *20*, 1307–1320.

Kagan, S., and Madsen, M. C. Experimental analysis of cooperation and competition of Anglo-American and Mexican children. *Developmental Psychology*, 1972, *6*(1), 49–59.

Kanter, R. M. *Men and women of the corporation*. New York: Basic Books, 1977.

Katz, I. Review of evidence relating to effects of desegregation on the performance of Negroes. *American Psychologist*, 1964, *19*, 381–399.

Katz, P. A. The acquisition of racial attitudes in children. In P. A. Katz (Ed.), *Toward the elimination of racism*. New York: Pergamon Press, 1976.

Kaufman, A. S. *Intelligence testing with the WISC-R*. New York: Wiley-Interscience, 1979.

Kaufman, M. Agard, J., and Semmel, M. (Eds.). *Mainstreaming: Learners and their environments*. Baltimore: University Park Press, 1978.

Kentucky Commission on Human Rights. *Six ways to avoid busing*. Louisville, Ky.: Kentucky Commission on Human Rights, 1975.

Kentucky Commission on Human Rights. *Blacks moving to suburban apartments*. Louisville, Ky.: Kentucky Commission on Human Rights, 1980a.

Kentucky Commission on Human Rights. *Housing and school desegregation increased by section 8 move: Under public housing program most black families chose Jefferson County suburbs*. Staff report 80-1. Louisville, Ky.: Kentucky Commission on Human Rights, 1980b.

Kerckhoff, A. C., and Campbell, R. T. Black-white differences in the educational attainment process. *Sociology of Education*, 1977, *50*, 15–27.

Kimbrough, J., and Hill, P. *The aggregated effects of federal education programs*. Santa Monica, Calif.: Rand Corporation, 1981.

Kirby, D., Harris, T., and Crain, R. L. *Political strategies in northern school desegregation*. Lexington, Mass.: D. C. Heath, 1973.

Klausmeier, H. J., Rossmiller, R. A., and Saily, M. (Eds.). *Individually guided elementary education: Concepts and practices*. New York: Academic Press, 1977.

Knight, G. P., and Kagan, S. Acculturation of prosocial and competitive behaviors among second- and third-generation Mexican-American children. *Journal of Cross-Cultural Psychology*, 1977, *8*, 273–284.

Koslin, S., Amarel, M., and Ames, N. A distance measure of racial attitudes in primary grade children: An exploratory study. *Psychology in the Schools*, 1969, *6*, 382–385.

Koslin, S., Koslin, B. L., and Pargament, R. *Efficacy of school integration policies in reducing racial polarization*. New York: Riverside Research Institute, 1972. (ERIC Document Reproduction Service no. ED 068 610.)

Koslin, S., Koslin, B., Pargament, R., and Waxman, H. Classroom racial balance and students' interracial attitudes. *Sociology of Education*, 1972, *45*, 386–407.

Kramer, B. M. Residential contact as a determinant of attitudes towards Negroes. Unpublished doctoral dissertation, Harvard University, 1950.

Krol, R. A. A meta analysis of comparative research on the effects of desegregation on academic achievement. Unpublished doctoral dissertation, Western Michigan University, 1978. *Dissertation Abstracts International*, 1978, *39*, 6011A. (University Microfilms no. 79-07 962.)

Kurtz, H. *The educational and demographic consequences of four years of school deseg-*

regation in the Pasadena Unified school district. Pasadena, Calif.: Pasadena Unified School District, 1975.

Lachat, M. A description and comparison of the attitudes of white high school seniors toward black Americans in three suburban high schools: An all white, a desegregated and an integrated school. Unpublished doctoral dissertation, Teachers College, Columbia University, 1972.

Larkin, J. School desegregation and student suspension: A look at one school system. *Education and Urban Society,* 1979, *11*, 485–495.

Larkins, G. A., and Oldham, S. E. Patterns of racial separation in a desegregated high school. *Theory and Research in Social Education,* 1976, *4*(2), 23–28.

Larson, J. C. *Takoma Park magnet school evaluation.* Rockville, Md.: Montgomery County Public Schools, 1980.

Lefcourt, H. M. Internal versus external control of reinforcement: A review. *Psychological Bulletin,* 1966, *65*, 206–220.

Lemke, E. A. The effects of busing on the achievement of white and black students. *Educational Studies,* 1979, *9*, 401–406.

Lessing, E. E., and Clarke, C. C. An attempt to reduce ethnic prejudice and assess its correlates in a junior high school sample. *Educational Research Quarterly,* 1976, *1*(2), 3–17.

Levin, B. School desegregation remedies and the role of social science research. *Law and Contemporary Problems,* 1978, *42*(4), 1–36.

Levine, D. U., and Meyer, J. K. Desegregation and white enrollment decline in a big city school district. In D. U. Levine and R. J. Havighurst (Eds.), *The future of big city schools.* Berkeley, Cal.: McCutchan, 1977.

Lezotte, L. W. Voter behavior as an expression of community attitudes toward desegregation. Paper presented at the annual meeting of the American Educational Research Association, San Francisco, April 1976.

Litcher, J. H., and Johnson, D. W. Changes in attitudes toward Negroes of white elementary school students after use of multiethnic readers. *Journal of Educational Psychology,* 1969, *60*(2), 148–152.

Lombardi, D. N. Factors affecting changes in attitudes toward Negroes among high school students. Unpublished doctoral dissertation, Fordham University, 1962.

Longshore, D. The control threat in desegregated schools: Exploring the relationship between school racial composition and intergroup hostility. Unpublished manuscript, System Development Corporation, Santa Monica, Calif., 1981.

Lopez, M. Bilingual education and the Latino student. In L. Valverde (Ed.), *Bilingual education for Latinos.* Washington, D.C.: Association for Supervision and Curriculum Development, 1978.

Lord, D. J. School busing and white abandonment of public schools. *Southeastern Geographer,* 1975, *15*, 81–92.

Lord, D. J. School desegregation policy and intra-school district migration. *Social Science Quarterly,* 1977, *57*, 784–796.

Lord, D. J., and Catau, J. C. School desegregation, busing, and suburban migration. *Urban Education,* 1976, *11*, 275–294.

Lucker, G. W., Rosenfield, D., Sikes, J., and Aronson, E. Performance in the interdependent classroom: A field study. *American Educational Research Journal,* 1976, *13*, 115–123.

Lunemann, A. Desegregation and student achievement: A cross-sectional and semi-longitudinal look at Berkeley, California. *Journal of Negro Education*, 1973, *42*, 439–446.

Lunn, J. C. *Streaming in the primary school*. London: National Foundation for Educational Research in England and Wales, 1970.

McClintock, C. Development of social motives in Anglo-American and Mexican children. *Journal of Personality and Social Psychology*, 1974, *29*, 348–354.

McConahay, J. The effects of school desegregation upon students' racial attitudes and behavior: A critical review of the literature and a prolegomenon to future research. *Law and Contemporary Problems*, 1978, *42*(3), 77–107.

McConahay, J. Reducing prejudice in desegregated schools. Paper presented at the meeting of the National Panel on School Desegregation Research, Key West, October 1979.

McConahay, J. B., and Hawley, W. D. *Attitudes of Louisville and Jefferson County public school students toward busing for school desegregation: Preliminary results*. Durham, N.C.: Duke University, Institute of Policy Sciences and Public Affairs, 1976.

McConahay, J. B. and Hawley, W. D. *Attitudes of Louisville and Jefferson County citizens toward busing for public school desegregation: Results from the second year*. Durham, N.C.: Duke University, Institute of Policy Sciences and Public Affairs, 1977a.

McConahay, J. B., and Hawley, W. D. *Is it the buses or the blacks? Self-interest versus symbolic racism as predictors of opposition to busing in Louisville*. Durham, N.C.: Duke University, Institute of Policy Sciences and Public Affairs, 1977b.

McConahay, J. B., and Hawley, W. D. *Reactions to busing in Louisville: Summary of adult opinions in 1976 and 1977*. Durham, N.C.: Duke University, Institute of Policy Sciences and Public Affairs, 1978.

Mackey, W. F., and Beebe, V. N. *Bilingual schools for a bilingual community: Miami's adaptation to the Cuban refugees*. Rowley, Mass.: Newbury House, 1977.

McNab, A. G. Project earn and learn: A community involvement approach to improving student behavior. In C. D. Moody, J. Williams, and C. B. Vergon (Eds.), *Student rights and discipline*. Ann Arbor: University of Michigan, School of Education, 1978.

McPartland, J. M. Testimony before the Subcommittee on Separation of Powers of the Committee on the Judiciary, U.S. Senate, 97th Congress, 1st Session, on Court-Ordered School Busing, September 30, 1981. Washington, D.C.: Government Printing Office, 1982.

McPartland, J., and Crain, R. L. Racial discrimination, segregation and processes of social mobility. In V. T. Covello (Ed.), *Poverty and public policy*. Boston: G. K. Hall, 1980.

McWhirt, R. A. The effects of desegregation on prejudice, academic aspiration and the self-concept of tenth grade students. Unpublished doctoral dissertation, University of South Carolina, 1967.

Madsen, M. C., and Shapiro, A. Cooperative and competitive behavior of urban Afro-American, Anglo-American, Mexican-American, and Mexican village children. *Developmental Psychology*, 1970, *3*, 16–20.

Mahan, T. W., and Mahan, A. M. The impact of schools on learning: Inner city children in suburban schools. *Journal of School Psychology*, 1971, *9*, 1–11.

Mahard, R. E., and Crain, R. L. The influence of high school racial composition on the academic achievement and college attendance of Hispanics. Paper presented at the annual meeting of the American Sociological Association, New York, 1980.

Maniloff, H. Community attitudes toward a desegregated school system. Paper presented at the annual meeting of the American Educational Research Association, Toronto, March 1978.

Mann, D. The politics of training teachers in schools. In D. Mann (Ed.), *Making change happen?* New York: Teachers College Press, 1978.

Marascuilo, L. A., and McSweeny, M. Tracking and minority student attitudes and performance. *Urban Education*, 1972, *6*, 303–319.

Martinez-Morales, E., and Cook, V. J. Cultural sensitivity and nondiscriminatory assessment: Toward a transactional model of assessment for Hispanic children. Unpublished manuscript, Vanderbilt University, George Peabody College for Teachers, 1981.

Maruyama, G., and Miller, N. Reexamination of normative influence processes in desegregated classrooms. *American Educational Research Journal*, 1979, *16*, 273–283.

Maruyama, G., and Miller, N. Does popularity cause achievement? A test of the lateral transmission of values hypothesis. Paper presented at the annual meeting of the American Educational Research Association, Boston, April 1980.

Massachusetts Research Center. *Education and enrollments: Boston during Phase II*. Boston: Massachusetts Research Center, 1976.

Meketon, B. The effects of integration upon the Negro child's response to various tasks and upon his level of self-esteem. Unpublished doctoral dissertation, University of Kentucky, 1966.

Mercer, J. R. *Labelling the mentally retarded*. Berkeley, Calif.: University of California Press, 1973.

Mercer, J. R., and Lewis, J. F. *System of multicultural pluralistic assessment*. New York: Psychological Corporation, 1978.

Mercer, J. R., and Scout, T. H. *The relationship between school desegregation and changes in the racial composition of California school districts, 1966–73*. Riverside, Calif.: University of California, 1974.

Merton, R. *Social theory and social structure*. New York: Free Press, 1957.

Meyers, C. E., Sunstrom, P. E., and Yoshida, R. K. The school psychologist and assessment in special education. *School Psychology Monograph*, 1974, *2*, No. 1.

Mills, R., and Bryan, M. M. *Testing . . . grouping: The new segregation in southern schools?* Atlanta: Southern Regional Council, 1976. (ERIC Document Reproduction Service no. ED 131 124.)

Milne, A. *Demonstration studies of funds allocation within districts: A report*. Washington, D.C.: National Institute of Education, 1977.

Miracle, A. W. Factors affecting interracial cooperation: A case study of a high school football team. *Human Organization*, 1981, *40*, 150–154.

Molotch, H. Racial change in a stable community. *American Journal of Sociology*, 1969, *75*, 226–238.

Moody, C. D., and Ross, J. D. *Costs of implementing court ordered desegregation*. Ann Arbor: University of Michigan, School of Education, Program for Educational Opportunity, 1980.

Moore, L. The relationship of selected pupil and school variables and the reading achievement of third-year primary pupils in a desegregated school setting. Unpublished doctoral dissertation, University of Georgia, 1971. *Dissertation Abstracts International*, 1972, *33*, 4843A. (University Microfilms no. 72-11 018.)

Moorehead, N. F. The effects of school integration on intelligence test scores of Negro children. Unpublished doctoral dissertation, Mississippi State University, 1972. *Dissertation Abstracts International*, 1972, *33*, 193A. (University Microfilms no. 72-20 270.)

Morgan, D. R., and England, R. E. *Assessing the progress of large city school desegregation: A case survey method.* Norman: University of Oklahoma, Bureau of Government Research, 1981.

Morgan, D. R., and England, R. E. School desegregation and white enrollment change: Community, district and political effects. Paper presented at the annual meeting of the Midwest Political Science Association, Milwaukee, April–May 1982.

Morgan, P. R., and McPartland, J. M. The extent of classroom segregation within desegregated schools. Report no. 314. Baltimore: Johns Hopkins University, Center for Social Organization of Schools, 1981.

Morrison, G. A., Jr. An analysis of academic achievement trends for Anglo-American, Mexican-American, and Negro-American students in a desegregated school environment. Unpublished doctoral dissertation, University of Houston, 1972. *Dissertation Abstracts International*, 1972, *33*, 6024. (University Microfilms no. 73-08 927.)

Mumpower, J. L., and Cook, S. W. The development of interpersonal attraction in cooperating interracial groups: The effects of success-failure, race and competence of groupmates, and helping less competent groupmate. *International Journal of Group Tensions*, 1978, *8*, 18–50.

Munford, L. White flight from desegregation in Mississippi. *Integrated Education*, 1973, *11*(3), 12–26.

Murnane, R. J., and Phillips, B. R. *Effective teachers of inner city children: Who they are and what they do.* Princeton: Mathematica Policy Research, 1979.

Narot, R. E. Teacher prejudice and teacher behavior in desegregated schools. In *Southern schools: An evaluation of the Effects of the Emergency School Assistance Program and of desegregation.* Chicago: National Opinion Research Center, 1973.

Nashville-Davidson County Public Schools. *Achievement performance over seven years.* Nashville, Tenn.: Nashville-Davidson County Public Schools, 1979.

National Assessment of Educational Progress (NAEP). *Three national assessments of reading: Changes in performance, 1970–80.* Report no. 11-R-01. Denver: Education Commission of the States, 1981.

National Center for Education Statistics. *The condition of education: Statistical report.* Washington, D.C.: Government Printing Office, 1981.

National Education Association. *Ability grouping: Research summary.* Washington, D.C.: National Education Association, 1968.

National Institute of Education. *Evaluating compensatory education: An interim report on the National Institute of Education compensatory education study.* Washington, D.C.: National Institute of Education, 1976. (ERIC Document Reproduction Service no. ED 132 238.)

National Institute of Education. *Desegregation and education concerns of the Hispanic community* (conference report). Washington, D.C.: Government Printing Office, 1977a.

National Institute of Education. *Implications of "follow-the-child" proposals.* Washington, D.C.: National Institute of Education, 1977b.

National Institute of Education. *Violent schools—safe schools: The Safe School study report to the Congress,* vol. 1. Washington, D.C.: Government Printing Office, 1978.

National Institute of Education. *In-school alternatives to suspension* (conference report). Washington, D.C.: National Institute of Education, 1979.

National Opinion Research Center (NORC). *Southern schools: An evaluation of the effects of the Emergency School Assistance Program and of school desegregation,* vol. 1. Chicago: University of Chicago, National Opinion Research Center, 1973.

National Public Radio. Pushouts: New outcasts from public school. Transcript of Options in Education program, GWU-IEL/NPR, September 9, 1974. (ERIC Document Reproduction Service no. ED 096 373.)

Natkin, G. L. The effects of busing on second grade students' achievement test scores. Research and Evaluation, Jefferson County, Kentucky Public Schools 1980.

Newcomb, T. M. *The acquaintance process.* New York: Holt, Reinhart & Winston, 1961.

Noblit, G. Patience and prudence in a southern high school: Managing the political economy of desegregated education. In R. C. Rist (Ed.), *Desegregated schools: Appraisals of an American experiment.* New York: Academic Press, 1979.

Nunn, C., Crockett, H., and Williams, J. A. *Tolerance for non-conformity.* San Francisco: Jossey-Bass, 1978.

Oakes, J. Tracking and inequality within schools: Findings from a study of schooling. Paper presented at the annual meeting of the American Educational Research Association, Boston, April 1980.

Oakes, J. Limiting opportunity: Student race and curricular differences in secondary vocational education. Paper presented at the annual meeting of the American Educational Research Association, New York City, March 1982.

Oakland, T. Research on the adaptive behavior inventory for children and the estimated learning potential. *School Psychology Digest,* 1979, *8,* 63–70.

Oakland, T., and Ferginbaum, D. Comparisons of the psychometric characteristics of the adaptive behavior inventory for children for different subgroups of children. *Journal of School Psychology,* 1980, *18,* 307–316.

Olsen, M. E. Two categories of political alienation. *Social Forces,* 1969, *47,* 288–299.

Olson, G. E. *The relationship of student racial prejudice to a variety of classroom dimensions in sixteen racially mixed classes.* Chicago: Roosevelt University, 1977. (ERIC Document Reproduction Service no. ED 139 884.)

Orfield, G. Response II. In N. Epstein (Ed.), *Language, ethnicity, and the schools: Policy alternatives for bilingual-bicultural education.* Washington, D.C.: George Washington University, Institute for Educational Leadership, 1977.

Orfield, G. *Must we bus? Segregated schools and national policy.* Washington, D.C.: Brookings Institution, 1978a.

Orfield, G. Report to the court, *Crawford* v. *Los Angeles,* Los Angeles, Calif., 1978b.

Orfield, G. *Desegregation of black and Hispanic students from 1968 to 1980.* Washington, D.C.: Joint Center for Political Studies, 1982.

Paige, J. M. Political orientation and riot participation. *American Sociological Review*, 1971, *36*, 810–820.

Patchen, M. *Black-white contact in schools: Its social and academic effects.* West Lafayette, Ind.: Purdue University Press, 1982.

Patchen, M., Davidson, J., Hofmann, G., and Brown, W. R. A summary of patterns and determinants of interaction in the Indianapolis public high schools. Unpublished manuscript, 1973. (Available from M. Patchen, Department of Sociology and Anthropology, Purdue University, West Lafayette, Indiana 47907.)

Patchen, M., Davidson, J., Hofmann, G., and Brown, W. R. Determinants of students' interracial behavior and opinion change. *Sociology of Education*, 1977, *50*, 55–75.

Patchen, M., Hofmann, G., and Brown, W. R. Academic performance of black high school students under different conditions of contact with white peers. *Sociology of Education*, 1980, *53*, 33–50.

Patchen, M., Hofmann, G., and Davidson, J. Interracial perceptions among high school students. *Sociometry*, 1976, *39*, 341–354.

Pearce, D. *Breaking down barriers: New evidence on the impact of metropolitan school desegregation on housing patterns.* Washington, D.C.: National Institute of Education, 1980.

Peretti, P. O. Effects of teachers' attitudes on discipline problems in schools recently desegregated. *Education*, 1976, *97*, 136–140.

Pettigrew, T. F. Social evaluation theory: Convergences and applications. In D. Levine (Ed.), *Nebraska Symposium on Motivation*, vol. 15. Lincoln: University of Nebraska Press, 1967.

Pettigrew, T. F. Rejoinder on racially separate or together. *Journal of Social Issues*, 1969, *25*(4), 201–205.

Popham, W. J., and Husek, T. R. Implications of criterion-referenced measurement. *Journal of Educational Measurement*, 1969, *6*, 1–9.

Poynor, H. *Instructional dimensions study, 1976–1977.* Washington, D.C.: Kirschner & Associates, 1977.

Pride, R. A. *Patterns of white flight: 1971–1979.* Nashville, Tenn.: Vanderbilt University, 1980.

Pride, R. A., and Woodard, J. D. Busing plans, media agenda and white flight. Paper presented at the annual meeting of the Southwestern Political Science Association, Houston, April 1978.

Project Student Concerns. Interim report. Louisville, Ky.: Jefferson County Education Consortium, 1977. (ERIC Document Reproduction Service no. ED 145 066.)

Proshansky, H., and Newton, P. The nature and meaning of Negro self-identity. In M. Deutsch, I. Katz, and A. R. Jensen (Eds.), *Social class, race, and psychological development.* New York: Holt, Rinehart, & Winston, 1968.

Pugh, M. D. Statistical assumptions and social reality: A critical analysis of achievement models. *Sociology of Education*, 1976, *49*, 34–40.

Radin, B. A. Equal educational opportunity and federalism. In M. F. Williams (Ed.), *Government in the classroom.* New York: Academy of Political Science, 1978.

Rajpal, P. L. Teacher judgements of minority children. *Integrated Education*, 1972, *10*(6), 33–36.

Ramirez, M., III. Cognitive styles and cultural democracy in education. *Social Quarterly*, 1973, *53*, 895–904.

Ramirez, M., III, and Castaneda, A. *Cultural democracy: Bicognitive development and education*. New York: Academic Press, 1974.

Raymond, L. Busing: Five years later—Test score trends: Blacks gain, whites hold. *Louisville Times*, May 13, 1980.

Read, F. Judicial evolution of the law of school integration since *Brown* v. *Board of Education. Law and Contemporary Problems*, 1975, *39*(1), 7–49.

Rentsch, G. J. Open-enrollment: An appraisal. Unpublished doctoral dissertation, State University of New York at Buffalo, 1967. *Dissertation Abstracts*, 1967, *28*, 1010A. (University Microfilms no. 67-11, 516.)

Richard, R., Knox, R., and Oliphant, T. The first year. *Boston Globe*, May 25, 1975.

Riordan, C. Equal-status interracial contact: A review and revision of the concept. *International Journal of Intercultural Relations*, 1978, *2*, 161–185.

Riordan, C., and Ruggiero, J. A. Producing equal-status interracial interaction: A replication. *Social Psychology Quarterly*, 1980, *43*, 131–136.

Rist, R. C. Student social class and teacher expectations: The self-fulfilling prophecy in ghetto education. *Harvard Educational Review*, 1970, *40*, 411–451.

Rist, R. *The invisible children*. Cambridge, Mass.: Harvard University Press, 1978.

Robbins, A. E. Fostering equal-status interaction through the establishment of consistent staff behaviors and appropriate situational norms. Paper presented at the annual meeting of the American Educational Research Association, New York, April 1977.

Roberts, B. F. Declining white enrollments and desegregation in central city public schools: Their immediate and long-term relationship. Honor's thesis, Harvard University, Department of Economics, 1978.

Roberts, B. J. Minority racial status, social marginality and social contact. Unpublished manuscript, 1980. (Available from the Department of Psychology, University of Florida, Gainesville, Florida 32611.)

Rock, W. C., Lang, J. E., Goldberg, H. R., and Heinrich, L. W. *A report on a cooperative program between a city school district and a suburban school district*. Rochester, N.Y.: City School District, 1968.

Rosenberg, M., and Simmons, R. *Black and white self-esteem: The urban school child*. Washington, D.C.: American Sociological Association, 1971.

Rosenfield, D., Sheehan, D. S., Marcus, M. M., and Stephan, W. G. Classroom structure and prejudice in desegregated schools. *Journal of Educational Psychology*, 1981, *73*(1), 17–26.

Rosenholtz, S. J. The multiple abilities curriculum: An intervention against the self-fulfilling prophecy. Unpublished doctoral dissertation, Stanford University, 1977.

Rosenholtz, S. J. Treating problems of academic status. In J. Berger and M. Zelditch, Jr. (Eds.). *Status attributions and justice*. New York: Elsevier, 1980.

Rosenthal, R., and Jacobson, L. *Pygmalion in the classroom: Teacher expectations and pupils' intellectual development*. New York: Holt, Rinehart, & Winston, 1968.

Ross, J. M. Resistance to racial change in the urban north: 1962–1968. Unpublished doctoral dissertation, Harvard University, 1973.

Ross, J. M. Does school desegregation work? A quasi-experimental analysis of parental attitudes toward the effect of desegregation on student achievement. Paper presented at the annual meeting of the Society for the Study of Social Problems, Chicago, September 1977.

Ross, J. M. The effectiveness of alternative desegregation strategies: The issue of voluntary versus mandatory policies in Los Angeles. Unpublished manuscript, 1981.

Ross, J. M., Gratton, B., and Clarke, R. *School desegregation and white flight reexamined: Is the issue different statistical models?* Boston: Boston University, 1981.

Rossell, C. H. The political and social impact of school desegregation policy: A preliminary report. Paper presented at the annual meeting of the American Political Science Association, San Francisco, September 1975a.

Rossell, C. H. School desegregation and white flight. *Political Science Quarterly,* 1975b, *90,* 675–695.

Rossell, C. H. *Assessing the unintended impacts of public policy: School desegregation and resegregation.* Washington, D.C.: National Institute of Education, 1978a.

Rossell, C. H. The effect of community leadership and the mass media on public behavior. *Theory Into Practice,* 1978b, *8,* 131–139.

Rossell, C. H. School desegregation and community social change. *Law and Contemporary Problems,* 1978c, *42*(3), 133–183.

Rossell, C. H. Magnet schools as a desegregation tool: The importance of contextual factors in explaining their success. *Urban Education,* 1979, *14,* 303–320.

Rossell, C. H. *Is it the distance or the blacks?* Boston: Boston University, 1980.

Rossell, C. H. The effectiveness of desegregation plans in reducing racial isolation, white flight, and achieving a positive community response. In W. D. Hawley (Ed.), *Assessment of current knowledge about the effectiveness of school desegregation strategies,* vol. 5. Nashville, Tenn.: Vanderbilt University, Institute for Public Policy Studies, Center for Education and Human Development Policy, 1981.

Rossell, C. H., and Ross, J. M. The long-term effect of court-ordered desegregation on student enrollment in central city public school systems: The case of Boston, 1974–1979. Report prepared for the Boston School Department. Unpublished manuscript, Boston University, 1979.

Rossi, R. J., McLaughlin, D. H., Campbell, E. A., and Everett, B. E. *Summaries of major Title I evaluations, 1966–1976.* Palo Alto, Calif.: American Institute for Research, 1977.

Rotter, J. B., Seeman, M., and Liverant, S. Internal versus external control of reinforcements: A major variable in behavior theory. In N. F. Washburne (Eds.), *Decisions, values and groups,* vol. 2. London: Pergamon Press, 1962.

Royster, E. C., Baltzell, D. C., and Simmons, F. C. *Study of the Emergency School Aid Act magnet school program.* Cambridge, Mass.: Abt Associates, 1979.

Rubin, D. P., and David, J. L. *The schoolwide projects provision of ESEA Title I: An analysis of the first year of implementation.* Palo Alto, Calif.: Bay Area Research Group, 1981.

Sagar, H. A., and Schofield, J. W. Integrating the desegregated school: Problems and possibilities. In M. Maehr and D. Bartz (Eds.), *Advances in motivation and achievement: A research annual.* Greenwich, Conn.: JAI Press, 1983.

St. John, N.H. De facto segregation and interracial association in high school. *Sociology of Education,* 1964, *37,* 326–344.

St. John, N. H. *School desegregation: Outcomes for children.* New York: John Wiley & Sons, 1975.

St. John, N. H., and Lewis, R. Race and the social structure of the elementary classroom. *Sociology of Education,* 1975, *48,* 346–368.

Samuda, R. J. *Psychological testing of American minorities: Issues and consequences.* New York: Dodd, Mead, 1975.

Samuels, J. M. A Comparison of projects representative of compensatory busing and non-compensatory programs for inner-city students. Unpublished doctoral dissertation, University of Connecticut, 1971. *Dissertation Abstracts International,* 1972, *32,* 6725A. (University Microfilms no. 72-14, 252.)

Sarason, S. B. *The culture of the school and the problem of change.* Boston, Mass.: Allyn & Bacon, 1971.

Sattler, J. M. *Assessment of children's intelligence.* Philadelphia: W. B. Saunders, 1974.

Schacter, S. Deviation, rejection and communication. *Journal of Abnormal and Social Psychology,* 1951, *46,* 120–207.

Scherer, J., and Slawski, E. J. Coping with desegregation: Individual strategies and organizational compliance. Unpublished manuscript, Oakland University, 1979.

Schofield, J. W. Social process and peer relations in a "nearly integrated" middle school. Final report, NIE Contract no. 400-76-0011. Unpublished manuscript, 1977. (Available from J. W. Schofield, Psychology Department, University of Pittsburgh, Pittsburgh, PA 15260.)

Schofield, J. W. School desegregation and intergroup relations. In D. Bar-Tal and L. Saxe (Eds.), *Social psychology of education: Theory and research.* Washington, D.C.: Hemisphere Press, 1978.

Schofield, J. W. The impact of positively structured contact on intergroup behavior: Does it last under adverse conditions? *Social Psychology Quarterly,* 1979, *42,* 280–284.

Schofield, J. W. Barriers to intergroup cooperation: The impact of unequal resources and in-group preference on task-oriented behavior. In S. Sharan, P. Hare, C. Webb, and R. Lazarowitz (Eds.), *Cooperation in education: Interdisciplinary perspectives.* Salt Lake City: Brigham Young University Press, 1980.

Schofield, J. W. *Black and white in school: Trust, tension or tolerance?* New York: Praeger, 1982.

Schofield, J. W., and McGivern, E. P. Creating interracial bonds in a desegregated school. In R. G. Blumberg and W. J. Roye (Eds.), *Interracial bonds.* Bayside, N.Y.: General Hall, 1979.

Schofield, J. W., and Sagar, H. A. Peer interaction patterns in an integrated middle school. *Sociometry,* 1977, *40,* 130–138.

Schofield, J. W., and Sagar, H. A. Unplanned social learning in an interracial school. In R. Rist (Ed.), *Inside desegregated schools: Appraisals of an American experiment.* San Francisco: Academic Press, 1979.

Schuman, H. Two sources of anti-war sentiment in America. *American Journal of Sociology,* 1972, *78,* 513–536.

Scott, W. *A study of bused and non-bused children.* Grand Rapids, Mich.: Grand Rapids Public Schools, 1970.

Seeman, M. On the meaning of alienation. *American Sociological Review,* 1959, *24,* 783–791.

Seeman, M. Alienation and social learning in a reformatory. *American Journal of Sociology*, 1964, *69*, 270–284.

Seeman, M. Alienation studies. In A. Inkeles (Ed.), *Annual review of sociology*, vol. 1. Palo Alto, Calif.: Annual Reviews, 1975.

Seeman, M. and Evans, J. W. Alienation and learning in a hospital setting. *American Sociological Review*, 1962, *27*, 772–782.

Seidner, J. Effects of integrated school experience on interaction in small bi-racial groups. Unpublished doctoral dissertation, University of Southern California, 1971.

Selznick, G., and Steinberg, S. *The tenacity of prejudice*. New York: Harper & Row, 1969.

Semmel, M. I., Gottlieb, J., and Robinson, N. M. Mainstreaming: Perspectives on educating handicapped children in the public school. In D. C. Berliner (Ed.), *Review of research in education*, vol. 3. Washington, D.C.: American Educational Research Association, 1979.

Serow, R. C., and Solomon, D. Classroom climates and students' intergroup behavior. *Journal of Educational Psychology*, 1979a, *71*, 669–676.

Serow, R. C., and Solomon, D. Parents' attitudes toward desegregation: The proximity hypothesis. *Phi Delta Kappan*, 1979b, *60*, 752–753.

Sharan, S. Cooperative learning in small groups: Recent methods and effects on achievement, attitudes, and ethnic relations. *Review of Educational Research*, 1980, *50*, 241–271.

Shaw, M. E. Changes in sociometric choices following forced integration of an elementary school. *Journal of Social Issues*, 1973, *29*(4), 143–157.

Sheatsley, P. White attitudes towards the Negro. *Daedalus*, 1966, *95*, 217–238.

Shuey, A. M. *The testing of Negro Intelligence*. 2d ed. New York: Social Science Press, 1966.

Silverman, I., and Shaw, M. Effects of sudden mass school desegregation on interracial interaction and attitudes in one southern city. *Journal of Social Issues*, 1973, *29*(4), 133–142.

Singer, D. Interracial attitudes of Negro and white fifth grade children in segregated and unsegregated schools. Unpublished doctoral dissertation, Teachers College, Columbia University, 1966.

Singleton, L. C., and Asher, S. R. Peer preferences and social interaction among third-grade children in an integrated school district. *Journal of Educational Psychology*, 1977, *69*, 330–336.

Slavin, R. E. *Effects of biracial learning teams on cross-racial friendship and interaction*. Report no. 240. Baltimore: Johns Hopkins University, Center for the Social Organization of Schools, 1977a.

Slavin, R. E. How student learning teams can integrate the desegregated classroom. *Integrated Education*, 1977b, *15*(6), 56–58.

Slavin, R. E. *Student learning teams and scores adjusted for past achievement: A summary of field experiments*. Report no. 227. Baltimore: Johns Hopkins University, Center for the Social Organization of Schools, 1977c.

Slavin, R. E. *Student team learning techniques: Narrowing the achievement gap between the races*. Technical report no. 228. Baltimore: Johns Hopkins University, Center for the Social Organization of Schools, 1977d.

Slavin, R. E. *Student teams and achievement divisions: Effects on academic performance, mutual attraction, and attitudes.* Report no. 233. Baltimore: Johns Hopkins University, Center for the Social Organization of Schools, 1977e.

Slavin, R. E. *Using student learning teams to desegregate the classroom.* Baltimore: Johns Hopkins University, Center for the Social Organization of Schools, 1977f.

Slavin, R. E. Multicultural student team instructional programs and race relations in desegregated schools. Paper presented at the annual meeting of the American Educational Research Association, Toronto, March 1978a.

Slavin, R. E. Student teams and achievement divisions. *Journal of Research and Development in Education,* 1978b, *12,* 39–49.

Slavin, R. E. Effects of biracial learning teams on cross-racial friendships. *Journal of Educational Psychology,* 1979a, *71,* 381–387.

Slavin, R. E. *Effects of individual learning expectations on student achievement.* Report no. 288. Baltimore: Johns Hopkins University, Center for the Social Organization of Schools, 1979b.

Slavin, R. E. Integrating the desegregated classroom: Actions speak louder than words. *Educational Leadership,* 1979c, *36,* 322–324.

Slavin, R. E. Student teams and achievement division. *Journal of Research and Development in Education,* 1979d, *12,* 39–49.

Slavin, R. E. Cooperative learning. *Review of Educational Research,* 1980a, *50,* 315–342.

Slavin, R. E. Cooperative learning in teams: State of the art. *Educational Psychologist,* 1980b, *15,* 93–111.

Slavin, R. E. *Cooperative learning.* New York: Longman, 1983.

Slavin, R. E., and Karweit, N. L. *Student teams and mastery learning: A factorial experiment in urban math nine classes.* Baltimore: Johns Hopkins University, Center for the Social Organization of Schools, 1982.

Slavin, R. E., and Madden, N. A. School practices that improve race relations. *American Educational Research Journal,* 1979, *16,* 169–180.

Slavin, R. E., and Oickle, E. Effects of cooperative learning teams on student achievement and race relations: Treatment by race interactions. *Sociology of Education,* 1981, *54,* 174–180.

Slawski, E. J. Pontiac parents, for busing or integration? *Education and Urban Society,* 1976, *8,* 477–498.

Sly, D. F., and Pol, L. G. The demographic context of school segregation and desegregation. *Social Forces,* 1978, *56,* 1072–1085.

Smylie, M. A. Reducing racial isolation in large school districts: The comparative effectiveness of mandatory and voluntary desegregation strategies. *Urban Education,* 1983, *17,* 477–502.

Smylie, M. A., and Hawley, W. D. *Increasing the effectiveness of inservice training for desegregation: A synthesis of current research.* Washington, D.C.: National Education Association, 1982.

Snyder, H. The effect of situational characteristics on the affiliation preferences of children in an integrated middle school. Unpublished doctoral dissertation, University of Pittsburgh, 1981.

Sobol, M., and Beck, W. W. Perceptions of black parents in an undesegregated subdistrict of an integrated school system. *Urban Education,* 1978, *12,* 411–422.

Sobol, M., and Beck, W. W. Phenomenological influence in minority attitudes toward school desegregation. *Urban Review,* 1980, *12,* 31–41.

Southern Regional Council. *The student pushout: Victim of continued resistance to desegregation.* Atlanta, Ga.: Southern Regional Council, 1973.

Southern Regional Council. A conflict of cultures. *Southern Exposure*, 1979, 7(2), 126–128.

Speelman, D., and Hoffman, C. D. Personal space assessment of the development of racial attitudes in integrated and segregated schools. *Journal of Genetic Psychology*, 1980, *136*, 307–308.

Stallings, J. *Study of the follow-through experiment.* Palo Alto Cal.: Stanford Research Institute, 1978.

Stearns, M. S., Green, D., and David, J. L. *Local implementation of P.L. 94-142: First year report of a longitudinal study.* Menlo Park, Calif.: SRI International, Education Research Center, 1980.

Stephan, W. G. Cognitive differentiation in intergroup perception. *Sociometry*, 1977, *40*, 50–58.

Stephan, W. G. School desegregation: An evaluation of predictions made in *Brown* v. *Board of Education. Psychological Bulletin*, 1978, *85*, 217–238.

Stinchcombe, A., McDill, M., and Walker, D. Is there a racial tipping point in changing schools? *Journal of Social Issues*, 1969, *25*, 127–136.

Stulac, J. The self-fulfilling prophecy: Modifying the effects of a unidimensional perception of academic competence in task-oriented groups. Unpublished doctoral dissertation, Stanford University, 1975.

System Development Corporation. *ESAA human relations study.* Santa Monica, Calif.: System Development Corporation, 1979.

System Development Corporation. *Human relations study: Investigations of effective human relations strategies.* Technical report, vol. 2. Santa Monica, Calif.: System Development Corporation, 1980.

Taeuber, K. E., and Wilson, F. D. *Analysis of trends in school segregation.* Madison: University of Wisconsin, Institute for Research on Poverty, 1979a.

Taeuber, K. E., and Wilson, F. D. *An analysis of the impact of school desegregation policies on white public and nonpublic school enrollment.* Madison: University of Wisconsin, Institute for Research on Poverty, 1979b.

Taylor, D. G. *Public reactions to a court order for metropolitan school desegregation: Detroit 1972.* Madison: University of Wisconsin, Institute for Research on Poverty, 1978.

Taylor, D. G. Sheatsley, P., and Greeley, A. Periods of change in American racial attitudes. *Scientific American*, 1978, *238*(6), 42–49.

Taylor, D. G., and Stinchcombe, A. *The Boston school desegregation controversy.* Chicago: National Opinion Research Center, 1977.

Taylor, D. R. A longitudinal comparison of intellectual development of black and white students from segregated to desegregated settings. Unpublished doctoral dissertation, University of South Florida, 1974.

Thernstrom, A. M. E pluribus plura: Congress and bilingual education. *Public Interest*, Summer 1980, *60*, 3–22.

Thiemann, F. C., and Deflaminis, J. A. Necessity's sharp pinch: Title I under conditions of merger and desegregation. Paper presented at the annual meeting of the American Educational Research Association, Toronto, March 1978.

Tobin, A., and Bonner, J. Elementary mathematics resource teacher program. *Arithmetic Teacher*, 1977, *24*, 329–332.

Tomlinson, T. M., and TenHouten, D. System awareness: Exploitive potential and ascribed status of elites. Paper presented at the annual meeting of the American Psychological Association, Montreal, September 1972.

Tompkins, R. Preparing communities for school desegregation. *Theory Into Practice*, 1978, *2*, 107–114.

Towson, S. Unpublished thesis proposal, University of Waterloo, 1980.

Treiman, D. Status discrepancy and prejudice. *American Journal of Sociology*, 1966, *71*, 651–664.

Trent, W. T. Expert opinion on school desegregation issues: Findings from the interviews. In W. D. Hawley (Ed.), *Assessment of current knowledge about the effectiveness of school desegregation strategies*, vol. 6. Nashville, Tenn.: Vanderbilt University, Institute for Public Policy Studies, Center for Education and Human Development Policy, 1981.

U.S. Bureau of the Census. *Current population reports, school enrollment: Social and economic characteristics of students, October 1975*. Series P-20, no. 294. Washington, D.C.: Government Printing Office, 1976.

U.S. Commission on Civil Rights. *Racial isolation in the public schools*. Washington, D.C.: Government Printing Office, 1967.

U.S. Commission on Civil Rights. *Five communities: Their search for equal education*. Washington, D.C.: Government Printing Office, 1972.

U.S. Commission on Civil Rights. *School desegregation in ten communities*. Washington, D.C.: Government Printing Office, 1973.

U.S. Commission on Civil Rights. *Toward quality education for Mexican Americans*. Mexican American Education Study, report no. 6. Washington, D.C.: Government Printing Office, 1974.

U.S. Commission on Civil Rights. *Fulfilling the letter and spirit of the law: Desegregation of the nation's public schools*. Washington, D.C.: Government Printing Office, 1976.

Uribe, O., and Levinsohn, F. H. (Eds.). *Desegregating Hispanic students*. Unpublished manuscript. National Institute of Education, 1978.

Van Every, D. F. Effect of desegregation on public school groups of sixth graders in terms of achievement levels and attitudes toward school. Unpublished doctoral dissertation, Wayne State University, 1969. *Dissertation Abstracts International*, 1970, *31*, 1559A. (University Microfilms no. 70-19, 074.)

Van Fleet, A. A. *Children out of school in Ohio*. Cleveland: Citizens' Council for Ohio Schools, 1977.

Vazquez, J. A. Bilingual education's greatest potential: Enrichment for all. *NABE Journal*, 1976, *1*, 23–26.

Wallace, G., and Larsen, S. C. *Educational assessment of learning problems: Testing for teaching*. Boston: Allyn & Bacon, 1978.

Walline, J. Solving student problems in the house system. *National Association of Secondary School Principals Bulletin*, 1976, *60*, 30–37.

Wang, M. C. Implications for effective use of instruction and learning. *Educational Horizons*, 1979a, *57*, 169–174.

Wang, M. C. Maximizing the effective use of school time by teachers and students. *Contemporary Educational Psychology*, 1979b, *4*, 187–201.

Watkins, S. Staff psychologist and coordinator for Emergency Aid Assistance Grant, Omaha Public Schools. Personal communication, 1980.

Weatherford, M. S. The politics of school busing: Contextual effects and community polarization. *Journal of Politics*, 1980, *42*, 747–765.

Weatherly, R. L. *Reforming special education: Policy implementation from state level to street level*. Cambridge: Massachusetts Institute of Technology Press, 1979.

Webster, S. W. The influence of interracial contact on social acceptance in a newly integrated school. *Journal of Educational Psychology*, 1961, *52*, 292–296.

Wegmann, R. G. Neighborhood and schools in racial transition. *Growth and Change*, 1975, *6*, 3–8.

Weigel, R. H., Wiser, P. L., and Cook, S. W. The impact of cooperative learning experiences on cross-ethnic relations and attitudes. *Journal of Social Issues*, 1975, *31*, 219–245.

Weinberg, M. The relationship between school desegregation and academic achievement: A review of the research. *Law and Contemporary Problems*, 1975, *39*, 240–270.

Weinberg, M. *Minority students: A research appraisal*. Report to the Department of Health, Education and Welfare, National Institute of Education. Washington, D.C.: Government Printing Office, 1977.

Wellisch, J. B. *Characteristics and contexts of ESAA basic human relations programs*. Santa Monica, Cal.: System Development Corporation, 1979.

Wellisch, J. B., Marcus, A., MacQueen, A., and Duck, G. *An in-depth study of Emergency School Aid Act (ESAA) schools: 1974–1975*. Report to the Department of Health, Education and Welfare, Office of Education. Washington, D.C.: System Development Corporation, 1976.

White, R. Sense of interpersonal competence: Two case studies and some reflections on origins. In R. White (Ed.), *The study of lives*. New York: Atherton Press, 1966.

Williams, F. E. An analysis of some differences between Negro high school seniors from a segregated high school and a non-segregated high school in Brevard County, Florida. Unpublished doctoral dissertation, University of Florida, 1968. *Dissertation Abstracts*, 1969, *30*, 1388A. (University Microfilms no. 69-17, 050.)

Williams, R. The BITCH-100: A culture-specific test. *Journal of Afro-American Issues*, 1975, *3*, 103–116.

Willie, C. V. *Race mixing in the public schools*. New York: Praeger, 1973.

Willie, C. V., and McCord, A. S. *Black students in white colleges*. New York: Praeger, 1972.

Winds of change. *The Boston Globe*, November 4, 1981.

Wisdom, J. Random remarks on the role of social sciences in the judicial decision-making process in school desegregation cases. *Law and Contemporary Problems*, 1975, *39*(1), 135–149.

Wolf, E. P. The tipping point in racially changing neighborhoods. *American Institute of Planners Journal*, 1963, *29*, 212–217.

Wolman, T. G. Learning effects of integration in New Rochelle. *Integrated Education*, 1964–1965, *2*(6), 30–31.

Wood, B. H. The effects of busing vs. non-busing on the intellectual functioning of inner city, disadvantaged elementary school children. Unpublished doctoral dissertation, University of Massachusetts, 1968. *Dissertation Abstracts*, 1969, *29*, 3432A. (University Microfilms no. 69-05, 186.)

Worchel, S. Cooperation and the reduction of intergroup conflict: Some determining factors. In W. G. Austin and S. Worchel (Eds.), *The Social Psychology of Intergroup Relations*. Monterey, Cal.: Brooks/Cole, 1979.

Wrinkler, D. R. Unequal achievement and the schools. *Integrated Education*, 1976, *14*(1), 24–26.

Wulfsberg, R. M. Testimony before the Subcommittee on Elementary, Secondary and Vocational Education of the Committee on Education and Labor of the House of Representatives, September 1980.

Wynn, C. Black and white Bibb County classrooms. *Integrated Education*, 1971, *8*(4), 10–16.

Zdep, S. M. Educating disadvantaged urban children in suburban schools: An evaluation. *Journal of Applied Social Psychology*, 1971, *1*(2), 173–186.

Ziegler, S. The effectiveness of cooperative learning teams for increasing cross-ethnic friendships: Additional evidence. *Human Organization*, 1981, *40*, 264–268.

Zoloth, B. The impact of busing on student achievement: A reanalysis. *Growth and Change*, 1976, *7*, 43–52.

Index

Aaronson, S., 97

Abernethy, V., 136

Ability grouping: and achievement, 131–132; alternatives to, 152–156; in elementary schools, 129; minority representation in, 129: persistence of, 131–132; and race relations, 70; and resegregation, 128–132, 161; rigidity in, 129, 131; and self-esteem, 131–132; student assessment and, 146–149, 161; teacher attitudes and, 131; teacher expectations and, 132. *See also* Cooperative learning techniques; Individualized instruction; Peer tutoring; Tracking

Abney, G., 41, 42, 43

Abramson, M., 137, 150

Achievement: ability grouping and, 131–132; of average-achieving students, 171–172; black-white gap in, 4, 104; central city desegregation and, 118; compensatory education programs and, 134; cooperative learning techniques and, 153; distribution of resources and, 121, 169–170; faculty desegregation and, 119; grade-level of first desegregation and, 109, 110, 113, 124; of high-achieving students, 171; impact of busing on, 7; impact of resegregation on, 126; length of desegregation experience and, 109, 113; metropolitan desegregation and, 117–119, 124, 125; minority, 4, 103–125, 168–171; peer influence on, 169; race relations and, 60; racial composition of school and, 119–121, 124, 125; school cli-

mate and, 114–117; socioeconomic desegregation and, 118, 120, 121; student conflict and, 7, 21; student efficacy and, 122–123; teacher attitudes and, 105, 170; teacher expectations and, 105, 122, 170, 171; white, 171. *See also* IQ scores

Acland, H., 87, 88, 90

Adelman, L., 79, 153

Agard, J., 150

Ahmadjian-Baer, J., 153

Alexander, D., 138

Alker, H. A., 19

Allen, V. L., 155, 156

Allport, G., 67, 68, 69, 93, 172

Alvarez, C. M., 80

Amarel, M., 63, 99

American Institutes for Research, 139, 140

Ames, N., 63, 99

Amir, Y., 67, 74, 98, 173

Anderson, L. V., 112

Ann Arbor, Mich., 112, 116

Archambault, F. X., 154

Arciniega, T., 131

Armor, D. J., 16, 28, 30, 32, 36, 37, 38, 63, 69, 70, 98

Arnez, N. L., 142, 144, 158

Arnove, R. F., 158, 159

Aronson, E., 79, 98

Asher, S. R., 84

Aspira of America, Inc., 136, 138, 139, 140, 142, 143

Ayling, R., 78, 97